Another
YEAR
of
WONDER

CLASSICAL MUSIC
FOR EVERY DAY

ALSO BY CLEMENCY BURTON-HILL

NON-FICTION

Year of Wonder: Classical Music for Every Day

FICTION

All The Things You Are
The Other Side of the Stars

Another
YEAR
of
WONDER

CLASSICAL MUSIC
FOR EVERY DAY

CLEMENCY BURTON-HILL

First published in 2021
by HEADLINE HOME
an imprint of HEADLINE PUBLISHING GROUP

First published in trade paperback in 2022
by HEADLINE HOME
an imprint of HEADLINE PUBLISHING GROUP

1

All chapter openers: manuscript score of the violoncello part of the B-Minor Mass by
J. S. Bach. Dresden, Sächsische Landesbibliothek – Staats und Universitätsbibliothek,
D-Dl Mus.2405-D-21. Photo: Alfredo Dagli Orti/REX/Shutterstock.

Cataloguing in Publication Data is available from the British Library

ISBN 978 1 4722 5938 7
eISBN 978 1 4722 5936 3

Typeset in ScalaOT 10/14.5pt by Jouve (UK), Milton Keynes

Printed and bound in Great Britain by Clays Ltd, Elcograf S.p.A.

HEADLINE PUBLISHING GROUP
An Hachette UK Company
Carmelite House
50 Victoria Embankment
London EC4Y 0DZ

www.headline.co.uk
www.hachette.co.uk

To Dr Christopher Kellner, for everything

'Clemency Burton-Hill makes classical music absolutely accessible, magical and medicinal. *Another Year of Wonder* is, indeed, another wonder.' Dolly Alderton, broadcaster, writer and bestselling author of *Everything I Know About Love*

'*Another Year of Wonder* is a gorgeous compendium of a piece of classical music for every day of the year. The perfect start to 2022, which we all hope will be brighter than the last two.' Elizabeth Day, bestselling author and host of the *How to Fail* podcast

'Clemmie is single-handedly the reason I have multiple classical music playlists, having always assumed that it wasn't for me. In Clemmie's world, everyone is invited to the classical party and that's what makes her books so beautiful and her words so welcoming. Clemmie's recommendations have broadened my mind, sharpened my imagination, tugged on my heartstrings and given me a song for every mood. Read this book and let yourself float away for a moment or two. What a gift.' Emma Gannon, bestselling author and host of the *Ctrl Alt Delete* podcast

'Clemmie writes about each piece of music with such energy and passion that you can't help but immediately want to stop what you're doing and seek it out. It's a fascinating book which I hope many will enjoy.' Eddie Redmayne

Contents

Foreword

When the first volume of *Year of Wonder* was published in 2017, I bought it for almost everyone I knew. The recipients ranged from my then ten-year-old god-daughter to my seventy-something father. Despite the six-decade age gap and their entirely different upbringings and preoccupations (one of them loves TikTok; the other prefers a Bach variation played on vinyl), it proved to be the perfect book for both of them.

As anyone who has read that volume will know, and as anyone who holds this precious book in their hands will soon come to realize, the extraordinary gift of the *Year of Wonder* series is that there is something in these pages for everyone. However you're feeling, at whatever time of year, you will be able to find what you need. You can read the whole lot in one go or dip in as you wish. You can be inspired by a composer you've never previously heard of or be comforted by an old favourite. Within these pages are people with extraordinary lives and astonishing gifts. You will find solace. You will find love. You will find heartbreak, grief, compassion and understanding. In short, you will find what it is to be human. You will find yourself.

On this journey, Clemency Burton-Hill is the best kind of guide: someone who eloquently communicates her own passion for classical music while making it accessible, joyous and wholly unthreatening for the rest of us. She writes with both knowledge and fluency, and her informed enthusiasm spills into every sentence. Classical music can so often feel shrouded in elitist mystique, as if it can only be understood by white men in dinner jackets playing at spotlit grand pianos in formal auditoria. It can feel exclusive and closed-off – especially if, like me, you have only ever been to a handful of concerts and barely managed to scrape through Grade 6 trumpet.

Reading *Year of Wonder* changes all that. It reminds us that music is one of the most direct forms of connection, and that one doesn't need to analyze it in order to feel it. It is not just an academic discipline; it is the experience of life itself – in all its glorious, messy complexity. And this volume of *Year of Wonder* picks up where the first left off, introducing us to a dazzling array of diverse voices.

Clemency knows the power of classical music all too well. Professionally, she has devoted her life to its passionate communication, in multiple forms – from radio shows to documentaries, articles, books and podcasts. Perhaps you've already listened to an episode of her award-winning podcast series *Classical Fix*, on BBC Sounds, where she mixes a specially curated playlist for a weekly interviewee, who invariably knows nothing about the genre. Perhaps you've heard *The Open Ears Project*, a critically acclaimed podcast she launched at New York Public Radio, in which she welcomed extraordinary guests from all walks of life to choose a piece of classical music that had meaning for them. The guests included everyone from Hollywood movie stars to 9/11 firefighters. Much of her work is shaped by the same purpose: to break down barriers and to help us each plug into the intangible, unparalleled, miraculous capacity that music has to connect.

But Clemency's understanding of the music she writes about is not purely professional. On 20 January 2020, just as she had almost completed the manuscript for the book you are now reading, she suffered a severe and life-threatening brain haemorrhage in New York. Her internal world went dark. She survived thanks only to timely intervention and the heroic efforts of her brain surgeon, Dr Christopher Kellner. She was in a coma for seventeen days.

During this time, her friends and family did not know if she would make it. If she did, we were warned, she would be radically altered and not the Clemmie we remembered. Powerless to do much, we tried to reach our beloved friend in the ways she had taught us to appreciate. We sent her music. By her bedside, it played continuously – an eclectic diet of hip-hop, soul, jazz, pop, Bach, Mozart, Beethoven and others.

When Clemmie regained consciousness, she rapidly set about defying every single medical expectation made of her. As she embarked upon the agonizing and interminably difficult business of recovery as an in-patient at a neuro-rehabilitation centre, she continued to listen to music like her life depended on it – and perhaps it did. I remember visiting her there for a week in February 2020 and being astounded every single day by her grace under unimaginable pressure. She had to relearn how to walk and talk. Her communication – arguably the most important part of her life – was horribly impeded. Yet not once did she show any sign of self-pity. She was constantly grateful for having another chance at life. She was full of love. In the evenings, when I left the hospital, I would often see her pressing play on her phone. Once, I glanced at the screen to see what was playing. It was Max Richter.

When, in early March 2020, the pandemic put paid to all visitors – including Clemmie's husband and two young sons, as well as her closest family and friends – she listened to music even more fiercely. When she, too, contracted COVID, she carried on listening as she had done since she was a tiny child. She relied on hearing music every single day, even if occasionally it proved to be a painful reminder of all she had lost.

Today, Clemmie has regained some of her speech and much of her movement. Although she would deny this (her self-effacement survives wholly intact) the scale of her recovery is testament to her heroic courage and determination. It is an ongoing process but, wonderfully for all the many people who love her, she is still indubitably, gloriously herself. Thank goodness.

According to Dr Kellner, music has been a vital part of her rehabilitation. The extent to which she has restored both her language and cognitive faculties is, in his view, largely thanks to the effect on her brain of the musical training she had earlier in life. Although the brain injury robbed Clemmie of so much, it could have been considerably worse.

'If ever there was proof in my own lived experience of music's extraordinary, supernatural power to heal, to restore, to comfort, this is it,' Clemmie says. 'It has been my steadfast companion in utmost sorrow and grief. And more generally, music is a constant, stubborn *proof*, in miraculous soundwaves, that life is not just worth living, but a way of showing you back to yourself, whoever you are.'

There could be no greater testament to the wonder of music. This book is your portal to that magical world. Prepare to be changed for ever by reading it.

Elizabeth Day
London, August 2021

Introduction

⌒

When I wrote the first volume of *Year of Wonder* in 2017, my motivation was straightforward: I believed that music – all music – is a potential source of solace, connection and joy, and that 'classical music', so often reserved for a so-called 'elite', should be available to anyone who might want to listen to it. I realized that we were in the beginning of a seismic technological shift which could transform the way that people, of all different backgrounds and ages and cultures, could access the music that largely gets labelled 'classical'. That was very exciting to me. Since the book's publication, it has been the wonder of my life to see it find such an open-eared, big-hearted audience around the world. I have loved hearing from my readers – and listeners! – about how the book has helped them on their own journeys through the sometimes vexing art of being human.

Now, five years later, I am writing this introduction in an utterly transformed, post-2020 world. Over the past two years I have witnessed – and personally experienced, on the most profound level – how music has offered particular consolation and companionship in these times of extreme grief, distress and isolation. Somehow even when things fall apart, music endures.

And so, although it might sound ridiculous, the platitudinous equivalent of sticking a Band-Aid over a brain hemorrhage, I still believe music is, above all else, a source of hope. Of radical, robust hope. I am given hope by the many stories in this book of composers, aka normal people, who have been compelled to create something of beauty, of imagination, of meaning, of enquiry – even if they happen to be largely unsupported or uncelebrated in their efforts in their own times: cruelly disabled, or sidelined, or even worse, victims of abject prejudice. I am given hope by the idea, too, of such music generating a profound response in future listeners, maybe on the other side of the world or in altogether unrecognizable circumstances. I am given hope by the constancy and generosity of this human exchange, unfolding across space and time, so that perfect strangers are afforded a soundtrack to process big things, big emotions, in privacy, or possibly shared with their community, but in a way that has a real impact in their own lives. Most of all, I am given hope by the fact that humans have been doing this for so long – often facing even worse inequity or poverty or plague – and still it endures.

While in its written form music is just abstract dots on a page, once it is breathed alive by living, feeling humans, it connects the dots across time and space and geography and circumstance. Yes, the genre known as 'classical music' was largely born in Western Europe, in a largely Christian tradition, but it certainly hasn't stayed there, and thank goodness! It's like irrepressible laughter, or our ever-expanding universe: it can't be contained.

There is about a millennium's worth of classical music gathered here over 366 days. Many of the earliest composers that I have included, like Hildegard of Bingen or Pérotin, almost certainly composed their music 'to the glory of God'. I obviously can't be certain, but I believe those remarkably gifted eleventh-century humans were also trying to encapsulate and express their sense of wonder about *just being here* – which, by a process of extraordinary alchemy, gets transmuted, goes into the sound and the physical vibrations of their music and travels across time to markedly different cultures with markedly different belief systems (or none). So, for example, J. S. Bach, a very devout Lutheran who died many hundreds of years ago, is only 'J. S. Bach', the immortal legend, because his music contains something ineffable that resonates in other people, who then lovingly resurrect his music every moment of every day on every continent. And the more I think about this endless continuum of human beings sharing, exchanging, depending upon music and each other, the more awed I am.

In this way, music is like a living laboratory – a never-ending stream of mutual endeavour that gets recorded and re-created by performers and audiences who interpret it for their individual sensibilities, proclivities and particular moments in time. When music 'means' something to us, whoever we are, we often bypass any intellectual questions and go directly to a physiological and emotional response. You know how it goes: sudden goosebumps; an involuntary tingle-factor; a feeling of the hair rising on the back of your neck. Something in that particular song or piece or performance has connected with you and your own set of experiences and thoughts, beliefs, traumas, tragedies, disappointments, secrets, regrets, joys. Almost before we are even aware of it, *something* has connected.

Academic study of classical music has its place, of course. But classical music, as it is actually heard and experienced by the vast majority of people, is all about these chance moments. It is not some fossilized relic, fenced off in a dusty museum or glittering concert hall. And entry to this thing called 'classical music' is not reserved only for those humans who profess to 'understand' it – who, by some mixture of luck or privilege or history, can both afford it and feel welcome at it. That fiction, no, worse, that de facto cultural segregation, that despicable 'othering', has no role in the world today.

And yet. I understand why so many people feel alienated or made to feel ignorant by the very term 'classical music' – and its presumed associated rituals – which cut across intersectional lines of wealth, education, race and class. For a long time, and in many cultures, music education has been sidelined at the expense of more 'useful' subjects or pursuits, pushing access to it into the hands of the privileged few who can and want to pay for it. The perception remains, therefore, that 'classical music' is only for posh, rich, white people, or at least that it is an esoteric monolithic museum piece with zero relevance to modern life.

But I am convinced (by my twenty-plus professional years of working with music, in many different guises and formats) that anyone can respond and be moved and even fall in love with classical music – without understanding 'how' it works on them. Because, spoiler alert: *literally nobody knows*! There is no neuroscientist, let alone any composer or musician, who really knows how music works on an individual brain and consciousness and the glorious emotional collection of atoms that constitute a human being. And long may that be the case. I like to think of it as an eternal flame, shedding light on the human heart: any human heart, in any age.

Your preferred music may not be classical, of course. If you prefer the Bangles, circa 1989, that's terrific. (And I love that song, by the way.) But if you have a modicum of curiosity about classical, my mission here is to make sure you never feel sheepish and/or somehow 'less-than' if you don't know the first thing about it, especially by those forces who say, in subtle or not-so-subtle ways, 'no, sorry, only white men allowed' or 'if you're not rich enough to come to the opera then you don't deserve to come to the opera'. Those forces are pernicious, long-embedded, but they are nothing to with the music itself. They are nothing at all. They can be overcome.

Because music is powerful. Music is *not* just sonorous air. Millions of people, over millennia, have drawn robust hope through music. Hope that can then be directed into other things: action, activism, inspiration, consolation, even survival. To channel the poet Seamus Heaney and his beautiful observation about the great paradox and renewing force of the imaginative arts, in one sense the efficacy of music is nil: 'no lyric,' he wrote, 'has ever stopped a tank. In another sense it is unlimited.' Or playwright Bertolt Brecht, who asked, 'In the dark times/Will there also be singing? Yes, there will also be singing/ About the dark times.' Invariably human beings respond to tyranny, to horror, to despair, by making art and often, later, that's how we have been able to hope, and somehow to cope.

One late September afternoon in the *annus horribilis* that was 2020, going home from a hospital appointment, I came across a quartet playing on the street in New York. They were four wildly talented youngsters, possibly recently just out of college. They had probably spent the majority of their lives dedicated to the pursuit of making it as a musician, sacrificing much and quite possibly racking up many thousands in debt. And now – this. No concerts; no tours; no real prospects. Busking on the sidewalk for small dollar bills, Venmo details prominently displayed on a makeshift sign in one of their instrument cases. Yet a crowd of masked strangers, with their haunted pandemic expressions, were suddenly stopping, and listening, and smiling, and getting their phones out to record this moment (and hopefully, sending money electronically). The quartet were *so good*. And, perhaps this being New York, they were a mixture of white, Black, and Asian-American players. They were playing Beethoven: late Beethoven, as it happened, a piece written in 1826 when the composer was almost totally deaf. I listened to them for a while, felt the autumn sunshine on my face, and was quietly inspired – with the music, with the city, with the world, with history and time and love and with the persistent notion that beauty and art and music, *this* is what gives life its endless, stubborn courage. This is what gives life its resilience. This is what gives us hope.

This is something.

JANUARY

1 January

Jesu, nun sei gepreiset – Jesus, now be praised,
Cantata BWV 41
1: Chorus
by Johann Sebastian Bach (1685–1750)

And we're off! What a thing it is, to embark on an entire new journey around the sun. Simultaneously the most normal and predictable thing in the world, yet, if you really think about it, kind of a miracle. I try not to take it for granted.

But who to choose as our musical companion on day one? It has to be Johann Sebastian Bach. This will come as precisely no surprise to any of my previous readers/listeners, because I am, proudly and unashamedly, Bach's ultimate fangirl: I believe he is the godfather, the singular genius from which everything else springs. His music does it all, says it all, contains it all, elevates it all, can be a refuge from it all.

This rousing chorus is from a New Year's Day cantata, which he wrote in 1725.

For me, it abounds in joyful optimism while still acknowledging the hardships and 'necessary dangers' of the old year. Whoever you are, and wherever you are, I sincerely hope these words, and the sheer gladdening fact that human beings, whatever they have faced, have *always* come together to sing, will lift your spirits on the first day of January. We have a big year ahead of us: let us link arms on this adventure together; let us go!

2 January

Kinderscenen, op. 15
12: 'Kind im Einschlummern' – 'Child falling asleep'
by Robert Schumann (1810–1856)

Classical music suffers from the idea, often cultivated from within, that its practitioners occupy some distant, elevated plane; that composers are conduits for the gods, perhaps, but certainly not real human beings with noisy heads and messed-up minds. Yet the history of classical music is littered with people whose lives honestly don't look so very different from ours; I believe their music, as an expression of that, is all the more powerful for it.

Part of my mission with this book therefore is not only to demystify the music but to humanize those who created it. You know these people; I promise, you do. The story of Robert Schumann, one of German Romanticism's titans, never fails to move me. Sensationally gifted, brilliant at whatever he turned his hand to – performing, composing, writing, editing – but broken inside, he was wracked with a debilitating mental illness, a form of manic depression that plagued his entire life and eventually, via an attempted suicide, led to his untimely death at forty-six.

This piece is barely longer than two minutes and somehow it contains everything, from raw desperation to an almost unbearable sweetness – and lurching back again to despair. With its clashing tensions and radiant harmonies, its relentless pulse, its inconclusive refusal to tie anything neatly up, it seems to me to be a pretty pitch-perfect depiction of what sometimes feels like the impossibility of being human.

And it's beautiful. So beautiful.

3 January

O sacrum convivium!
by Olivier Messiaen (1908–1992)

It was probably Saint Thomas Aquinas, the hugely influential medieval theologian, who wrote the original text about the 'blessed sacrament' on which this motet is based, and which has proven such a temptation for composers throughout the centuries. Other major musical figures who have set these words include Franz Liszt (31 July), Palestrina (2 February) and Pergolesi (16 March), but none quite gives me the shivers as much as this setting by the twentieth-century French composer Olivier Messiaen, whose fiercely individualistic voice and worldview affords him a distinctive place in the history of classical music. His music is *'full of new chords'* that are, as one writer puts it, *'extraordinary in their diversity'*; he did a deep and profound dive into the nature of love and creation through works that frankly sound like nothing else; he even transcribed ornithological recordings to incorporate and emulate the sound of birdsong. He was a true original.

And he had profound personal faith, of which this is a sublime expression. Written in 1937, relatively early in his career, there is something in the sometimes shimmering, sometimes lurching 'chromaticism' of the choral writing that nails the ecstasy of spiritual elevation, however that may personally manifest in you. It is grace-giving, glory-pledging stuff indeed.

Mens impletur gratia,	*the mind is filled with grace,*
Et futurae gloriae, nobis pignus datur	*and a pledge of future glory is given us*

4 January

Asteroid 4179: Toutatis
by Kaija Saariaho (b. 1952)

Celestial bodies have long held a deep fascination for composers. While Gustav Holst, for example, famously riffed on the whole planetary system, and Joseph Haydn wrote an opera, *Il mondo della luna*, about an astronomer who mistakenly believes he's been transported to the moon, the contemporary Finnish composer Kaija Saariaho here focuses her terrific musical imagination on an asteroid. Specifically, the stony asteroid whose orbit passes closest to Earth. She says she became fascinated by 4179 Toutatis, which was discovered on this day in 1989, after seeing pictures of its unusual shape and learning about its 'complex rotation', namely how different areas of it rotate at different speeds. (Or, if you want to get really technical, how its rotation is the result of two different types of motion with periods of 5.4 and 7.3 Earth days.) 'One consequence of this,' she explains, 'is that Toutatis does not have a fixed north pole like the Earth; instead its north pole wanders along a curved path on the surface roughly every 5.4 days. The stars viewed from Toutatis wouldn't repeatedly follow circular paths, but would crisscross the sky, never following the same path twice.'

As a result, the slow-rotator Toutatis doesn't have anything that could be described as a 'day', and its orientation with respect to the solar system never repeats. I love the idea of this plucky, individualistic asteroid, our closest neighbour, doing its own thing, crisscrossing the sky in its own special time and colliding with other heavenly objects in its own, unrepeatable way.

5 January

'Triple Concerto' in C major for piano, violin and cello, op. 56
3: Rondo alla polacca
by Ludwig van Beethoven (1770–1827)

Although a concerto tends to be a showpiece for a single solo instrument set against an orchestra, many composers have explored the idea of multiple soloists sharing the spotlight simultaneously.

Beethoven only ever tried this trick once, but, characteristically, it was to magnificent effect, blending the best of both chamber and orchestral music. It's possible that his so-called 'Triple Concerto' from 1803 was composed with one of his young students in mind, Archduke Rudolph. The Austrian royal would remain a lifelong friend and patron to Beethoven (who also dedicated a number of other works to him including his lovely 'Archduke' trio), but at this point he was only around sixteen and might have needed a little back-up onstage from two other more experienced players. Certainly, compared to the rest of his output, Beethoven goes relatively easy on the piano part.

The combination of piano, violin and cello coming together before an orchestra in this way was, as Beethoven wrote to his publisher, 'really something new'. And what I love is how he is clearly having such fun with it: the vibe is markedly less dramatic than some of his more famous works, including the epic 'Eroica' symphony, which he was composing at exactly the same time. I find this polonaise-style third movement to be a particularly jovial soundtrack to a January day.

6 January

Andante spianato and *Grande polonaise brillante* by Frédéric Chopin (1810–1849)

Yesterday we heard Beethoven riffing on a 'polonaise', a traditional Polish dance in ¾ time which was ultra-fashionable in the Romantic era. Indeed, a polonaise was the first musical form that today's composer, the Polish-born Frédéric Chopin, turned his prodigious genius to: he was then just seven years old. By the time he wrote his *Grande polonaise* in 1830, he was all of twenty; shortly afterward, he would leave his beloved homeland, first for Vienna, and then Paris, where he would spend the rest of his all-too-brief life. And it was here that he added the dreamy 'Andante spianato' section of this piece, which opens proceedings before giving way to the splendid fanfare of the polonaise.

With his dazzling talents and dashing looks, Chopin was instantly embraced by Paris and its glittering artistic society, becoming almost an overnight celebrity. Yet for all he became something of an adopted Frenchman, his roots ran deep. The polonaise, uniting as it did all strata of Polish society, from nobles to townsfolk, was inextricably linked to the tradition of his homeland, and Chopin remained deeply patriotic to the end. Before succumbing to tuberculosis (and leaving generations of piano-lovers to imagine what else he might have contributed to the piano repertoire had he only lived longer), he went on to write dozens more polonaises, only eighteen of which survive.

7 January

Sonata for cello and piano
2: 'Cavatine'
by Francis Poulenc (1899–1963)

Poulenc, who died on this day, was the son of a prosperous pharmaceuticals manufacturer who fully expected him to join the family firm. Despite his son's evident love of music, Poulenc *père* forbade his gifted son to enter the Paris Conservatoire, insisting instead that he attend a local school, the Lycée Condorcet.

Poulenc was therefore effectively forced to teach himself the piano and composition. But after his parents died in quick succession when he was still in his teens, the pianist Ricardo Viñes became his mentor. Viñes greatly encouraged his compositional gifts. Poulenc later fell in with Erik Satie (1 July), describing his influence as *'immediate and wide, on both the spiritual and musical planes'*, and became a member of the group of avant-garde Parisian composers known as Les Six, which also included Germaine Tailleferre (10 January).

Poulenc's music divides people: some view it as 'unserious', as if it is rather too melodic and pleasing on the ear to be considered progressive. Personally, I prefer Igor Stravinsky's take. The great Russian composer wrote to the Frenchman in 1931 to say: *'You are truly good, and that is what I find again and again in your music'*.

Poulenc led a complex, colourful life: he was openly gay, was possibly active in the French resistance, and the early levity and lightheartedness you can hear in his earlier music was later tempered by a gravity produced perhaps by the difficult experiences life had thrown his way. He began sketching out this richly sensuous cello sonata in 1940: written in the shadow of the war, it seems driven by those darker modes, yet as is so often the case with his music, the piece is also lit with a certain inner radiance. I think it's beautiful.

8 January

again (after ecclesiastes)
by David Lang (b. 1957)

Happy birthday to one of contemporary music's greats: the Pulitzer-winning composer David Lang. With characteristic self-deprecation, the American has described himself as a *'weirdo . . . the biggest nerd in the world'*. But don't be fooled: his is a music of fierce humanity and, for all its cerebral intelligence, he peddles in immediate emotional connection. *'If you use these pieces to figure out who you are and what you believe,'* he says, *'you can dedicate a huge amount of energy to really trying to figure out what's true.'*

It's that essential truth that I think shines through his music. In this arresting choral piece from 2005, Lang liberally adapts a few lines from the beginning of the Book of Ecclesiastes, whose eponymous prophet (called 'Kohelet' in Hebrew) is associated with harvest. *'Kohelet'*, he explains, *'moves powerfully from the cycling of the seasons to other endless natural and human cycles, creating a strange equilibrium of hope and futility . . . I wanted to make a piece that might convey the weariness of all these endless cycles, concentrating on the weight of things repeating again. And again.'*

9 January

Sonata in F Minor for two pianos, op. 34b
2: Andante, un poco adagio
by Johannes Brahms (1833–1897)

Classical music is often perceived to be an art form that is mired in the past, isolated from contemporary life: regressive – or at the very least conservative – museum pieces. But this is to do a real disservice to the fact that throughout history, composers have often been at the cutting edge of scientific advance. Take the piano, for example. Today we might think of it as pretty ordinary, an instrument that has been around for ever, but the keyboard has, in fact, been a constantly evolving piece of sophisticated technology that the most curious musical minds of the day have always enthusiastically embraced.

Some of the earliest major composers to play around with the 'piano' as we might recognize it today were Mozart and Haydn – and Mozart in particular was quickly keen to explore the possibility of throwing more than two hands into the mix at once: in 1765, aged nine, he performed a four-hand sonata with his sister at a concert in London, which would have been considered a radical act at the time. The piano duet as a genre has provided a rich vein of possibility ever since, whether for more than one piano, or for four hands (or more) playing the same keyboard – which would have been physically impossible on the much smaller harpsichord and clavier keyboards that preceded the instrument we know today.

In the Romantic era, it was indubitably Johannes Brahms who contributed most significantly to the genre. This piece actually began life as a string quintet, and was subsequently rearranged again as a popular piano quintet, but it's this version, for two pianos, that really does it for me. The ravishing second movement in particular encapsulates both the passionate fervour and formal grace that is, I think, the hallmark of Brahms's eternal genius.

10 January

Violin Sonata no. 2
1. Allegro non troppo
by Germaine Tailleferre (1892–1983)

Today, we have a fresh and lovely violin sonata from one of the coolest cats of twentieth-century music. Born Marcelle Germaine Taillefesse, she changed her name in a deliberate act of resistance against her father, who – as, to be fair, most bourgeois fathers of daughters of the day would probably have done – forbade her from pursuing her great passion: music. Not to be deterred, she kept taking piano lessons from her enlightened mother (hats off, Mrs T!) and ended up winning a place at the storied Paris Conservatoire, where she rubbed shoulders with many of the most interesting musical talents of the day, including Francis Poulenc (7 January) and Maurice Ravel (5 April), who actively encouraged her as a composer.

Tailleferre lived a long and richly productive life, composing everything from ballets for the bad boy of modernist dance, Sergei Diaghilev, to film scores which boldly incorporated African themes, and concert works for unlikely instruments, including classical saxophones. As the only female member of the avant-garde Parisian group Les Six, she met the prevailing prejudice against women composers head on, by all accounts simply refusing to let it stop her. I love the fact that she was apparently still to be found composing at her piano right up to the day she died, in her early nineties.

11 January

Ave, dulcissima Maria
by Morten Lauridsen (b. 1943)

Among the most curious paradoxes about the place that classical music occupies – or fails to occupy – in contemporary life is this: that even as our Western societies become ever more secular, there is a real and growing hunger for spiritually-inflected music that seems to fill a void or meet a real human need. On digital music-streaming platforms, sacred choral playlists abound, often being voraciously streamed and consumed by the very same people who say they no longer align themselves with an organized religion.

The reasons for this curious state of affairs are complex and intersected, and too knotty to explore in depth today, but suffice it to say: I believe that the overwhelming power of the sound of human voices coming together, sometimes in discord, sometimes in harmony, resonates with something fundamental about who we are as a species. It might sound overstated, but I honestly believe that for people of all faiths or none, works, such as this modern setting of the ancient '*Ave Maria*' text by the contemporary American composer Morten Lauridsen, offer nothing less than a vital public service for the times in which we live.

And so – whoever you are, whatever you're up to – I hope you can find eight or so minutes to carve out the space to simply let this into your life today. I promise you'll thank yourself for it.

12 January

Anno
'Solstice: Light Out'
by Anna Meredith (b. 1978)

Another musical birthday to celebrate today: that of the multi-talented London-born, Scottish-raised composer Anna Meredith, whose diverse musical language is impossible to classify and all the more exciting for it. Classically trained, Meredith is completely at home in that world, working with leading symphony orchestras, winning awards and appearing at prestigious classical events such as The BBC Proms. Yet she is equally fluent in the sound worlds of electronics, pop, film and even avant-garde jazz. In other words, she is a terrific advocate for the idea – which echoes my own heartfelt belief – that 'music is music'; that all this stuff is connected via the same sonic DNA.

For her 2018 album *Anno/Four Seasons* Meredith riffs, as many other composers have also been tempted to do, on one of the most famous pieces of classical music ever written, Vivaldi's *Four Seasons*. And true to form she brings her own unique swagger and wit to proceedings. *Pitchfork* described it – and let's take a moment to consider how cool it is that *Pitchfork* even cared enough to review it – as doing 'all kinds of interesting little things'; her notes 'smudge the borders between movements, offer ambivalent shades of feeling, comment on the themes themselves'. It is 'if not a mind meld . . . at least as fun as Face Swap filter on Instagram'.

Purists, you might want to look away. The rest of us: enjoy!

13 January

Deux arabesques, L. 66
1: Andantino con moto in E major
by Claude Debussy (1862–1918)

Debussy is one of the towering geniuses of French music: a maverick who dissolved age-old rules about harmony and, by invoking ancient musical forms and languages, paradoxically created a bold and brilliant expression of what modern European music could be.

Thanks to his undulating and intensely lyrical phrases, which invariably call to my mind shimmering French landscapes, smoky Parisian cafes, perhaps a lonesome woman drinking absinthe at a bar, Debussy is also synonymous with musical 'impressionism', though he himself was resistant to the term. He was only in his twenties when he wrote this pair of 'arabesques', which reflect his interest in an earlier musical era when, as he described it, *'music was subject to the laws of beauty inscribed in the movements of Nature herself'*. This supremely graceful vignette is about four minutes long, a snap, yet has the ability to instantly slow down my world; to drench everything in light. And if that's not a precious quality for a cold winter day, I don't know what is.

(By the way: any Alicia Keys fans out there, you might recognize this as the opening riff of her song 'Like the Sea' from her 2009 album *The Element of Freedom*. Yet more proof that classical music has more to say to contemporary popular music genres than we usually give it credit for.)

14 January

~~~

Reverie
by Angela Morley (1924–2009)

Angela Morley's musical career might have been very different had her grandfather not been such a prankster. Having already tried her hand at the banjo ukulele and upright piano, at the age of ten she fell in love with the violin. But it was to be a short-lived thing: after a *'month-long love affair'*, as she described it, her grandfather took matters into his own hands. He *'smeared butter on my bow and very effectively brought my career as a violinist to an end'*.

The violin world's loss was composition's gain: Morley (who was born Walter Stott and underwent gender confirmation surgery in 1972) went on to become an important figure in twentieth-century British music across multiple genres, including TV shows and film scores, as well as orchestral and so-called 'light' music. A gifted conductor, she was also a musical arranger extraordinaire, able to provide orchestral accompaniments or transpose melody from one canvas onto another to fantastic effect. No wonder she became the arranger of choice for leading singers of the day, including Shirley Bassey and Dusty Springfield.

With two Emmy awards under her belt, Morley made history when she became the first openly transgender person to be nominated for an Oscar, in 1974. (She was nominated again in 1976.) It's easy to overuse the word pioneer, but I feel like we should just let that fact rest there for a moment. She died on this day in 2009.

15 January

String Quartet in D major, op. 64 no. 5 ('The Lark')
1: Allegro moderato
by Franz Joseph Haydn (1732–1809)

Being a musician is, and always has been, a precarious job. For most composers throughout history, your best shot at security was probably bagging some kind of wealthy benefactor, supportive patron or, perhaps best yet, a court gig with benefits. That of course might mean compromising your own creative freedom, having to write to order and indulge the whims of whoever was, so to speak, paying the piper. But it was also a necessary bulwark against penury.

Haydn is a composer who became closely associated with a particular noble court – the Esterházy of Hungary – where he worked for almost thirty years. He wrote prolifically whilst in its employ, producing one magnificent work after another across various musical forms: symphonies, oratorios, concertos, opera, and, perhaps most significantly, the string quartet, of which he is generally acknowledged to be the father. (His nickname among fellow composers, including his contemporary Mozart, was 'Papa Haydn'.)

Interestingly, however, by 1790, the year Haydn produced this particularly uplifting example of the form, he had recently been released from his contract after the death of his patron Count Nicholas, and was working as a freelancer. A trip to London showed him the possibilities of writing for bigger, less intimate audiences than the court, and you can almost hear the shift in his musical language as certain confines get released, shackles get shaken off, and everything opens up. Glorious.

16 January

20 Exercices et Préludes
1: Vivace
by Maria Szymanowska (1789–1831)

One of the great joys of the *Year of Wonder* project for me has been discovering so many inspiring musical humans whom I'd really quite like to have known in real life. Maria Szymanowska, daughter of a Polish pub landlord and brewer, sounds ace. She became one of the first professional concert pianists (of any gender) of her era, finding huge success at a time when prejudice would have been stacked against female musicians. She toured extensively around Europe, where she dazzled audiences with her ambitious decision to play from memory (very rare, if not unprecedented, at the time). She was also a highly respected teacher, a direct musical influence on a whole new generation of Romantic composers including Frédéric Chopin. And she ran her own St Petersburg salon, which was frequented by all sorts of artistic luminaries of the day, including superstar Russian composer Mikhail Glinka (6 May) and the great poet Alexander Pushkin. The leading literary light Johann Wolfgang von Goethe wrote poetry for her and is said to have been madly in love. All that, and she was also, following her divorce in 1820, a single mother of three. Oof, that juggle must have been real.

Szymanowska also somehow found the time to compose at least a hundred pieces, mostly for her own instrument. I find this fizzy little prelude a perfect pick-me-up: a quick musical fix that instantly gets me in the mood to channel Maria and get things done.

17 January

Adelita
by Francisco Tarrega (1852–1909)

Look, sometimes what I really need in life is an epic symphony with all the bells and whistles, and sometimes what I need is a tiny little shot of musical perfection, small but perfectly formed, such as this miniature by one of the founding fathers of the classical guitar. Lyrical, bittersweet, touching, it does what it does in under two minutes and is all the more delicious for it.

18 January

Habanera
by Emmanuel Chabrier (1841–1894)

This one's for anybody who's ever slogged their way through a job they hate whilst still doing all they can to keep a creative dream alive on the side. I see you. And so, I like to think, would the French romantic composer Emmanuel Chabrier, who was born on this day. Discouraged by his bourgeois family and lawyer father from following his heart into music, he dutifully studied law too and worked as a civil servant in the French Ministry of the Interior for many years. Meanwhile he kept up his musical side-hustle, composing as much as he could in his spare time, until, on the cusp of turning forty, he decided (and I paraphrase) that life's too short.

January can sometimes be a tricky time of year when it comes to wondering about our place and purpose in the world, so I hope you'll take inspiration from Chabrier's unwavering determination to do what he loved, unapologetically. Once he decided to take the plunge, he wrote often-effervescent music that seems almost drunk on life, and remained a full-time composer for the rest of his days. (Liberated from the bureaucratic drain of his day job, by the way, he and his wife immediately took a six-month jaunt around Spain which was to yield some of his most fruitful musical inspiration, including the sultry rhythms that infuse this habanera.)

Chabrier, in other words, never looked back. And he refused to worry about imposter syndrome. '*I am virtually self-taught,*' he once observed. '*I belong to no school. I live and breathe music, I write as I feel, with more temperament than technique, but what is the difference – I think I am an honest and sincere artist*'. Some critics have noted how his lack of formal training actually helped him cultivate an innovative musical language which paved the way for the following generation of French modernists. Vindication indeed!

19 January

～◌

Strum
by Jessie Montgomery (b. 1981)

Jessie Montgomery is a hugely talented American composer, violinist and educator who not only writes beautifully distinctive music but moves through the world like a real human. This might sound like no big deal, but it's actually crucial for a genre whose purist protectors often seem to want to *actively* alienate new potential audiences by promoting the idea that classical artists are somehow different from the rest of us. Montgomery lives a real life, like a real person – Instagramming her cocktails and paying homage on social media to her mother's home cooking. She also believes in the power of music as a catalyst for social change, and is impressively committed to education initiatives in under-served communities which try to effect precisely that change.

Her music is hard to describe, in the best possible way: it has its own language and dynamic energy, and it does that wonderful thing where it makes you *think* you know what world you're in, then pretty much immediately wrongfoots you, sonically speaking. This piece, she explains, '*draws on American folk idioms and the spirit of dance and music. Strum has a kind of narrative that begins with fleeting nostalgia and transforms into ecstatic celebration*'.

And hey, it's mid-January. I reckon we could all do with a little ecstatic celebration, no?

20 January

On the Nature of Daylight
by Max Richter (b. 1966)

'*A meditation on violence and its repercussions*' is how composer Max Richter described this gut-wrenchingly beautiful track in the sleeve notes to his seminal album *The Blue Notebooks*, which was released in 2004 as a '*protest*' about the invasion of Iraq the previous year. I find it not at all surprising that the piece has subsequently been co-opted by film-makers of many stripes, including Denis Villeneuve (in *Arrival*, 2016) and Martin Scorsese (in *Shutter Island*, 2010); its sustained and lilting strings and aching harmonies provide a singular sonic canvas, somehow mournful yet radiant, for visual flights of the imagination.

The actress Elisabeth Moss, of *The Handmaid's Tale* fame, starred in a video for the track when it was re-released in a fifteenth anniversary version. She admitted, '*My work has been inspired by his music for so many years and not a day goes by on set where I don't have Max's music playing in my ears before a take.*' Hers is an unusual day job, to be sure, but truly this music could soundtrack any sort of life scene, any undertaking, and I mean that as the highest possible compliment. Like the very greatest works of art, it contains multitudes: beauty and grief, love and loss, interiority and presence; everything.

21 January

Berceuse
by Amy Beach (1867–1944)

Today's spotlight shines a light on a classical pioneer – a woman who refused to let the casual but total bias against her gender stop her. Amy Beach is the first female American composer to have attained anything like public recognition. She was certainly the first American woman to publish a symphony – a major achievement, to be sure – although the current reckoning about centuries of sexism in classical music is helping, albeit slowly, to unearth forgotten stories of female composers who long predate her.

A prodigious talent and virtuoso pianist, Beach was essentially forbidden by her husband, an eminent doctor who was much older than her, from performing in public or publishing her work. But that did not stop her from writing reams of music, of which this gorgeous lullaby is a particularly luscious example.

22 January

Piano Sonata
2: Lent
by Henri Dutilleux (1916–2013)

Unless you've been living under a rock, you'll most likely be aware of the enthusiastic modern embrace of the ancient practice of meditation. Hardly a day goes past without some article or other extolling the virtues of its almost-miraculous effects on our brain chemistry.

I want to get on the meditation bandwagon. I really do. But the truth is: I struggle. My brain is noisy as hell and, although I realize that makes me even more of an ideal candidate for what it can do, I often end up feeling even worse after an attempted meditation session than I did before I started.

Enter music.

To me, this piece is like a secret free hack to get me in the same headspace, if I really open up my ears and allow it to do its work. The net effect is similar, and it costs nothing. Incredible.

23 January

Sure on this shining night
by Samuel Barber (1910–1981)

To a titan of American arts today. Samuel Barber was a professional baritone, a highly respected conductor, and, most importantly, an iconic composer, much lauded even in his own lifetime.

Although some of Barber's progressive contemporaries derided his instinct for 'old-fashioned' or Romantic-era qualities (like, er, *tonality*) the fact remains: he was a wonderful composer, with an innate gift for direct and emotive melody. (If you don't believe me, watch Oliver Stone's 1986 Vietnam-war-era film *Platoon*, the soundtrack of which features Barber's timeless *Adagio for Strings* . . . Exactly!)

Barber was all of ten years old when he composed his first operetta, *The Rose Tree*, and he went on to produce at least one major composition in nearly every musical genre – collaborating with many of twentieth-century America's most prominent artists, including songwriters Irving Berlin and Richard Rodgers, and choreographer Martha Graham.

But Barber – who died on this day – struggled with depression and alcoholism, and his creative life was dogged by many periods of writer's block. Perhaps this was why he seemed particularly drawn to short, small-scale art songs, setting dozens of verses by James Joyce, Emily Dickinson, Rainer Maria Rilke, Stephen Spender, and as we hear today, Barber's contemporary, James Agee – who as it happens, wrote one of my all-time favourite lines: *'I weep for wonder'* . . .

> *Sure on this shining night*
> *Of starmade shadows round,*
> *Kindness must watch for me*
> *This side the ground . . .*

24 January

Ubi caritas
by Ola Gjeilo (b. 1978)

It was as a high school student that the Norwegian composer Ola Gjeilo first sang in a choir – and the experience made an immediate impact on him. '*I loved it from the very first rehearsal,*' he recalls, noting that the first piece they sang was a setting of the Latin motet 'Ubi caritas et amor' by Maurice Duruflé. It was love at first sing: he was duly awestruck. '*It will always be one of my favourite choral works of all time,*' he admits. '*To me, it's the perfect a cappella [unaccompanied] piece.*'

Duruflé's incomparable setting of the text, which was based on an iconic sliver of ancient Gregorian chant, provided a powerful source of inspiration for Gjeilo, whose own take echoes Duruflé's elegant form and profoundly expressive dynamic range. I find this 2009 setting, with its almost weightless depth, to feel timeless; as such it takes a richly deserved place in the canon and continuum of human musical history.

25 January

Scottish Fantasy, op. 46
4: Finale (Allegro guerriero)
by Max Bruch (1838–1920)

For Burns Night, music from a German composer who had no obvious personal connection to bonny Scotland but was so taken by the richness and vibrancy of its folk music tradition that he wrote an entire fantasia based on some of its best tunes – including, in this movement, 'Hey Tuttie Tatie', from the unofficial anthem 'Scots Wha Hae', for which Robert Burns (1759–1796) wrote the words.

When I first got to know this piece, as a young violinist, I had visions of Bruch, one of music's great Romantics, wandering around Scotland, drinking in those magnificent mountains, deep glens and glittering lochs, and pouring his heart back out onto the page. I subsequently discovered that most of his inspiration had in fact come from a 1780s' anthology of Scottish folk songs that he had discovered in Munich Library. He wrote the whole thing at home in Germany.

I kind of love that. Even if you, too, have no link with Scotland or you can't think of anything less appetizing than haggis and tatties for dinner tonight, I hope Bruch's musical shout-out to Robert Burns's Scotland will be enough to get your feet tapping and perhaps have you marvelling anew at ways in which music can connect us across space, geography and time.

26 January

Symphony no. 4 in G major, op. 33
1: Allegro
by Napoléon-Henri Reber (1807–1880)

A bit like the examples of Poulenc (7 January) or Chabrier (18 January), both of whom we met earlier this month, today's composer was 'supposed' to follow his family's wishes to go into a 'proper' career. In Reber's case, that was in industry, and he studied sciences accordingly. But his real calling was for music, and against the odds, which must have been considerable, he began teaching himself flute, piano and composition. At the grand old age of twenty-one, he won a place at the Paris Conservatoire – only to be dismissed with an unexceptional record. Poor guy.

(Not to be deterred, Reber finally got the last laugh: in 1851 he was appointed professor of harmony at the same institution; a decade later, in 1862, he was made professor of composition; and from 1871, he became the official inspector of the Conservatoire's branches!)

Despite that grit – and I think, real talent – lasting success, either commercial or critical, eluded him. These days, his name is largely forgotten. Possibly, Reber was just a man out of step with his own time. His altogether more famous friend, Camille Saint-Saëns (3 February), wrote:

> With his predilection for the past and his exquisite courtesy of manner, he evoked a bygone age; his white hair looked as though it were powdered; his frock-coat had an air of period dress about it; he seemed like a forgotten man from the eighteenth century, wandering through the nineteenth as a contemporary of Mozart might have done, surprised and somewhat shocked by our music and our ways.

27 January

The Violin
6: 'Resting in the Green'
by Anna Clyne (b. 1980)

It's hard to categorize the music of London-born, New York-based, Grammy-nominated composer Anna Clyne. She frequently collaborates with artists from other disciplines including film, visual art and dance, with the *'intention'*, she says, *'to create music that complements and interacts with other art-forms, and that impacts performers and audiences alike'*.

This atmospheric track comes from her album suite *The Violin*. Shortly after her mother died in 2008, Clyne chanced upon a random violin in the UK charity shop Oxfam. *'It was in a dusty old case leaning up against a pile of vinyl records in the basement,'* she notes. Priced at £5.99, the European baroque-style violin, dating from the late 1800s, with a hand-carved lion's head scroll, was a massive bargain. The instrument needed some work, so she had it restored by a luthier in exchange for composition lessons, then headed back to Brooklyn, where she bartered another canny deal with two violinist friends: she would write them a new duet, called *Blue Hour*, in exchange for lessons.

Clyne admits that one of her favourite pieces of music for violin is the presto from Bach's Violin Sonata No. 1 in G minor. *'On the anniversary of my mother's death,'* she explains, *'I composed six more pieces to make a suite alongside Blue Hour, which became the opening movement for* The Violin *– composing one piece an evening . . . finishing on the day of her anniversary.'* Bach's music is quoted throughout the album.

Later, Clyne collaborated with the visual artist Josh Dorman to create seven stop-motion animations to accompany each of the work's movements. You can see these online if you're interested.

28 January

'What power art thou' ('Cold Song')
from *King Arthur*
by Henry Purcell (1659–1695)

Well, I don't know how *you* react to being rudely awakened from a deep sleep, but on the off-chance you're somebody who might struggle with being wrenched from your slumbers, spare a thought for Purcell's 'Cold Genius', who in this air from Act III of *King Arthur* (1691) is awoken by the call of Cupid and is so furious about the situation that he promptly demands to go underground and back to sleep (and freeze to death, which seems a little extreme).

Sometimes the greatest power comes from simplicity. Purcell pretty much builds the whole thing around a single note, ramping up tension through the repeated bassline (his trademark) and driving John Dryden's words hypnotically forward through evocative frosted strings and shimmering, chromatic harmony (which, simply put, means notes which don't belong in the home key signature). It's an immediately arresting, weird and unforgettable work, a fitting example of the sort of brilliance which made Purcell one of the most significant musicians the UK has ever produced.

> *What power art thou, who from below*
> *Hast made me rise unwillingly and slow*
> *From beds of everlasting snow?*
> *See'st thou not how stiff and wondrous old,*
> *Far unfit to bear the bitter cold,*
> *I can scarcely move or draw my breath?*
> *Let me, let me freeze again to death.*

29 January

'Time Lapse' – piano version
by Michael Nyman (b. 1944)

Musical snobs often turn their noses up at film scores, imagining that movie music is somehow inferior to 'real' classical music. This is to conveniently disregard the fact that some of the greatest classical composers have been drawn to tell stories on celluloid – from Saint-Saëns (3 February) who wrote the first ever film score, in 1908, to the likes of Shostakovich (25 September), Prokofiev (1 December) and Benjamin Britten (22 June). It's also nonsense.

Michael Nyman, the multi-talented pianist, composer and conductor, is one of living music's powerhouses. This piece was originally written for the 1985 film *A Zed & Two Noughts*, and remarkably, director Peter Greenaway actually asked for the music to be written and recorded *before* he started shooting. He then planned the film specifically with the mood of Nyman's music in mind.

This haunting track is a stunningly beautiful work, whose solemn power derives from Nyman's superb use of what's known in music as 'ground bass', a repeating 'ostinato' chord sequence that becomes, essentially, the music's pulse, its beating heart. This was a musical device much relied upon by composers in the Baroque era such as Purcell, whom we also heard at it yesterday. It has been taken up by pretty much every decent songwriter ever since. (Check out, for example, rap giant Coolio's 'C U When U Get There', or the Jackson Five masterpiece 'I Want You Back'.)

Nyman tells us that he deliberately set the style of the music against what would be happening on-screen and that, tellingly, the emotional content 'was my private affair, not really related to the requirement of the film'. It certainly packs a punch.

30 January

Lowak Shoppala' – Fire and Light
Act I: VIII: 'Koni'
by Jerod Impichchaachaaha' Tate (b. 1968)

Born in Oklahoma, the distinguished composer Jerod Impichchaachaaha' Tate is a citizen of the Chickasaw Nation, the thirteenth-largest federally recognized Native Peoples group in the US. (His middle name, i.e. his inherited traditional Chickasaw 'house name', means 'his high corncrib'.)

Music is a hugely significant element in Native American life, as it is in most human cultures, intimately and spiritually connected to rituals around birth, death, religion, healing, games, leisure, exploring the supernatural and contemplating the great beyond. According to the *New Grove Dictionary of Music*, *'explorers and settlers'* since the sixteenth century have written *'descriptions of Native American songs and dances, marking the frequency of musical activities, and noting that, often, a musical celebration would last an entire night'*.

Today's piece is from a visionary work expressing Chickasaw culture, history and identity through modern classical music, children's voices, art and drama, which Tate created with three other Chickasaw artists. He cites the composers Claude Debussy, whom we heard earlier this month (13 January), Béla Bartók (25 March) and Stravinsky (4 April) as personal inspirations, precisely because of their ability to, as Tate hears it, express something profound about their national character – yet universally human too. I find this very moving.

31 January

Four Impromptus, op. 90, D. 899
No. 3 in G flat
by Franz Schubert (1797–1828)

Let us mark the close of this first month of the year with a piece that celebrates a major musical birthday.

Franz Schubert, born on this very day, is one of the heroes of the Romantic era: in his tragically short life (he died at thirty-one), he pretty much single-handedly established the German art song ('Lieder') tradition, writing more than six hundred of them, many of which remain shining masterpieces of the form; he also composed symphonies, piano sonatas, song cycles, masses, operas and dozens of miniatures such as today's short piano work.

The 'impromptu' was all the rage in nineteenth-century musical circles, and Schubert deftly turned his own hand to the form. He wrote two sets of impromptus, each containing four apiece, the second set of which was only published after he died. For all their brevity and economy, Schubert, one of the greatest musical storytellers of all time, spins an entire narrative world in just a few minutes. I struggled to choose which impromptu to select for today, but honestly they're so short, and so very sweet, you could do far worse than to enjoy the whole lot.

FEBRUARY

1 February

Oboe Concerto in D minor, op. 1
2: Adagio
by Alessandro Ignazio Marcello (1673–1747)

For my money, this is quite simply one of the most beautiful pieces ever written for one of the most beautiful instruments out there. Mournful, yet somehow hovering on the edges of an exquisite hopefulness at the same time, I find it all the more moving when I listen to it today, the day Marcello died. I'll say no more and let the music speak for itself.

2 February

Alma redemptoris mater
by Giovanni Pierluigi da Palestrina (1525–1594)

Today we shuttle back through the centuries to the radiant peak of Renaissance 'polyphony' (which is a fancy-ish way of saying 'many voices') and one of its poster boys, Giovanni Pierluigi da Palestrina – whose prolific achievements in music are all the more remarkable when you learn of his other busy side-hustles: he also made a good living selling sacramental wine, running a leather and fur business, and renting out multiple properties. (He was apparently a decent land-lord too, even personally unblocking his tenants' toilets.)

Palestrina died on this day, having written five hundred motets as well as almost one hundred masses, multiple books of madrigals and assorted other church music. We'll hear one of those motets today, his setting of a Marian hymn praising 'the Mother of our Saviour'; the text of which was likely written by a man known rather unfortunately as Hermann the Cripple, as referenced by the great medieval writer Geoffrey Chaucer in *The Prioress's Tale*.

The simple words of the text have been set by dozens of composers, and in Palestrina's deft hands they are woven into a serene, quiet mas-terpiece. I am often amazed by how something that sounds so ethereal and otherworldly can connect us in such a grounding way to some-thing so fundamentally human. Again and again, I marvel at this irrefutable fact: that human beings come together, and sing. In dark times, in all times, I find it offers such simple but profound consolation.

3 February

Bassoon Sonata in G major, op. 168
1: Allegretto moderato
by Camille Saint-Saëns (1835–1921)

Compared to certain attention-hogging instruments like the violin and piano, the humble members of the woodwind family don't tend to get much time in the spotlight, especially the larger and darker-timbred ones. Despite their often gorgeous, sensual tones, players of these lovely instruments enjoy relatively slim pickings when it comes to solo repertoire.

The great French Romantic Camille Saint-Saëns was heroically determined to right this wrong. In 1920 he set out to write a sonata apiece for all the woodwind family; what he could not, alas, have known was that he was already in the final year of his life. He managed to deliver the goods for the clarinet, oboe and bassoon, but sadly died before he was able to produce the flute and cor anglais works he had also planned to write.

Bassoonists must have been thankful ever since: Saint-Saëns writes with such sensitivity and intelligence, allowing players to show off the range of everything a bassoon might do. Right off the bat, the richness and poignancy of this simple melody hits me every time.

4 February

Schlaflied
by Sven Helbig (b. 1968)

What might this thing called 'classical music' mean in our modern age? The label remains unhelpful, full of elitist connotations, but meanwhile the thing itself continues to evolve and develop in all sorts of thrilling ways. I could not – as I hope is obvious! – feel more reverent about or respectful towards the masterpieces of the past, but I also believe that, contrary to its stuffy image, classical music is a vital, evolving, alive art form, and that if we are to engage and excite new audiences from all backgrounds then we have to loudly cheerlead for the composers who are creatively tackling that issue head on.

Today's composer is a case in point. As well as being a gifted composer, the German musician Sven Helbig is also a director, instrumentalist, arranger and producer, as fluent in electronics and other digital technologies as he is in traditional counterpoint and harmony. He co-founded the Dresden Symphony Orchestra specifically with a mission to perform only contemporary music, and his dynamic versatility across multiple platforms has led him to create some of the most interesting work of our time – including ambitious choral works that incorporate electronics and visual arts, contemporary dance takes on much-loved old stories (including Peter Pan), and theatrical, multi-media musical events that take place in site-specific venues, such as the balconies of vintage apartment buildings in the former East Germany.

This little piece is a lullaby, and while it calls for rather more modest forces than that, I always find it to be a thing of quiet and lovely joy. I hope you'll agree.

5 February

12 Fantasias for flute without bass
1: Fantasia in A major
by Georg Philipp Telemann (1681–1767)

After our encounter with the bassoon a couple of days ago, today's piece features another woodwind instrument revelling in a spot of rare solo glory: the flute. Telemann was a talented flautist, which is presumably why he was able, in this set of fantasias, to concoct musical forms that seem impossibly complex for an instrument that looks so simple. (At its most basic, a flute is literally just a pipe of material with some holes in it, and humans have been playing a version of this for at least 35,000 years.)

Hold up. Humans have been playing flutes *for thirty-five thousand years?*

That's right. Cast your mind, if you will, way back in time to the Hohle Fels Cave in the hills west of Ulm in what is now south-western Germany. It would have been the depths of the Ice Age, and while some homo sapiens were busy carving figurative sculptures not far from here, others of the species were apparently filling their caves with the sound of music produced by bone and ivory flutes. Archaeologists who discovered fragments of a five-holed flute made from the bone of a griffon vulture in 2008 described the find as demonstrating *'the presence of a well-established musical tradition at the time when modern humans colonized Europe'.*

The thought of this, of these early people and their well-established musical traditions, gives me actual shivers: something to ponder, perhaps, as you listen to Telemann's swirling, freewheeling virtuosics. Aren't humans amazing?

6 February

Elégie in C minor, op. 24
by Gabriel Fauré (1845–1924)

'A direct expression of pathos' is how one of Fauré's biographers describes this unashamedly lush yet quietly intimate work. As a composer, Fauré bridges an interesting moment in musical history, with pieces such as this one exemplifying a sort of high French Romanticism which would soon give way to the cooler stance and more intellectual approach of *avant-garde* modernism. But whichever style he was writing in, what unites all of his music, I think, is its beguiling authenticity. Where many of his Parisian peers were keen to show off their cleverness in every note they wrote, Fauré's music, as his student Charles Koechlin once wrote, '*never mocks or sneers . . . It is varied by the thousand sentiments touching love . . . but often, too, it is the intimate mingling of a hidden melancholy with a certain serenity . . . Grief is not far from this essentially human work*'.

And maybe it's just *that* which always moves me when I hear this piece; its fleeting sonic expression of an oh-so-human truth: that grief, inevitably, is the price we always pay for love.

7 February

Piano Concerto no. 1 in C major, op. 15
1: Allegro con brio
by Ludwig van Beethoven (1770–1827)

People sometimes ask me whether it matters if they don't know what certain words connected to classical music mean. It's not surprising the genre can seem so daunting, given how much of it is delivered in language that is unfamiliar to most. In general, I would answer: no, it does not matter. Is your response to a piece going to be affected because you don't, say, know what an *'appoggiatura'* is? Probably not. Would an in-depth understanding of contrapuntal techniques or a recognition of *'passus duriusculus'* affect your decision on whether to stick a piece on your playlist or not? Chances are, no. But today I really do want to draw your attention to Beethoven's instruction that this movement be played 'con brio'. 'Brio' is such a great word, I think, evoking the sort of sparkling panache or élan that cannot fail to brighten a February day. And for me that's what this music delivers, every time: peak *brio*. I'll take it.

Beethoven had actually attempted at least two other piano concertos before this, but as his first to actually be published, it gets the glory of being called the 'piano concerto number one'. (I make this point merely so you can beware of certain classical folks who might want to correct you if you were to drop into conversation, for example, that this is 'Beethoven's first piano concerto'. They may also be the sort of folk who want to make you feel silly for not talking fluent *appoggiatura*. Such people are not to be given a second's thought.)

8 February

Piano Trio
1: 'Pale Yellow'
by Jennifer Higdon (b. 1962)

This American Grammy- and Pulitzer-winner, who started composing relatively late in life, says she has always been fascinated with the connection between painting, colours and music. '*In my composing,*' Jennifer Higdon reveals, '*I often picture colors as if I were spreading them on a canvas, except I do so with melodies, harmonies, and through the instruments themselves.*' She goes on to ponder: '*. . . can colors actually convey a mood?*'

I'm no scientist, I can't give you a technical answer, but after listening to this meditative piano trio in all its pale yellow glory I'm tempted to say: yes. For me, it conveys a mood of absolute reflection, and thus delivers me into a sort of state of grace. And that's no small feat.

9 February

'For Jóhann'
by Vikingur Ólafsson (b. 1984)

It was on this day in 2018 that the contemporary music world lost one of its most distinctive voices, the Icelandic composer Jóhann Gunnar Jóhannsson. Perhaps you heard his music on a film score (he was twice Oscar-nominated, for his scores for *Sicario* and *The Theory of Everything*); perhaps on television, in theatre or dance. Such were his eclectic gifts. He died of an accidental drug overdose, aged just forty-eight.

This touching tribute from his countryman, the brilliant young pianist Vikingur Ólafsson, takes music by J. S. Bach as its principal inspiration but pays subtle homage to Jóhannsson's own style, including his predilection for mixing traditional orchestration with contemporary touches such as electronics and otherworldly sound effects. I find it to be intensely moving: three short minutes that, with so little, do so much.

10 February

4 Romantic Pieces, op. 75, B. 150
1: Allegro moderato
by Antonín Dvořák (1841–1904)

A lyrical gem today from a Czech musical star, in which a simple violin melody soars over a rippling piano accompaniment – and that's pretty much that. No drama, no darkness, just a few minutes of pure, unabashed sweetness. Dvořák was one of the great symphonists of his day, often writing music on an epic scale, but he saw nothing shameful in composing miniatures such as these; in a letter to his publisher about this set of 1887 vignettes, he declared: *'My work brings me as much pleasure as if I were writing a major symphony . . . didn't Beethoven and Schumann also once write little pieces, and look what they came up with!'*

11 February

Nunc dimittis
by Arvo Pärt (b. 1935)

To a piece of sacred choral music today that was composed this century but feels somehow eternal, as if suspended in space and time. As I write, the Estonian-born Arvo Pärt is the most frequently performed living composer in the world. And it's not hard to hear why: his aesthetic is beautifully minimalist, all shimmering vocal textures and radiant harmonies, with a gentle intensity that seems to inspire devotion, irrespective of faith. No wonder it has such widespread appeal.

The *Nunc dimittis* is a fourth-century-BC text from the Gospel of Luke that has been set by many composers and captured the imagination of such literary giants as T. S. Eliot, Roald Dahl and John le Carré. Pärt's ravishing treatment creates what I can only describe as a sonic structure of great spaciousness and clarity. It literally seems to 'open up'. He starts with a low, almost drone-like note that draws you in, gradually expanding the closely layered harmonies, line by vocal line, until that glowing nimbus of sound erupts, at around four minutes in, into an ecstatic collective cry on the word *'lumen'* – meaning 'light'. It's a properly goose-bump-inducing moment. Never, I would argue, has a single chord of music matched so perfectly a word of text. Pärt's interplay between silence and space is also breathtaking and generates a sort of electrically charged stillness. The composer once remarked: *'On the one hand, silence is like fertile soil, which, as it were, awaits our creative act, our seed. But on the other hand, silence must be approached with a feeling of awe.'*

Well, awe is certainly the feeling that this piece instils in me. If you can spare around seven minutes of your day to close your eyes, hit pause on everything else and let this piece in, truly in, I'm quite sure you won't regret it.

12 February

3 Preludes and Fugues, op. 16
No. 2: Prelude and Fugue in B flat major
by Clara Schumann (1819–1896)

One of the great pleasures of writing and curating my previous book *Year of Wonder* and this companion volume has been the opportunity to dive deeper into the lives of the people behind the music I've loved for a long time. I've become inspired and intrigued by so many stories along the way, but perhaps none more so than Clara Schumann. Pioneering pianist, composer, teacher, muse, critic, diarist, activist, wife, mother, grandmother, housekeeper, book-keeper, nurse; the list of her attributes and side-hustles would put a millennial 'multi-hyphenate' to shame.

It is, of course, a gross understatement to say that the classical world has been, by and large, a pretty inhospitable place for any aspiring composer identifying as female until relatively recently (and some might argue, still is). I feel wretched, then, when I think of Clara Schumann and the vast amounts of stunning music she managed to produce in the face of what must have felt like seemingly insurmountable pressures at that time. Daughter of a tyrannical father; wife of a much more famous composer (Robert, whom we met last month, and who suffered from devastating mental illness; see 2 January); a mother of *eight* children and the main breadwinner in the household. Perhaps it's no surprise that, despite her extravagant gifts, Clara gave up composing at the age of just thirty-six. Later in life, she mused:

> *I once believed that I possessed creative talent, but I have given up this idea; a woman must not desire to compose. There has never yet been one able to do it, should I expect to be the one?*

Oh, Clara. Of course you should have. Of course.

13 February

The Currents
by Sarah Kirkland Snider (b. 1973)

Yesterday we were celebrating a female composer who, despite being largely sidelined in her own era, did much to indirectly or directly pave the way for future generations of women in classical music. Today we'll meet one of the beneficiaries of Schumann's legacy: a contemporary female composer who, like Clara, is also a pianist who is keen to stretch the expressive as well as technical boundaries of what might be possible for her beloved instrument (which she describes as her *'musical passion'*).

Sarah Kirkland Snyder wrote this lovely meditative piece on commission from the American Pianists Association, and says she sees in it a challenge to the performer *'to be at their most expressive, poetic and lyrical'* as well as showing off *'formidable technique'*. It is a piece, she says, that rewards *'attention to detail and sensitivity to pacing and narrative . . . my hope is that* The Currents *allows the performer to focus on storytelling as well – skills that, to my mind, are just as essential'*.

I love her emphasis on storytelling and narrative; it's a reminder of one of the great gifts of music in all its evocative abstraction: you can listen, let your mind wander, and map your own story onto whatever you hear. There are no rules.

The title, by the way, and what Kirkland Snyder describes as the *'emotional impetus'* of the piece, was inspired by the poetry of Nathaniel Bellows, whose work she had set in a previous piece.

> *But like the hidden current*
> *somewhere undersea*
> *you caused the most upheaval on the other side of me.*

14 February

Étude no. 2
by Philip Glass (b. 1937)

I don't wish to dwell upon the fact that today is Valentine's Day – a needlessly difficult day for many, thanks to the over-commodified nature of modern life, *sigh* – but I hope you will forgive me a little indulgence, in the form of a short musical love-gift to myself. An act of 'self-care', if you will.

Because: my adoration for this piece knows no bounds.

I know! There are many, many people who will not agree with me, who might think I am crazy, who do *not* love Philip Glass's music. That's okay. That is the beauty of music, and love, and being human.

See you tomorrow.

15 February

Fandango
by Santiago de Murcia (1673–1739)

As is probably clear by now, I'm pretty fanatical about trying to shine a spotlight on composers who have been largely ignored by the mainstream classical canon. Often, inevitably, that means women and composers from non-white backgrounds, but sometimes it can even mean white European males. Today's composer has been virtually ignored by history, despite the fact that he made a vital contribution to the history of guitar music. As such, we don't know much about Santiago de Murcia, other than that he was born and died in Madrid, but it seems likely that he also had occasion to travel to the New World: some of his compositions have been discovered as far away from Spain as Mexico and Chile.

Creatively way ahead of his time, de Murcia was fascinated by music both old and new, and he blended aspects of popular dance music from Europe, South America and North Africa into a mash-up of musical fusion that must have sounded pretty radical at the time – and that even, to this day, has a rhythmic effervescence that reliably gets my feet tapping. The collections of his work that survive also shed light on the performing techniques, styles and musical theory of the late Baroque period.

And yet, despite all this vision and inventiveness, de Murcia died a pauper in Madrid, having signed a declaration of poverty in 1729. There are stories like this that come up again and again in the history of music: these towering creative minds, ignored in their time, who could never have imagined how their music might live on and light up future lives. It always gives me pause, that. Something to think about as you press play.

16 February

'Cremona, The Red Violin'
from *The Red Violin*
by John Corigliano (b. 1938)

Happy birthday to an American great: the much-garlanded, triple Grammy-, Oscar- and Pulitzer-winning John Corigliano, who has written prolifically for the concert hall, opera house and silver screen, always with his signature blend of Romantic grandeur and modernist bite. The 1999 film from which this track comes takes as its inspiration a particular Stradivarius violin, whose whereabouts were unknown for some two hundred years and whose distinctive red colour is a result of Stradivarius opting for a darker varnish rather than the usual golden gloss. (I know, it sounds pretty niche – but this kind of detail is the stuff of violin-nerd *dreams*. Guilty as charged.)

In this track, Corigliano's haunting and dramatic melody transports us to Cremona, an iconic northern Italian town that, since the sixteenth century, has been the epicentre of global violin-making excellence; so much so that in 2012, UNESCO declared its traditional craftsmanship of violin-making an 'intangible cultural heritage', along with things like Argentinian tango, Belgian beer culture or Chinese calligraphy. This track is over almost before it's begun, barely ninety seconds long, but it leaves its mark: I find one listen is rarely enough.

17 February

Will There Really Be a Morning?
by Ricky Ian Gordon (b. 1956)

Ricky Ian Gordon is a New York-based composer of contemporary opera and classical art song who is also steeped in the traditions of American musical theatre and cabaret, which give his music a gigantic sense of heart. Tackling themes both intimate and epic, from the AIDS epidemic (he lost his lover to the disease) to the American Civil War, he is often drawn to literary settings, working with the words of John Steinbeck, Marcel Proust, Langston Hughes, and, in this case, another great American poet, Emily Dickinson (1830–1886), who was herself a musician before she began writing poems.

The words are full of yearning anticipation for what the future may hold; the music matches its bittersweet sense of longing to perfection.

> *Will there really be a morning?*
> *Is there such a thing as day?*
> *Could I see it from the mountains*
> *If I were as tall as they?*

18 February

Psalm 42, op.42
1: 'Wie der Hirsch schreit' – 'As the hart longs'
by Felix Mendelssohn (1809–1847)

Another beautiful text setting, this time of words by Martin Luther, who died on this day, from the major Romantic composer Felix Mendelssohn. It was composed in 1837 and made an immediate impression: Mendelssohn's fellow composer Robert Schumann described it as *'the highest point recent church music has reached at all'*, and even the composer himself, whose correspondence reveals a touching degree of humility, thought it his finest sacred piece; the *'best thing I have composed in this manner'*. He said, simply: *'I hold (it) in higher regard than most of my other compositions.'* (Which is really saying something, as his other compositions are almost all stunning.)

Wie der Hirsch schreit nach frischem Wasser,	*As the hart cries out for fresh water,*
So schreit meine Seele, Gott, zu dir.	*so my soul cries, Oh God, for you.*

19 February

Hiraeth
by Grace Williams (1906–1977)

To a completely different sound world today, as we mark the birth of the Welsh composer Grace Williams with this atmospheric piece for solo harp. Williams, who studied with Ralph Vaughan Williams and counted fellow composers Benjamin Britten and Elizabeth Maconchy among her friends, was a trailblazer: in 1949 she became the first British woman ever to score a feature film (with *Blue Scar*), and towards the end of her life she was offered an OBE in the New Year's Honours for services to music (which she turned down).

Like so many female composers throughout history, though, Williams suffered from prejudice against her gender. There is a moving letter she writes to a friend, having finally been commissioned to write a major work, that I suspect will resonate with many a female creator: *'You know, it was a marvelous sensation being asked to write something: someone wanting your music'* (emphasis mine). Much of her music has been lost or neglected, but a renewed interest in her work is bringing more and more of her pieces to light, revealing a distinctive musical voice, and one that was much influenced by the idioms and cadences of Welsh folk music and poetry.

Shortly before her death from cancer, she wrote to Maconchy with zero self-pity, counting her blessings: *'. . . that I've had such a run of good health, able to go on writing, and just being me with my thoughts and ideas and sensitivity'*. I love that she had reconciled herself to a central truth – *'just being me with my thoughts and ideas and sensitivity'* . . . I find that phrase so touching and inspiring.

Hiraeth is a hard word to translate from the Welsh, but it denotes a sort of nostalgic longing. I think you can hear that quality laced throughout the piece.

20 February

Passaggio
by Ludovico Einaudi (b. 1955)

If it were a story, it would be set on the seafront of a long beach. A beach without beginning and without end. The story of a man who walks along this shore and perhaps never meets anyone. His gaze lingers occasionally to look at some object or fragment brought from the sea. The footprints of a crab or a solitary seagull. I always take the sand, the sky, some clouds, the sea. Only the waves change, always the same and different, smaller, larger. Shorter. Longer.

So reads a passage from the sleeve notes of the 1996 album *Le Onde*, by Ludovico Einaudi, his first for solo piano, from which this piece comes. Inspired by Virginia Woolf's classic modernist text, *The Waves*, the music's undulating arpeggios and sonic glitter do a beautiful job of evoking that beach without beginning or end. I listen and am instantly transported; I hope you will be too.

21 February

Cello Sonata in G minor, op. 19
3: Andante
by Sergei Rachmaninov (1873–1943)

I'm a great believer in what I call (somewhat unimaginatively) 'before and after' pieces of music: works that, once heard, change everything.

This was one of those pieces, and it makes me happy every time I think about it. I'm lucky enough to have been so steeped in classical music all my life that I have literally thousands of beloved pieces I can riffle through in my mental library, but even so I'm on a constant journey of discovery: I love nothing more than hearing brand new things. And sources of new music can come from all sorts of places: a recommendation from a friend, a serendipitous algorithmic nudge, a radio programme or podcast, a fleeting reference in a book. In this case, it was a moment in Patrick Gale's lovely 2018 novel *Take Nothing With You*. At one point, Gale's main character Eustace, a young cellist, is learning this piece, and his teacher declares:

> *Regret. The whole movement expresses regret. One day you'll understand the kind of thing he means but for now just, well, think of how you feel when you remember a perfect day that you can never, ever have again.*

Not being able to recall the cello sonata off the top of my head, I went straight online and found it, and listened, and that was that. I simply could not believe the wrenching beauty of what I was hearing.

22 February

Verschwiegene Liebe – Silent Love
by Hugo Wolf (1860–1903)

Long before there were the Beatles or Stevie Wonder or Beyoncé or Adele, there were the great lieder writers of the nineteenth century: the star songwriters of their time ('Lieder' literally just means 'songs') who figured out that a three-minute ballad, invariably about love or loss or both, could, funnily enough, really resonate with a wide audience. Although lieder could in some ways be said to have been around since the troubadours of the twelfth or thirteenth century, the tradition reached a glorious classical zenith in Romantic-era Germany and Austria, thanks to the likes of Franz Schubert, Johannes Brahms, Robert Schumann – and Hugo Wolf, who died (of syphilis) in Vienna on this day, having attempted suicide a few years previously. I hope it isn't too glib to say he knew a thing or two about love and loss.

Wolf wrote some three hundred songs of great expressive intensity, setting words by many different writers, including Michaelangelo, Goethe, and, in this case, Joseph von Eichendorff, one of the leading poets of the day.

Errät es nur eine,	*If only she could guess*
Wer an sie gedacht	*Who has thought of her*
Beim Rauschen der Haine,	*In the rustling groves,*
Wenn niemand mehr wacht	*When no one else is awake*
Als die Wolken, die fliegen –	*But the scudding clouds –*
Mein Lieb ist verschwiegen	*My love is silent*
Und schön wie die Nacht.	*And lovely as night.*

23 February

När natten skänker frid – When night confers repose by Karin Rehnqvist (b. 1957)

If you live in the northern hemisphere and the dark days of late February are by any chance getting you down by now, here's another dose of luminous contemporary choral music that might just help. This time it's from one of Sweden's finest composers (who also happens to be the first woman to hold a professorial post at the Royal College of Music in Stockholm).

'*As a composer,*' Rehnqvist says, '*I am the consummate listener. I make my ears as big as I can, and I listen in on the world. I listen to people, to the earth, to roots and skies. I send feelers even further, far out into the universe. What needs to be said? What needs to take shape as music? What do we, the people living right now, need to hear?*'

I am wildly in love with this idea of 'making your ears as big as you can': what a way to go about life! This piece is highly atmospheric, simultaneously evoking the icy climes of the composer's native Scandinavia yet glowing with something akin to fire. It's like the sonic equivalent of a really good whisky: listening to it is a gift.

24 February

'Lascia ch'io pianga' – 'Let me lament my cruel fate' from *Rinaldo* by George Frideric Handel (1685–1759)

It was on this day in 1711 that the first performance of an opera called *Rinaldo* took place, at London's Haymarket Theatre. *Rinaldo* was revolutionary for being the first Italian language opera written specifically for the London stage, and despite the fact that Handel dashed it off in a hot minute, borrowing here and there from previous works he had written, it was an immediate hit with audiences and became the most-performed opera of his lifetime.

Set during the Crusades, *Rinaldo* concerns those small matters of love, war and redemption, and contains a number of arias, or songs, that are so good they have become stand-alone concert works in their own right. This one might just be the most popular of all. Taking place in Act 2, it is sung by the character of Almirena, who has been abducted and imprisoned by the sorceress Armida and separated from her fiancé and love of her life, Rinaldo. Here she is addressing the Saracen chief, Argante, who has just confessed his love at first sight. (Unlike many opera plots, this one does actually end happily ever after, but we don't know that yet . . .)

Lascia ch'io pianga	*Let me lament*
Mia cruda sorte,	*My cruel fate,*
E che sospiri	*And that I*
La libertà.	*Long for freedom.*

25 February

12 Sonatas, op. 16: Sonata prima
5: Soli violini
by Isabella Leonarda (1620–1704)

To one of the most productive and prolific composers of her time: Isabella Leonarda, who died on this day. Having entered an Ursuline convent in Novara, Italy, aged sixteen, and later becoming Mother Superior, it was many decades before Leonarda began to produce music regularly; most of her works seem to have been written after she turned fifty. Despite that, she managed to produce around two hundred pieces that we know of, so far. (I say 'so far', because long-overdue scholarship into many female composers from history is uncovering works at a rate that is both gratifying – for the music we now have at our disposal and can bring back to life – and depressing, for what it reminds us about the historical marginalization of women in classical music for so long.)

It's hard to imagine what sort of odds Leonarda must have overcome to have published as much music as she did in her lifetime. The set of gentle sonatas that make up her opus 16, from which this lovely, lyrical movement comes, became, when they appeared in Bologna in 1693, the earliest published instrumental works by a woman. That fact alone, I hope you agree, makes them worth a little celebration.

26 February

Overture from *L'amant anonyme*
1: Allegro presto
by Joseph Boulogne, Chevalier de Saint-Georges (1745–1799)

Often dubbed – inevitably, if unimaginatively – 'the Black Mozart', Joseph Boulogne is one of classical music's true trailblazers. Generally regarded as the first major classical composer of African ancestry, he was born in the French colony of Guadeloupe, the son of a wealthy planter who owned a 250-acre plantation with sixty slaves, and the planter's wife's sixteen-year-old slave, Nanon. (I know!) Unlikely as it may sound, Boulogne, who was educated in France, went on to become a fine dancer, a colonel in Europe's first all-Black army regiment during the French Revolution, and a champion swordsman, one of the biggest fencing stars of the day. This was quite the trajectory, given his background as the son of a slave.

For all his sporting celebrity, however, it was music that was his greatest passion. When he made his public debut as a violinist in a new orchestra called the Concert des Amateurs in 1769, audiences went wild. He went on to become a star performer and then conductor of the ensemble: even Queen Marie Antoinette was a fan and later supported him personally when systemic racism kept him out of a position at the Paris Opera for which he would have been ideally suited.

As a composer, Boulogne wrote string quartets that were directly inspired by Haydn's (15 January), violin concertos aplenty, and six comic operas of which only this one, *The Anonymous Lover*, survives in its entirety. The opening section of the overture is a cheerily upbeat and zingy affair, three-and-a-half minutes of elegant instrumental interplay and narrative momentum. I find it a highly motivating soundtrack to a morning; I hope you do too.

27 February

Fantasia in F minor for Piano 4 hands, op. 103
by Franz Schubert (1797–1828)

Written in the last year of his tragically short life, and published only after his death, this is Schubert at his most melodically endearing yet quietly sophisticated. The format of the work reflects the vogue in nineteenth-century Europe for 'four-hand' music that enabled social music-making without the need for a second piano; incredibly, for all its complexity and drama, this piece requires only one keyboard. During Schubert's lifetime the bulk of his income was in fact made through the publication of such '*Hausmusik*', or house-music.

The piece is dedicated to the woman generally regarded to be the (unrequited) love of Schubert's life, Countess Karoline of Esterházy, to whom he had taught piano a decade previously. Apparently, she once jokingly chastised him for not dedicating anything to her and he allegedly replied: '*What is the point? Everything is dedicated to you anyway.*' Oof.

28 February

Ô Abre Alas – Open, wings
by Francisca Edviges Neves 'Chiquinha' Gonzaga (1847–1935)

An iconic carnival anthem today, from Brazil's first professional female composer and a true pioneer. Living in the patriarchal society she did, it would have been considered bad enough that this spirited female, who was the daughter of a freed Black woman slave and a strict military father, wanted to make music her career. That Gonzaga was also a two-time divorcée, shunned by her community, only added insult to injury to those forces who would keep her irrepressible creative talents at bay.

Nevertheless, she persisted, remaining politically active – advocating for such causes as the abolition movement, copyright law and suffragism – as well as defiantly creatively productive in the face of unrelenting prejudice. In her long and vibrant life, Gonzaga produced some two thousand works that helped to put Brazilian classical music on the map; pieces that, in their inventive fusion of European dance forms and Afro-Brazilian rhythms, still sound thrillingly fresh.

Gonzaga died on this day, at the age of eighty-seven – having recently finished what was to be her final opera, *Maria*, and with her much younger lover at her side.

29 February

Overture
from *The Barber of Seville*
by Gioachino Rossini (1792–1868)

There aren't too many classical composers whose music is so popular they can claim to be legit celebrities in their own time (in ours, Max Richter, whom we heard last month, may be a rare exception). But Rossini, who was born on this day, was not only outrageously gifted (writing thirty-nine operas before his fortieth birthday) and successful (he was one of the few composers who made a decent living from his work); he was also the creator of music so mainstream it might feasibly be described as the pop music of its day. His fellow composer Felix Mendelssohn may have described him as a 'genius', but for once this wasn't just a critical assessment: apparently Rossini's catchy melodies were whistled on the streets, and one Dr Cotugno, a well-regarded physician in Naples, reported over forty cases of women dying of excitement while watching one of his operas, *Moses in Egypt*. (I have not actually been able to verify the anecdote, but its widespread existence sort of tells you all you need to know.)

Unpretentious, unashamedly commercial, epicurean, Rossini was apparently as much a dab hand in the kitchen as he was in the opera house: his reverence towards food, especially the pasta of his home town, Bologna, is the stuff of legend.

Whether or not you are reading this in a leap year, I hope you'll raise a toast to the anniversary of the birth of one of music's great individuals.

MARCH

1 March

Ave verum corpus
by Karl Jenkins (b. 1944)

On St David's Day, music written by one Welsh musical superhero for another (its dedicatee is the great bass-baritone Bryn Terfel). Jenkins is one of the most performed of all contemporary composers, his music adored by people around the world, and yet he remains remarkably modest, saying it is *'gratifying and humbling'* that his work has found such an enormous audience.

Describing his style as having *'a classical base but [drawing] on other cultures that flavour the music'*, he often builds on the exceedingly rich musical traditions of his Welsh homeland to incorporate aspects of Eastern music and mysticism. (As he puts it, rather brilliantly, he is something of a *'musical tourist'*.) Of his setting of the sorrowful thirteenth-century text *Stabat Mater*, from which this movement comes, he explains: *'I was trying to give the grief a broader, global picture than Western Christian culture – universal, embracing all cultures. It's a bit of a crusade I have – to give my work a universal message.'*

The piece is classic Jenkins: emotionally direct, harmonically rich, instantly accessible. And I mean 'accessible' in an entirely positive way, although many purist classical critics might turn up their noses; for these folks, 'accessible' inevitably means 'dumbing down'. I have no tolerance with such a position, and neither does the composer: Jenkins once said of the classical music world that *'It's the snobbery, stuffiness and elitism of the culture that needs working on.'* A sentiment with which I can only agree.

2 March

Lento
by Aleksey Igudesman (b. 1973)

As one half of the musical comedy duo Igudesman & Joo, today's multi-talented composer Aleksey Igudesman has racked up almost fifty million views on YouTube, with audiences lapping up the '*inspired lunacy*' of the duo's schtick, which blends musical virtuosity with comedic zaniness in equal measure. It is hard to overstate how rare it is for classical performers to cross over into the mainstream like this, but, as well as being a violinist, conductor, comedian, film-maker, producer, actor and poet, the Russian-born Igudesman is also a tech entrepreneur and, as today's beautifully meandering, meditative piece proves, a talented composer in his own right. His music has been performed by some of the world's leading ensembles, including the New York Philharmonic and the Vienna Symphony Orchestra.

3 March

Three Dream Portraits
2: 'Dream Variation'
by Margaret Bonds (1913–1972)

Today we mark the birthday of an extraordinary American musician who became one of the first Black classical performers to gain recognition in the US. A prodigy who composed her first work at the age of five and went on to become the first African-American soloist with the Chicago Symphony, Margaret Bonds learned the piano from her mother and later attended Northwestern University in Illinois. There, as one of its first Black students, she experienced racial discrimination at first hand. (The university did not provide housing for African-American students; as a Black female she was also forbidden from using certain facilities, including, for example, the swimming pool.) '*It was in this prejudiced university, this terribly prejudiced place . . .*' she later wrote, '*I was looking in the basement of the Evanston Public Library where they had the poetry. I came into contact with this wonderful poem, "The Negro Speaks of Rivers", and I'm sure it helped my feelings of security . . .*'

The life-saving poem in question was by Langston Hughes, whom she later befriended in New York and with whom she collaborated on many projects, including the 1959 song collection *Three Dream Portraits*, of which this is the second part. Bonds was a lover of words: she set poetry by the likes of W. E. B. DuBois and William Shakespeare. Nothing, though, in my view, comes close to her fabulous setting of Hughes.

To fling my arms wide
In some place of the sun,
To whirl and to dance
Till the white day is
    done.

Then rest at cool evening
Beneath a tall tree
While night comes on gently,
    Dark like me –
That is my dream!

81

4 March

Lauda Jerusalem
by Antonio Vivaldi (1678–1741)

According to legend, an earthquake struck Venice on this day in 1678, and it was certainly a date, if you'll excuse the terrible pun, that would have seismic sonic implications. Happy birthday to the one and only Antonio Vivaldi, a composer who has so much more going on than merely the snatched phrases of *The Four Seasons* you may have heard piped over a phone line while on hold to your internet provider, when sitting in the dentist's office or eating spaghetti at any number of generic Italian restaurants. In many ways that piece has become the audio equivalent of the red-check tablecloth, a cliché which does a disservice to Vivaldi's singular genius and the immeasurable contribution he made to the music of the Baroque period and beyond.

An ordained priest who yet battled with some of the most complex questions about what it is to be an earthbound and flawed human being, Vivaldi wrote some eight hundred works, including five hundred concertos, forty-six operas, and assorted sacred music, including this setting of Psalm 147 – which he offered to the orphanage of young girls where he worked for much of his life, the Ospedale della Pietà, in 1739, just a couple of years before he died. It's not one of Vivaldi's best known works; in fact I have still never seen or heard it performed live, but right from the potent drama and energy of its opening bars, sung by double choir, through to the soaring lines of the two soprano solos who enter later, I find it simply magnificent – seven or so minutes of music so rich and rewarding I can lose myself in it completely.

5 March

Prelude no. 1 in E minor
by Heitor Villa-Lobos (1887–1959)

Villa-Lobos was a conductor, cellist, pianist and guitarist, often described along the lines of 'the single most significant creative figure in twentieth-century Brazilian art music'. It was as a composer, though, that his legacy is most significant.

Deeply curious about the extraordinarily rich musical tradition of his homeland, Villa-Lobos also had a sharp ear on the music coming out of Europe and the USA, especially that by the likes of Debussy, Satie and Stravinsky. With his phenomenal grasp of both musical cultures and a singular way of blending them, he was the first composer to really put Brazilian classical music on the map. (Speaking of which, one of my favourite insights from any composer ever is Villa-Lobos declaring his first harmony teacher to be '*a map of Brazil*'. Just fantastic.)

I love this sensuous and sultry 'sentimental melody', written in 1940 as part of a set of guitar preludes that he dedicated to his beloved partner, Arminda Neves d'Almeida, for whom he left his wife. Although he and 'Mindinha', as she was fondly known, never married, they remained together for the rest of his life.

6 March

Sonata for violin and piano no. 5 in F major, op. 24 ('Spring')
1: Allegro
by Ludwig van Beethoven (1770–1827)

It was not Beethoven himself who dubbed this 1801 piece for violin and piano the 'Spring Sonata'; that nickname was applied many years later, after his death. But my goodness is it appropriate: this is music as joyous and fresh and life-affirming as you can get, brimful of beautiful melodies and animated by a spirit that truly does feel like a musical rebirth. It reveals Classical-era Beethoven poised on the cusp of the incoming world of Romanticism, exploring the modern possibility of a truly equal partnership between the two instruments and unleashing not only radically expansive, emotional expression in his melodic lines but rhythmic gestures that prefigure, by well over a century, the general loosening up of form that would result in jazz and the blues.

Wherever you are in the world, and whether or not spring has yet sprung round your way, I hope you feel newly awakened and energized by this amazing music.

7 March

'Morning on the Limpopo; Matlou Women' from *Limpopo Songs* by Paola Prestini (b. 1975)

'*An artistic visionary*' is how fellow American composer Philip Glass (14 February) describes Paola Prestini. '*There is a kind of energy system that follows her/her work wherever she goes.*' You might say it takes one to know one: such an imprimatur is not something that the iconic Glass, I imagine, throws around all too casually. Prestini is certainly a force of nature: an accomplished composer who has also shaken up the contemporary classical scene in the US. In recent years she has launched National Sawdust, a performing arts space in Williamsburg, Brooklyn that is also a hub for curation, criticism, recordings and vital initiatives such as the annual Hildegard competition which celebrates and directs critical resources to composers who identify as female, trans or non-binary. She is a boundary-pusher all right, a distinctive compositional voice and generous spirit who represents, for the classical world, a proper breath of fresh air.

8 March

Prelude, op. 73
by Mana-Zucca Cassel (1885–1981)

Today is International Women's Day and, it happens, the day that one inordinately talented – and now largely forgotten – musical woman died. 'Mana-Zucca' (or Gussie Zuckermann) was born in New York on Christmas Day, 1885, and her life played out in parallel with the twentieth century, with all of its extraordinary progress, and its unspeakable horrors. Just think about it: the year she was born, Franz Liszt was still alive, Adolf Hitler was yet to be born, a little-known author named Mark Twain had recently published a story called *Adventures of Huckleberry Finn*, and the French bacteriologist Louis Pasteur had just proven the theory of vaccination by administering an anti-rabies shot to save a nine-year-old boy's life. In the year she died, the first Space Shuttle was returning to earth, MTV had started broadcasting pop music videos, IBM was selling the first Personal Computer and the AIDS epidemic was officially underway. *Mind-spinning . . .*

Anyway, I digress. By the age of three, this fabulous female was performing in public; by eight, she was appearing as the piano soloist in front of the New York Symphony Orchestra; and before too long, she was much in demand as a star soloist, delighting audiences as far away as England, France, Germany, Holland and Russia. Closer to home, meanwhile, Mana-Zucca was starring in several musical comedies, appearing on Broadway as an actress and singer, and writing the smash hit song 'I Love Life' . . . All the while being drawn to compose wonderfully textured classical pieces, like this prelude which, despite being just a few minutes long, I hope you will agree is a true delight.

9 March

Abendlied – Evening Song
by Josef Rheinberger (1839–1901)

Rheinberger is one of those composers whose name has slipped from history, although he was prolific and taught a handful of twentieth-century German musical heavyweights, including the *Hansel and Gretel* composer Engelbert Humperdinck and the legendary conductor Wilhelm Furtwängler. Many years before he became a teacher, though, he wrote this sacred anthem, on this day in 1855, when he was just fifteen years old. I came across it by chance on a stunning album of 'Music for the Close of Day' from the Cambridge Singers and conductor John Rutter, who translates the text thus:

Bleib' bei uns, denn es will Abend werden;	*Bide with us, for evening shadows darken,*
Und der Tag hat sich geneiget.	*And the day will soon be over.*

It goes without saying it's a piece that could be enjoyed at any time of day, but, if you can, I would recommend that you take four-and-a-half minutes, on this or any evening, to listen to this serene, supremely peaceful work. For me it always sets the day just passed in a different light, and I'm invariably grateful for that change in perspective.

10 March

Spanish Dances, op. 23
2: Zapateado
by Pablo de Sarasate (1844–1908)

To an almost direct contemporary of yesterday's composer Josef Rheinberger, today: the great Spanish violin virtuoso Pablo de Sarasate, who
was born on this day. A child prodigy, like many of the composers we
are encountering in this book, he made his first public appearance at
the age of eight and started composing, especially for his own instrument, the violin, in his teens. In fact, he wrote such fiendishly difficult
pieces – like this one, from a collection of Spanish Dances that he published in 1880 – that the playwright and music critic George Bernard
Shaw once remarked that his talents *'left criticism gasping miles behind
him'*. What a way to put it!

11 March

History of Tango
2: 'Café 1930'
by Astor Piazzolla (1921–1992)

Another musical birthday to celebrate today, that of the Argentine tango master Astor Piazzolla who, as well as being synonymous with the dance traditions of his homeland, was also steeped in classical music (as well as almost every other musical genre you could care to name: after his family moved from Argentina to Greenwich Village, New York, when he was a child, he soaked up everything he could get his ears on, from Bach to early jazz and beyond).

This piece comes from Piazzolla's seminal work *History of Tango*, which might therefore raise an eyebrow as to what it's doing here, but its mournful melodic lines fit right in with the rest of the music in this book, so who's to say it's not 'classical'? In fact, as far as I'm concerned, a piece such as this is another powerful argument against the policing of musical genre boundaries at all.

12 March

Violin Concerto in F sharp minor
2: Adagio ma non troppo
by José Silvestre White Lafitte (1836–1918)

Also known as Joseph White, today's composer, who died on this day, was born in Cuba of mixed Spanish and Afro-Cuban heritage. Having shown great musical promise from an early age, he was encouraged to continue his studies by the American composer Louis Moreau Gottschalk, who happened to accompany him in a recital whilst visiting Cuba and promptly felt compelled to raise the money for White to travel to Paris for study. White went on to win first prize in violin at the storied Paris Conservatoire and his compositions, including this unashamedly romantic and lyrical violin concerto, received critical acclaim from the likes of arguably the most famous and celebrated composer of the day, Gioachino Rossini (29 February).

That hasn't stopped White's name and contribution to music history from being mostly overlooked until recent years. Thankfully, the systemic prejudice that has long relegated composers of colour to the sidelines is being actively addressed, and incremental progress is being made to bring many forgotten musical talents out of the shadows. It's a long road ahead, but it's something.

13 March

Concerto for violin concertato, strings and basso continuo
1: Allegro
by Georg Philipp Telemann (1681–1767)

Actively discouraged from becoming a musician by his family, Telemann dutifully studied for a career in the law, but was so passionate about music that he effectively, as a sort of side-hustle, taught himself how to play multiple instruments including the violin, recorder, oboe, viola da gamba, chalumeau (a sort of early clarinet) and clavier (an early keyboard), as well as how to compose. And, boy, did he compose: some 3,600 works (that we know of) across a dizzying array of styles and forms, including opera, sacred music, secular cantatas, instrumental concertos, oratorios, a symphony and some stellar organ music.

Telemann has had a bit of a chequered history when it comes to musical reputation. A notoriously hard-to-please contemporary critic, Johann Mattheson, wrote during his lifetime that '*Telemann is above all praise*', but such a glowing assessment has not always been universally held. He fell largely out of favour in the nineteenth century, and it was only in the mid-twentieth century that a renewed interest in his intricate, melodic and often highly expressive music re-elevated him to a status that, for what it's worth, I believe he is well deserving of.

14 March

The Road Home
by Stephen Paulus (1949–2014)

It was a 2001 commission from a choir asking for a short 'folk'-type choral arrangement that led American composer Stephen Paulus to discover (and susbsequently 'fall in love' with) a tune called 'The Lone Wild Bird'. Collected in *The Southern Harmony Songbook* of 1835, the melody is built on a scale called the 'pentatonic' that has existed for centuries in all musical cultures around the world; in other words, it is one of humanity's most common and unifying musical expressions.

Having found the tune he would work with, Paulus then approached the Minnesota-based writer and librettist Michael Dennis Browne about writing some words; to his delight, Browne came up with an equally 'universal' theme. '*He writes,*' says Paulus, '*so eloquently about "returning" or "coming home" after being lost or wandering . . . often the most powerful and beautiful message is a simple one.*'

> *Tell me, where is the road*
> *I can call my own*
> *That I left, that I lost*
> *So long ago?*

15 March

Reflets – Reflections
by Lili Boulanger (1893–1918)

It was on this day in 1918 that the music world lost one of its most promising talents. Lili Boulanger was only twenty-four when her life was claimed by intestinal tuberculosis, or what we would now term Crohn's Disease. In her short time on earth she had proved spectacularly gifted: in 1913, she became the first woman, aged just nineteen, to win the most eminent composition prize of the day – the Prix de Rome, whose other recipients include such luminaries as Claude Debussy (13 January) and Henri Dutilleux (22 January). When she died she left behind instrumental works, choral pieces, an unfinished opera, and a handful of songs, including this dark but radiant setting of words by Maurice Maeterlinck.

Sous l'eau du songe qui s'élève	*Beneath the water of the dream that rises,*
Mon âme a peur, mon âme a peur.	*My soul is afraid, my soul is afraid.*
Et la lune luit dans mon coeur	*And the moon shines into my heart*
Plongé dans les sources du rêve!	*That is bathed in the dream's source!*
Sous l'ennui morne des roseaux,	*Beneath the sad tedium of the reeds,*
Seul le reflets profonds des choses . . .	*Only the deep reflection of things . . .*

Boulanger's older sister, Nadia (16 September), lived into her nineties and became one of the most important figures in twentieth-century music, teaching many of the greatest composers of the day. It hardly bears thinking about, what Lili might also have gone on to achieve had she lived, but at least – at least – there's this.

16 March

Salve regina in C Minor
1: 'Salve regina'
by Giovanni Battista Pergolesi (1710–1736)

Speaking of musical lives cut drastically short, today we mark the death from tuberculosis of an Italian Baroque genius. (The twenty-six-year-old Pergolesi died, it also breaks my heart to say, in abject poverty.) In the six short years he was active as a composer, he wrote highly original and achingly beautiful sacred music such as this, one of two settings of the Marian hymn *Salve regina*, as well as operas, oratorios, cantatas, masses and instrumental works. Although when he died he was hardly known outside his native Italy, his name achieved almost overnight posthumous fame in 1752, when an opera troupe performed one of his works, *La serva padrona* (*The Maid Turned Mistress*) in Paris. Something of a feeding frenzy for his music ensued, with certain unscrupulous publishers scribbling the name 'Pergolesi' over whatever they fancied in order to cash in on the sudden trend for his work. It's only since the late 1970s that scholarship has been undertaken to come up with a complete edition of his authentic works.

Along with a ravishing setting of the *Stabat mater*, this would have been among the very last music that Pergolesi wrote, stricken, having withdrawn in the last year of his life to a Capuchin monastery in Pozzuoli to try and preserve his last vestiges of strength. I find it heart-wrenchingly exquisite music; the knowledge that it was composed by a human being at the very close of a life that should, if things were just, have continued for many more decades, only makes it more moving.

17 March

Lorica of St Patrick
by Charles Villiers Stanford (1852–1924)

With words attributed to St Patrick (372–466) and his Irish ministry from the fifth century, this seems a fitting work for today, St Patrick's Day. Written in the style of a Druid's incantation, it's a prayer of protection for anyone who faces a long journey, invoking layer upon layer of blessings. The Dublin-born Stanford took the words and worked them into his own arrangement of an old melody from the Ancient Irish Church; the effect, I think, is beautiful.

We all need our protections. Whatever your personal belief system, or even if you have none, I hope you'll find solace not only in the blessings at the heart of the hymn but also in the simple consolations of the music.

18 March

Miocheries, op. 126, no. 13
'La toute petite s'endort' – 'The littlest falls asleep'
by Mel Bonis (1858–1937)

'*This is the borderland,*' says pianist Bertrand Chamayou, '*haunted by the most varied of emotions, from tenderness to fear, from the feeling of completeness that engenders peace of mind to the anguish of nothingness and fear of the dark*' . . . Oof! Chamayou – who I have to thank for introducing me to today's piece – says he wanted to explore the lullaby or 'berceuse', a very familiar musical trope, *because* it is too easily dismissed as a mere trifle – and I think he is fully vindicated.

'*It is here that the springs of delight and anxiety well up,*' he argues, '*where every being, in one way or another, experiences an overriding need for closeness and reassurance. It is these overlapping feelings, this emotional confluence, that I wanted to illustrate . . . No other musical genre communicates this so well as the berceuse. Behind its apparent simplicity, it expresses the quintessence of the human soul. It touches the hearts of children as much as it reawakens the innocence lying dormant beneath our adult shells.*'

It twists my heart, reading that and listening to Mel Bonis's very beautiful but also quietly devastating take on the berceuse, especially on this date. She died on this day, having never got over the death of her beloved younger son, five years previously.

19 March

Four Studies
3: 'Slow Canons'
by Nico Muhly (b. 1981)

'*It takes courage and confidence to leave out so much*' is how *Gramophone* magazine's critic Pwyll ap Siôn put it, with admirable pith, in a review of this 2014 work. Certainly courage and confidence are two qualities it is hard not to associate with the brilliant American composer Nico Muhly, a protégé of Philip Glass (14 February), who has worked across many different genres and with collaborators as varied as Anonhi, Sufjan Stevens and Björk but who cites Renaissance English polyphony as one of his greatest obsessions.

In this arresting and intriguing piece, Muhly employs the device of a musical drone – a technique which has existed, in many different musical cultures, for centuries – and intricately laces two minimalist solo violin lines around it to create a luminous and eerie soundscape. It's only a few minutes long but unlike anything I've heard.

20 March

Suite no. 2 in F major, HWV 427
1: Adagio
by George Frideric Handel (1685–1759)

Given that Handel was a legit celebrity of his day, an enterpreneurial game-changer who created such epic musical works as the *Music for the Royal Fireworks*, the *Water Music*, the *Messiah* and spectacular Coronation anthems that are still very much in use today, there is something almost heartbreakingly intimate about this fleeting little keyboard piece. It sounds almost improvised, impromptu; I hear in it a sort of private plea, something so tender and so human it's almost difficult to listen to. You wonder what's being exposed.

It's invariably a foolhardy and futile exercise to speculate about the possible connections between a composer's interior state of mind and the music they produce, but I can't help but think about the fact that Handel, for all his success and for all the emotion in his operas and oratorios, never married. What was going on in that heart of his? We know almost nothing about his private life, which is curious given he was such a prominent public figure in the dynamic musical scene of eighteenth-century London (he settled in the capital, having arrived from Germany in 1712, and became a naturalized British citizen in 1727; he was given a full state funeral and is buried in Westminster Abbey). Says Jacqueline Riding, director of London's Handel House Museum: *'None of his friends wrote much about him and apart from the fact he ate and drank too much and had a bad temper we don't know much about his feelings.'*

But maybe, just maybe, the music tells us all we need to know. Listen to the note of longing on which this movement ends: whatever inspired such wistfulness, it's hard to imagine music more deeply felt than this.

21 March

Vergnugte Ruh', beliebte Seelenlust – Delightful rest, beloved pleasure of the soul, BWV 170
1: Aria
by Johann Sebastian Bach (1685–1750)

Depending on whether you're consulting the old (Julian) or new (Gregorian) calendar, J. S. Bach was either born today, or on 31 March, so I have taken no chances and we'll be hearing his music on both days.

What to say about Bach that can possibly be sufficiently captured in mere words? One can spout platitudes like 'he is the father figure of Western music' and to be sure, he is: a single human being who contributed around three thousand pieces of music to the canon, each and every one of them extraordinary, arguably changing all of music for all time. But that doesn't even come close to it. There are innumerable reasons why he is supreme, but for me, speaking as a confused agnostic, a spiritually convinced non-believer, I think it ultimately comes down to the fact that Bach is quite simply the closest I come to the divine. When nothing makes sense, or when everything makes sense, there's Bach. From the most eviscerating tragedy to the purest elation, there's Bach. For everything in between, there's Bach. For every one of us, too, there's Bach. As the great keyboardist András Schiff put it, writing in 1999 on the eve of the 250th anniversary of Bach's death:

Bach was a deeply religious man. You don't have to share his belief, but the unique spirituality of his music unites players and listeners in a sense of community. That power has in no way diminished . . . since Bach's death, and it is sure to maintain its full force as long as music holds meaning for humanity.

As long as music holds meaning for humanity! Happy birthday to the greatest.

22 March

Recomposed: Vivaldi Four Seasons
'Spring 3'
by Max Richter (b. 1966)

After celebrating Bach's birthday (round one) yesterday, we have another birthday today: that of one of contemporary music's towering minds and a man who in many ways represents the peak of a tradition that draws its lineage right back to Bach. To be fair, you'd be hard pressed to find any composer writing today who doesn't connect in some way to Bach, whether consciously or not, but Max Richter exhibits this debt of gratitude with his own singular genius: like his predecessor, he is a phenomenal synthesizer of all that he hears around him, soaking up influences from a rich variety of sources. And yet everything he writes has its own distinctive, Richterian essence that sets it apart from the countless imitators who have since sprung up in his shadow.

In response to the statement that Bach was the *'supreme arbiter and law-giver of music'*, Richter once said: *'I wouldn't argue with that. I always feel like Bach is in a special case, really. If somebody says, "Well, what are your favorite composers?" really what they are saying is, "What are your favorite composers apart from Bach?" Because obviously Bach is your favorite composer if you are involved in music at all. It's a little bit like Mount Everest. There's Mount Everest and then there are all the other mountains. And Bach is the universal gravitation of music.'*

That being said, in today's piece, which I hope by now is appropriate for the season (at least in the northern hemisphere), Richter happens to be paying homage to another Baroque master (and Bach contemporary), Antonio Vivaldi. Taken from his phenomenal 2012 reworking of *The Four Seasons*, this 'Spring section' is three minutes of astonishing music that floors me every single time I hear it.

23 March

'Befreit' – 'Liberated'
from Five Songs, op. 39 no. 4
by Richard Strauss (1864–1949)

It was on this day that the German composer Richard Strauss first met his contemporary and countryman Richard Dehmel (1863–1920). It was an encounter which was to prove creatively fruitful: Dehmel was a poet and Strauss went on to set eleven of his poems to music, including this one, a moving text which evokes a couple in the midst of a parting. Dehmel explained that it might allude '*to any kind of loving couple. Such mutual elevations of the soul – at least noble souls – apply not only to death, but to any parting for life; for every leave taking is related to death, and what we give up for ever, we give back to the world . . .*'

Ich habe sie dir zur Welt geweitet;	*I made it our world, our joy to own it!*
O Glück!	*O Bliss!*

Strauss apparently said that he liked his songs best of all of his output, which also includes some of the era's most iconic operas and instrumental music. I remember the first time I ever heard one of his songs (see also 1 September); I couldn't believe that music – especially 'old' classical music like this – was capable of doing what it was doing, harmonically and melodically. It felt so bold, so jazzy, so almost-imperfect, so human. I basically fell in love on the spot, and in love I remain.

24 March

Spanish Dances, op. 37
1: 'Danza lenta'
by Enrique Granados (1867–1916)

Music by one of Spain's greatest composers today, and a man whose ability to draw on the colourful musical traditions of his homeland at the same time as keeping an ear on those of others would inspire many later Spanish musicians, including Manuel de Falla (26 December) and Pablo Casals; he was also much admired by other composers of the day who had an interest in how to incorporate folk music into original work – including Edvard Grieg and Camille Saint-Saëns.

This lush and lilting slow dance is undercut by a note of poignant melancholy. Having learned more about Granados' life – and death – I can never hear it without thinking of the tragic circumstances of this day in 1916. A man who was reluctant to travel, Granados had nevertheless been on tour in the USA and, after a last-minute decision to extend his trip, was finally on his way back home to Europe. But it was 1916, wartime hostilities were rife, and the boat he was travelling in across the English Channel, the *Sussex*, got torpedoed by a German U-boat. He managed to scramble into a lifeboat, but after spotting his wife, Amparo, flailing in the waters nearby, he leapt out to try to save her. They both drowned.

25 March

3 Hungarian Folksongs from Csík, BB 45b
1: Rubato
by Béla Bartók (1881–1945)

Speaking of an interest in folk traditions, we have a happier event to commemorate today: the birth of the man who would not only become the leading Hungarian composer of his day, but one of the most important and pioneering collectors of folksong in musical history.

It was in 1907 that Béla Bartók set off by train for a two-month sojourn in the Eastern Carpathian mountains with a mission to listen, record and gather folk music from the Székely people he encountered there. The trip was incredibly fruitful, and among the countless melodies he picked up in the Csík district, in what was then Transylvania, were three simple tunes played to him on a peasant flute, which he duly set for piano. Such music was elemental, for sure, yet extraordinarily powerful: as *The New Yorker*'s critic Alec Ross notes, it offered Bartók '*a deeper understanding of folk style, which led to a transformation of his own musical language*'. That language in turn has gone on to shape a raft of twentieth-century composers – and so it goes on: the continuum of human inspiration and influence.

26 March

Double Sextet
1: Fast
by Steve Reich (b. 1936)

'*I do think it's one of the better pieces I've done in the past few years*' is how today's composer Steve Reich modestly reacted to the news that this piece had won the 2009 Pulitzer Prize for Music.

The twentieth century had seen a vogue in European and American classical music for atonality, if not a complete turning on its head of almost a millennium's worth of tonal status quo in the 'serialism' or 'twelve-tone music' that emerged from the Second Viennese School, thanks to composers such as Arnold Schoenberg (13 September), Anton Webern and Alban Berg. Reich, along with the likes of Philip Glass (14 February), represents a musical return to something far more tonal, rhythmic, emotionally meditative and even melodic, without sacrificing a jot of intellectual vibrancy or spirit of sonic adventure: this is music that is far from 'conservative'. Indeed, Reich often utilizes technology as another musical voice, setting live playing against tape recording and loops, as in groundbreaking works such as 1967's *Violin Phase* or this piece, which is composed for two identical sets of sextets, each comprised of flute, clarinet, violin, cello, vibraphone and piano, and in which he specifies that it can either be performed by twelve live humans or by six playing against a recorded tape.

Reich, Glass and other 'first-generation minimalists', as they are sometimes known, created a revolution, changing not only American music but, I would argue, *all* music, from pop and rock to jazz and hip-hop. Those chill beats you might hear at a yoga class? Those are, in a big way, down to Reich. That gently looping piano vibe on a movie soundtrack that really got under your skin? That too. As one critic puts it simply: '*He is a universal composer.*'

27 March

'Bevo al tuo fresco sorriso' – 'I drink to
your intoxicating smile'
from *La Rondine*
by Giacomo Puccini (1858–1924)

Today we revel in a straight-up unabashed love song, opera-style, with a gorgeous moment from one of Puccini's least-performed operas, *La Rondine* (*The Swallow*), which was premiered in Monte Carlo on this day in 1917. If the opera itself lacks the greatness of some of Puccini's other hits – think *La Bohème*, *Tosca*, *Madama Butterfly* – this soaring quartet more than holds its own. As two couples come together towards the end of one of opera's least overblown plots they raise a toast which I think we can all get behind: *Let us drink to love!*

Inneggiamo alla vita	*Let us sing to life*
che ci donò l'amor!	*that gave us love!*

28 March

10 Preludes, op. 23
No. 10 in G flat major: Largo
by Sergei Rachmaninov (1873–1943)

A hauntingly lovely piece today, marking the death on this day of one of music's all-time greats, Sergei Rachmaninov. The phenomenal Russian composer and pianist, who fled to the USA after the Russian Revolution and finally settled in California, was experiencing financial difficulty in 1903 when he holed up in a Moscow hotel to write the set of preludes from which this gorgeous closing movement comes. But if the motivation to produce this music was largely driven by financial necessity, in no way is the art compromised: even in this fleeting vignette, Rachmaninov harnesses the gifts of soaring melody, exalting expressiveness and rich musical colour that are the hallmarks of his more expansive works such as the great symphonies and piano concertos.

Rachmaninov was a gigantic-handed prodigy with a memory bordering on genius, who produced his first piano concerto at the age of eighteen and went on to create some of the most wonderful music ever written for the piano. But the critics were not always kind and the harshest of all critics was undoubtedly himself: he suffered from crippling bouts of depression, writer's block and self-doubt throughout his whole life. '*A composer's music should express the country of his birth, his religion, his love affairs,*' he once said. '*It should be the sum total of his experience.*' Rachmaninov certainly had a whole lot of life experience to express, and we are the lucky beneficiaries of the fact he could do so through music as beautiful as this.

29 March

Waltz
from *Eugene Onegin*
by Pyotr Ilyich Tchaikovsky (1840–1893)

After yesterday's Rachmaninov, today a cheery and uplifting waltz by one of the composers who was most directly influential to him, Pyotr Ilyich Tchaikovsky. It was on this day in 1879 that Tchaikovsky's magnificent take on Pushkin's verse-novel *Eugene Onegin* was premiered, at the Maly Theatre in Moscow. Although the initial critical response was lukewarm, the opera – or 'lyric scenes in three acts', as the composer described it – was later acknowledged as a masterpiece, a bold work that rejected the fashion of the time for grand plots focusing on Russian history or mythology by instead daring to turn inward towards a more domestic, emotional, intimate setting. As one musicologist puts it, the *'radically new' Eugene Onegin 'rails against the societal conventions its composer loathed'*. Tchaikovsky was certainly unashamedly sympathetic towards his spurned heroine, Tatyana, and openly scornful of the 'cad' Onegin who rejects her; in many ways he wears his own highly emotional heart on his sleeve, which is why the music packs such a punch.

30 March

Ave generosa
by Hildegard of Bingen (c. 1098–1179)

To one of the most extraordinary figures from the Medieval era today, the polymathic Christian visionary, medic, writer, poet, composer and very early feminist Hildegard of Bingen. Hildegard was just a young girl when her parents offered her up to the church, as was apparently the custom for the tenth child in a family. Having experienced visions since she was three years old, she was sent to a remote hilltop monastery called Disibodenberg where she was to spend almost forty years sequestered with a group of other nuns in a stone cell, away from the monks.

Hildegard was a prolific writer, producing books on theology, medicine and natural healing as well as over four hundred letters. We know that it was sometime after 1136 that she began producing music, presumably for her fellow nuns, but we know very little about the circumstances in which she could compose: whether she wrote her songs on a tablet or slate or parchment, or whether someone else notated them for her; whether she wrote the words first. But she was dedicated to the cause: her extraordinary collection of music and poetry, *Symphonia armonie celestium revelationum*, brings together seventy-seven songs and poems that make up a liturgical cycle for the church year, as well as a morality play called *Ordo virtutum*, which explores the tussle between seventeen Virtues and the Devil for the destiny of a female soul.

Hildegard's music is characterized by an almost improvisatory melodic freedom, creating an ethereal sound world that points far forward into the distant future; it is perhaps this that gives her compositions such a sense of timelessness.

31 March

Herr, gehe nicht ins Gericht – Lord, do not pass judgement on your servant, Cantata BWV 105
3: Aria: 'Wie zittern und wanken Der Sünder Gedanken' – 'How the thoughts of the sinner tremble and waver'
by Johann Sebastian Bach (1685–1750)

An unapologetic second celebration of Bach's birthday today (see also 21 March) with a cantata that he apparently dashed off in just a couple of days. Although Bach wrote many thousands of pieces across different forms and genres, it is in his vocal music, reckons conductor John Eliot Gardiner, that the *'beating heart'* of the man is revealed. I'm inclined to agree: here he is, yes, a man wrought through with the divine – and exploring, in this cantata as in many others, the complex intricacies of a Christian faith – but also defiantly and gloriously human. A man who loved and lost and laughed and had friends and made mistakes and picked himself up and went on, as we all do. It might sound crazy, but I think one of the things I love most about Bach's music is how non-judgmental, how tolerant, it somehow is. It creates something like a safe space, in today's parlance, in which to show up with your whole self, wrestle with the most profound questions about what it is to be human, what it is to be. And it offers consolation. I can't explain why, but it does.

Happy birthday, again, my hero.

APRIL

1 April

Nautilus
by Anna Meredith (b. 1978)

Fresh fanfare beats for a brand new month today from one of British music's brightest lights, the Scottish-born Anna Meredith MBE. A former Composer-in-Residence with the BBC Scottish Symphony Orchestra, Meredith's magnificently distinctive work has been performed everywhere from the BBC Proms to the 2012 Cultural Olympiad. The '*classical polymath*', as the music website *Pitchfork* puts it, works across multiple genres with a wide array of collaborators; as such her music is gratifyingly hard to categorize and her approach to sound has been described as '*a playground*'. As one interview notes: '*Using years of classical training and a decade-long career in composition, she manipulates the tools in her toybox to bend sound and create challenging new forms that dance on the edges of genre.*'

I love that phrase '*dancing on the edges of genre*'. And Meredith seems to have embraced that category-elusion with glee. '*I love that there seems to be lots of places that this music can sit,*' she says. '*There's lots of options for where people want to take it . . . All of us want to try to contextualize things . . . that's totally human. But I try to filter most of it out.*' Above all, she says: '*I'm always looking for stuff that feels joyful.*' Hard to argue with that.

2 April

Alma redemptoris mater
by Dobrinka Tabakova (b. 1980)

After Anna Meredith yesterday, today we hear from another outstanding contemporary voice in British music, the Grammy-nominated composer Dobrinka Tabakova, and her setting of the timeless Marian hymn *Alma redemptoris mater* (we heard Palestrina's back in February).

'Accessible and communicative' is how one critic describes Tabakova's music; for her own part she says she is attracted to music *'that grabs you and has something to say'*. Although she writes in many different forms, for everything from the accordion to the violin, I find myself drawn again and again by the sustained lines of her choral writing – including this work, which was commissioned as part of the 750th anniversary celebrations of Merton College, Oxford, in 2014. *'Some of my fondest musical memories,'* Tabakova admits, *'are when I sang in school or chapel choir, so to be able to create a work which might become a great memory for some of the performers is a wonderful opportunity.'*

3 April

Piano Quintet in F sharp minor, op. 67
3: Allegro agitato – Adagio coma prima – Presto
by Amy Beach (1867–1944)

'. . . *she played the piano at four years, memorizing everything that she heard correctly*', wrote Amy Beach's mother. '*Her gift for composition showed itself in babyhood before two years of age. She could . . . improvise a perfectly correct alto to any soprano air I might sing.*'

Beach (née Cheney; she only published under her husband's name) is often described as the 'first' American female composer, which always gets my goat as there must have been many, many more Americans identifying as female who were compelled to write music before the late nineteenth century, but there we go. The precociously gifted Beach certainly blazed a trail: the premiere of this piece of chamber music, in Boston in 1908, led critics to proclaim it '*truly substantial, free, variously imagined and restlessly expressive music*' as well as '*truly modern*' and '*in the fashion of our time*'. It's hard to overstate what an achievement it was for a woman of Beach's well-to-do status to break through in this way. After she'd been married, at eighteen, to an eminent Bostonian doctor, he'd obliged her to withdraw from her budding career as a concert pianist. And although he oh-so-kindly allowed her to keep working on her composing behind closed doors, he forbade her from studying with a composition teacher.

The result is that the largely self-taught Beach's music has its own distinct language, even as it incorporates aspects of the Romanticism of the preceding era and the European composers she held in such high esteem, including Brahms. Far from conservative, even if it doesn't exactly push formal boundaries, her music brims with an energy and sincerity that I find hugely appealing.

4 April

Ave Maria
by Igor Stravinsky (1882–1971)

Completed in Paris on this day in 1934, this ravishing setting of the *Ave Maria* reflects a renewed interest from Stravinsky, one of the most influential composers of the twentieth century, in the Orthodox traditions of his Russian homeland. Exiled in Paris, by the mid-1920s he had begun to attend Orthodox services along with other Russian émigrés, and was moved to produce a selection of works based on church texts.

This is not, it's fair to say, one of Stravinsky's greatest hits – unlike, say, the infamous ballet *The Rite of Spring*, which was an absolute game-changer when it premiered in 1913, or other scores he wrote for Diaghilev's Ballets Russes such as *Petrushka* or *The Firebird*. But to me it is profoundly beautiful; its swaying, haunting vocal lines get me every time.

By the way – fun fact – it is thanks to Stravinsky's close friend, muse and fellow artistic powerhouse Nadia Boulanger (sister of Lili, whom we encountered last month) that we have this piece in our midst at all. While some of the other Orthodox-based works that he wrote around this time have not survived, Boulanger kept the autograph score in her possession and was an ardent public advocate for its brief but powerful impact, apparently describing it as one of her favourite Stravinsky works to conduct.

5 April

Pavane pour une infante défunte – Pavane for a Dead Princess
by Maurice Ravel (1875–1937)

I sometimes wonder what it must have been like, to have been sitting in the audience at the Société Nationale de Musique concert in Paris on this day in 1902, and to hear this extraordinary music unfold, note by note, for the very first time in public. What a gift!

A pavane is a form of slow, processional dance that was all the rage in the courts of Europe during the sixteenth and seventeenth centuries. The *infante* or *infanta* of the title refers to a young Spanish princess. Maurice Ravel, who was born right on the French border with Spain, always had an enthusiasm for Spanish culture and customs, and although he was not paying tribute here to any specific dead *infanta*, he described the piece as '*an evocation of a pavane that a little princess might, in former times, have danced at the Spanish court*'.

With its air of contained melancholy and alluring mystique, it's not quite typical of Ravel's early modernist style, but it's a stone-cold masterpiece, and was a smash hit from the outset. Such was the demand to hear it in all sorts of contexts, he arranged it in an orchestral version in 1910: both versions have remained enduringly popular; firm favourites among concert programmers and audiences alike.

6 April

More sweet than my refrain
by Howard Skempton (b. 1947)

A tender vocal miniature today from one of Britain's greatest contemporary composers, laying aside his usual adventures in experimentalism to set a radiant fragment by Ralph Waldo Emerson, the great American poet who celebrated the existence of the sublime in both humanity and nature.

> *More sweet than my refrain*
> *Was the first drop of April rain*

Enough said, really.

7 April

Night Bird
by Karen Tanaka (b. 1971)

Happy birthday to the Tokyo-born composer Karen Tanaka, protégé of the great French musician Pierre Boulez and one of Japan's leading contemporary composers.

This might sound crazy, but I find listening to this piece is like stepping over a threshold and falling into some sort of other dimension. It's so incredibly eerie and beautiful, with the mournful lines of the alto saxophone offset by an otherworldly backdrop of tape, electronics and gentle percussion effects.

Many of Tanaka's works reflect her passion for the natural world and concern for the environment, but this piece, which was composed in 1996, turns somewhat inward, towards a place of quiet human intimacy. 'Night Bird,' she tells us, *'is a love song filled with tender whispers of lovers. I have tried to weave colours and scent into the sound . . .'*

8 April

Berceuse in D flat major, op. 57
by Frédéric Chopin (1810–1849)

In the spring of 1917, during the Great War, the Anglo-Welsh poet Edward Thomas spent ten weeks in France on the Western Front, where he kept a war diary. Against a context of horror that is all but unimaginable to most of us, his writing reveals a soul still open to receiving beauty, and that in itself becomes something profoundly redemptive. After a terrible night of trench warfare, for example, he manages to observe, with somehow sharpened senses: '*Beautiful was Arras yesterday coming down from Beaurains and seeing Town Hall ruin white in sun like a thick smoke beginning to curl . . .*'

One of the most desperately moving details in Thomas's war diary is the revelation that one of his men had brought a gramophone to the Western Front. Amid the quotidian horrors of the war, with its relentless shell fire, its indescribable toll, there was music to be heard: billeted in those deserted, desolate houses behind the front line, the men would play records, and Thomas, in his diary, would make a note of what they heard each day. One of the pieces they played was this piano lullaby, a vignette of utmost tenderness composed, quite late in his life, by the great Polish Romantic composer Frédéric Chopin.

8 April 1917 would be Edward Thomas's last day on this earth. He was killed fighting in the Battle of Arras the very next day. I like to imagine the possible consolation that he might have drawn from this music in the days leading up to his futile death. It is music, as the writer Robert Macfarlane (who told me the story about Thomas) describes it, that has the power to work on us like a '*quiet kind of miracle*'.

9 April

Memory Mist
by Florence Price (1887–1953)

Today we celebrate the birth of the composer, organist and teacher Florence Price, a remarkable musician for whom the term 'pioneering' barely covers it. Born in Little Rock, Arkansas, she showed musical talent from an early age, but when local white piano teachers refused to teach her because she was African-American, it fell upon her mother to step in. In 1904, Price was accepted into the esteemed New England Conservatoire, where, although racism was rife (she allegedly passed herself off as Mexican to avoid the worst of it), she managed to attain not one but two diplomas. A local lynching in 1927 prompted her to flee from Little Rock to Chicago with her young family, and it was here, in 1933, that she became the first Black woman ever to have her music performed by a major American ensemble, when the celebrated Chicago Symphony Orchestra premiered her Symphony no. 1.

It is a work on a much more intimate scale with which we celebrate Price today: a brief and fleeting track that nevertheless contains multitudes. Price was sixty-two when she wrote this, which may account for the looking-back-in-time vibe of the title, but far from an abstract mist it rather evokes a sort of pristine statement of intent. It's somehow all here, in the dreamy melody, bluesy harmonies and inventive dissonances: the roots, the flowering, everything Price lived through; it's all here.

10 April

The Lamentations of Jeremiah the Prophet:
Lamentations for Holy Wednesday
Lamentatio 1
by Jan Dismas Zelenka (1679–1745)

Today we travel back to the era of Bohemian Baroque and a composer whose harmonic innovations, structural daring and dazzling way with counterpoint have been almost entirely – and I would argue, unfairly – forgotten. In his day, the Czech-born, largely Dresden-based composer Zelenka was friends with the likes of Telemann and a colleague of J. S. Bach; we know from letters that Zelenka even entrusted Bach's eldest son to work as a copyist on some of his music. Nevertheless, his idiosyncratic and zingy music – which exhibits many of the same qualities as standard German Baroque works with a dynamic nod towards Czech folk traditions – fell gradually out of favour; it is largely only down to the work, 150 or so years later, of another Czech composer, Bedřich Smetana (28 September), that interest in his music has picked up at all. In 1863, Smetana presented some of Zelenka's work in Prague, and he also delved through the archives of Dresden to rework some of the original Zelenka scores.

Despite Smetana's efforts, much of Zelenka's music remains unknown and unrecorded, but it is surely ripe for revival. This piece is almost thirteen minutes long, but it unfolds with such sustained drama, via such crunchy dissonances and such blissful resolutions, that I find it always rewards a listen handsomely.

11 April

Beyond
by Charlotte Bray (b. 1982)

A protégé of the late, great Oliver Knussen (8 July) and Mark-Anthony Turnage (10 June), two of contemporary British music's most significant composers, Charlotte Bray is fast snapping at their heels. Despite her relative youth, she has been commissioned by leading ensembles, including the London Symphony Orchestra, the City of Birmingham Symphony Orchestra and Britten Sinfonia, and has had her work performed at major institutions, including the Royal Opera House and BBC Proms.

The piece we'll hear today is an intimate work, calling not for large forces such as a symphony orchestra, but rather a single violin. First performed on this day in 2015, Bray wrote this brief, haunting solo violin work as a gift for a friend '*on his departure and return to his homeland of Israel*'. She explains: '*An impassioned melody flows freely and sweetly. I wanted to principally explore the dark lower register of the instrument, as well as the special sound quality found high on each string. Long questioning phrases hang in the air, yet a sense of closure is finally reached.*'

12 April

Mass in A minor
4: Sanctus – Benedictus
by Imogen Holst (1907–1984)

Imogen Holst – known to her friends as 'Imo' – was the only child of Gustav Holst, the man who composed *The Planets* and became a towering figure in early-twentieth-century British music. As such, her own achievements in music have been somewhat eclipsed (no pun intended), but her compositional voice was exceedingly fine; she was, according to fellow composer Colin Matthews, *'inimitable'*; a *'seemingly austere, thoughtful'* person who could nevertheless *'explode with enthusiasm'*.

As well as a talented composer, Imogen was a keen arranger of folk songs, a gifted writer, a conductor, administrator and amanuensis to the great composer Benjamin Britten (22 June), who became a close friend and associate. Her Mass in A minor shows her particular gift for writing vocal music that is spare and evocative and distinctive.

13 April

Piano Trio in D major, op.1
1: Allegro non troppo, con espressione
by Erich Wolfgang Korngold (1897–1957)

The publication in 1910 of this piece stunned the musical world at the time, written as it was by a thirteen-year-old boy. There is not a hint of juvenilia about the thing: with its playful rhythms and rather louche harmonies, it hints at a nocturnal sophistication that evokes the world of fin-de-siècle Vienna and its transformative revolutions in art, literature and music. No wonder Gustav Mahler declared the boy a genius and Richard Strauss was such a fan.

Having fled the Nazi regime in 1934, Korngold would go on to have a stellar career in opera in Hollywood, writing some of the most iconic movie scores of the era. I think those gifts for narrative and finely honed dramatic instincts are all on display in this first published work, which he sweetly dedicated to his father.

14 April

Avril 14th
by Richard D. James, aka Aphex Twin (b. 1971)
arr. Christian Badzura (b. 1977)

And breathe. This simple, lullaby-like piece has an instantly restorative effect on me. Originally written for piano, it also works a treat when arranged for violin. And in case you're wondering what on earth music by an electronic/dance producer like Aphex Twin is doing in a book about classical music, I actually discovered this gorgeous arrangement on the album *For Seasons* from leading classical violinist Daniel Hope and Deutsche Grammophon, which is arguably the most prestigious classical label in the world. As I've said before: music is music.

15 April

Partita for 8 voices
2: Sarabande
by Caroline Shaw (b. 1982)

It was on this day in 2013 that the American composer Caroline Shaw became the youngest ever winner of the Pulitzer Prize for Music, for the *Partita* from which this movement comes, and the world – including Kanye West – fell in love. Shaw is also a producer and a busy violinist, violist and vocalist, collaborating with many of New York's most dynamic performers, including the vocal ensemble Roomful of Teeth and the Attacca Quartet. She's humble, funny, quick to laugh and devoid of pretension; an idealist who believes that music represents a model of democracy and listening from which we could all potentially learn.

I was going to try to describe the effect of this fantastically original work, but it's almost impossible. It eludes words, in the very best possible way: referencing everything from Georgian male voice vocal traditions to Korean *p'ansori* singing, it is unlike anything I have ever heard. I hope you'll simply open your ears and your hearts to its strange and wonderful power.

16 April

Magnolia
Part 1, no. 1: 'Magnolias'
by R. Nathaniel Dett (1882–1943)

A spray of musical magnolia today, courtesy of the Canadian-American composer (Robert) Nathaniel Dett, who descended from escaped slaves, and became, in 1908, the first Black student to complete the Bachelor of Music degree at Oberlin Conservatory, winning Phi Beta Kappa honours. Dett's later education included a stint at Harvard University and in France under the tutelage of the legendary pedagogue Nadia Boulanger (16 September); other major influences in the evolution of his style included Samuel Coleridge-Taylor (15 August) and Antonín Dvořák (10 February), not to mention the traditional spirituals he heard growing up. Dedicating his life and work to music and education, Nathaniel Dett became a learned and highly respected pianist, organist, choral director, esteemed music professor and brilliant composer, as we shall hear today.

I find that whatever state I'm in, its aura of freshness and rebirth – complete with a quick April shower in the middle – cannot fail to improve my mood. Consider it a three-and-a-half-minute dose of musical springtime.

17 April

O Maria, tu dulcis
by Chiara Margarita Cozzolani (1602–c. 1676/8)

Believe it or not, seventeenth-century Italy was something of a hotbed when it came to producing outstandingly musical nuns, of which today's composer is a fine example. We don't know a huge amount about Margarita Cozzolani, who took 'Chiara' as a holy name, other than that she was cloistered, for her entire adult life, in the Benedictine convent of Santa Radegonda in Milan, just across the street from the duomo. Reports from the time testify to the crowds of people that would flock to the 'exterior church', which was open to the public, to hear groups of nuns singing her radiant music.

Between 1640 and 1650 Cozzolani wrote prolifically, producing at least four volumes of music, two of which survive complete. Later, when she became Abbess at Santa Radegonda, she seems to have stopped composing, but was nevertheless instructive in guiding the convent through a time of tension when the super-strict Archbishop Alfonso Litta sought to limit the nuns' 'irregular' contact with the outside world, including the practice of music.

It might sound unlikely that a composing nun could achieve a fanbase, but how's this for a review? In 1670, one Filippo Picinelli wrote: '*The nuns of Santa Radegonda are gifted with such rare and exquisite talents in music that they are acknowledged to be the best singers of Italy . . . Among these sisters, Donna Chiara Margarita Cozzolani merits the highest praise . . . for her unusual and excellent nobility of [musical] invention.*'

18 April

Requiem
5. Recordare
by Franz von Suppé (1819–1895)

History has not been kind to poor Franz von Suppé, who was born Francesco Ezechiele Ermenegildo Cavaliere Suppé Demelli in what is now Split, Croatia, on this day. A composer of some thirty operettas and at least 180 stage works, including ballets, comedies and farces, his music has sunk into near-obscurity, even despite featuring in episodes of *Bugs Bunny*, *Betty Boop*, *Popeye* and *Mickey Mouse*. (In *Popeye the Sailor*, for example, Popeye conducts a performance of Suppé's *Poet and Peasant Overture*, renamed the *Spinach Overture*).

Suppé was musically precocious, writing his first Mass by the age of thirteen, but like many composers he was discouraged by his bourgeois family from pursuing his passion, and instead ended up studying law. After his father died, however, all bets were off: he steeped himself in the fashionable Italian opera hits of the day, including those by Verdi (22 May), Rossini (29 February) and his own distant relative Donizetti, and threw himself into composition, more than making up for lost time.

His is certainly not music that's going to change the world, unless you're *really* into cartoon soundtracks, but there is a certain flamboyance to Suppé's style that I find rather charming and engaging.

19 April

A Boy and a Girl
by Eric Whitacre (b. 1970)

Setting words by the Mexican poet Octavio Paz, who died on this day in 1998, this is a brief choral work by the hugely popular Grammy-winning American composer Eric Whitacre.

'"A Boy and a Girl" is such a tender, delicate, exquisite poem,' says Whitacre. 'I simply tried to quiet myself and find the music hidden within the words. I'm often asked which of my compositions is my favorite. I don't really have one that I love more than the others, but I do feel that the four measures that musically paint the text "never kissing" may be the truest notes I've ever written.'

As far as I'm concerned, truth like this can be a veritable spiritual oasis in our lives: it may last only a moment, but it delivers a certain sense of peace and stillness that resonates far beyond its means.

Tendidos bajo tierra	*Stretched out underground,*
una muchacha y un muchacho.	*a boy and a girl.*
No dicen nada, no se besan,	*Saying nothing, never kissing,*
cambian silencio por silencio.	*giving silence for silence.*

20 April

Call
by Julianna Barwick (b. 1981)

Another contemporary American composer today, this time one whose music leans into the world of ambient experimentalism and is often mentioned in the same breath as the likes of Brian Eno. But Barwick's compositional aesthetic is rooted in a classical tradition. '*I was in choirs my whole life,*' she once told *The New Yorker*. '*Voice lessons in high school, an opera chorus after high school. I was always making stuff up, singing out the window, making myself cry while singing to myself. My favorite songs were the mournful, emotional, beautiful ones.*'

This certainly falls into that category for me. One critic described her work as '*articulating the ineffable*', which is, I think, a brilliant way to evoke the tender, meditative, occasionally hypnotic web of sound that Barwick's music invariably spins.

21 April

Messe de Nostre Dame
1. Kyrie
by Guillaume de Machaut (c. 1300–1377)

From the hyper-modernism of yesterday, today we will be transported way, way back in time with music by the most significant composer of the medieval era, Guillaume de Machaut. The fourteenth-century Frenchman was also a prolific and widely celebrated poet (Chaucer was a fan, emulating Machaut's technical innovations in his own verse) and a key figure in the movement known as Ars Nova, which represents such a tremendous flowering of music and art of the time.

For Machaut, music and poetry were intricately entwined: he viewed the lyric and its setting as a single entity. And this piece is extraordinary to me. It is somehow ancient and timeless at once, with its isorhythmic patterns (where a rhythmic phrase is repeatedly over-lapped in different melodic forms), dissonant polyphony and brazen blue notes. There are parts that sound as though they could have been written yesterday, when in fact the Mass from which this comes, prob-ably written for Rheims Cathedral sometime in the 1360s, is the earliest known complete setting of the Ordinary of the Mass attribut-able to a single composer.

When I think of the immeasurable musical significance of the Mass in Western culture, with all the towering examples that would follow, from Bach to Mozart to Beethoven to Bruckner to Dvořák and indeed, tomorrow's composer Dame Ethel Smyth, it sends shivers down my spine to think that this is the *very first one*.

22 April

Serenade in D major
2: Scherzo: Allegro vivace – Allegro molto
by Ethel Smyth (1858–1944)

Happy birthday to British composer Dame Ethel Smyth, whom Tchai-kovsky once declared was '*one of the few women composers whom one can seriously consider to be achieving something valuable in the field of musical creation*'. That statement probably tells you all you need to know about the context of the time, underlining what an achievement it was that a woman could manage to break into the wholly male-dominated world of classical music *at all*, let alone achieve even a modicum of success.

This terrifically upbeat serenade was the piece with which Smyth announced herself, as a serious composer of orchestral music. It was successfully presented, in 1890, at the Crystal Palace Concerts series – possibly to the chagrin of her family, who were dismayed by her 'inappropriate' choice of career. Smyth would go on to write operas, symphonies and choral works, including a celebrated Mass in D; away from music she also became a leading figure in the British suffragette movement. Her composition *The March of Women* became the official anthem of the Women's Social and Political Union, and in March 1912 Smyth was arrested, alongside more than 100 other feminists, and sent to Holloway Prison.

In her writings Smyth comes across as a fantastically pragmatic, courageous sort. During the World War One, she worked as an assist-ant radiologist in a French military hospital from 1915 to 1918; when increasing deafness compromised her compositional abilities, she turned to writing and penned memoir after memoir – recounting her life in classical music, feminist activism, and as an open lesbian, discussing her romantic involvements with a slew of fabulous women of the day, including Virginia Woolf.

23 April

Three Shakespeare Songs, op. 6
1: 'Come Away, Death'
by Roger Quilter (1877–1953)

More British music today, and indeed from a direct contemporary of yesterday's composer, Dame Ethel Smyth. Roger Quilter was just one of the countless composers, from all over the globe and across the centuries, who have been inspired to write music to the immortal words of William Shakespeare (1564–1616), who may have been born and certainly died on this day.

Quilter can hardly be described as a major composer, but he nevertheless had considerable gifts which are often unfairly overlooked. He composed no fewer than seventeen Shakespeare songs, and this one, using words from Act 2, scene 1 of *Twelfth Night*, is a particularly fine example of his great facility with text setting. It shows an ear perfectly attuned to the stress of the words; as one critic notes, '*the two verses are nearly strophic, but not quite, and the wrenching climax appears on the word Shakespeare surely designed for the purpose, "weep"*'.

I find it somehow sorrowful and redemptive all at once.

Come away, come away, death,
And in sad cypress let me be laid;
Fly away, fly away, breath;
I am slain by a fair cruel maid.
My shroud of white, stuck all with yew,
O prepare it!
My part of death, no one so true
Did share it.

24 April

'Curtain Tune'
from *The Tempest*
by Matthew Locke (1621–1677)

Okay, I couldn't resist. More Shakespeare. This time from the man who was arguably the leading composer for the stage of his era, and music for a 1674 production of an opera version of *The Tempest*. The 'Curtain Tune' depicts the fateful shipwreck from which the rest of the plot emerges, and is full of engaging musical twists and turns.

Locke served King Charles in an official capacity and was succeeded in his role by none other than Henry Purcell (28 January), who wrote a mournful memorial ode after he died entitled 'What hope for us remains now he is gone?' Quite the ringing endorsement from the man who would himself go on to be one of the greatest composers England has ever produced.

25 April

Keltic Suite, op. 29
2: 'Lament'
by John Foulds (1880–1939)

Foulds represents a moment in early-twentieth-century British culture sometimes described as the English Musical Renaissance. Born in Manchester, a vibrantly musical city then as now, his father played bassoon in the legendary Hallé Orchestra, and Foulds himself joined the ensemble as a cellist at the age of twenty.

Cosmopolitan in outlook and unpretentious in style, as a (largely self-taught) composer he wrote vast amounts of so-called 'light music' and theatre scores as well as traditional classical forms including string quartets, symphonic poems, concertos and a 'concert opera'. But he was highly curious and also drawn to more experimental modalities: some of his music goes on to anticipate later trends in minimalism and tonal adventurousness, and reflects his fascination with Eastern, especially Indian, folk music, of which he was an inveterate collector. Long before such a notion was made fashionable by the likes of Ravi Shankar and Yehudi Menuhin or the Beatles, Foulds had a dream of creating a musical synthesis between East and West. In 1935 he became Director of European Music for All-India Radio in Delhi, putting together an orchestra from the ground up and composing music for ensembles containing traditional Indian instruments. In 1939, he was invited to open a new branch of the station in Calcutta. Within a week of arriving, however, he contracted cholera and died on this day.

This piece is unashamedly romantic, encapsulating a certain essential British nostalgia which has proved enduringly popular. I listen and I can't help but see rolling hills, perhaps a train journey, steam rising off a cup of tea – yet it manages not to curdle into cliché.

26 April

Anthracite Fields
4: 'Flowers'
by Julia Wolfe (b. 1958)

Premiered in Philadelphia on this day in 2014, *Anthracite Fields* is the Pulitzer Prize-winning work by American composer Julia Wolfe.

Written for the unusual combination of chorus and sextet, the oratorio evokes Pennsylvania coal-mining life around the turn of the twentieth century. The local-born Wolfe, who has described the piece as '*almost a public history project*', spent over a year researching the work. '*I [have] this fascination . . . with labor history and somehow finding a way to tell that story in music,*' she told NPR. '*I wrote the text – I really gleaned the text – because I'm taking from oral histories and political speeches and texts of ballads . . . It's not a literal narrative. It really is getting at the story from many different angles.*'

Classical music is so often accused of being inward-looking and somehow elevated, unconcerned with the complex realities of human life as it is actually lived. Wolfe represents the opposite of such complacency. '*Here's this life and who are we in relationship to that? We're them. They're us. And, basically, these people, working underground, under very dangerous conditions, fueled the nation.*'

Small but revealing details abound. While speaking to a daughter and granddaughter of a miner, Wolfe heard that women in the small mining villages would try to bring a degree of colour and joy to their impoverished existences using flowers. Wolfe builds on that simple image, having the chorus sing a list of those flowers during this section, and it is so moving and powerful.

We're them. They're us.

27 April

Romance
by Alexander Scriabin (1871–1915)

Music by the Russian composer Scriabin today, a very unusual figure for his time. He was a mystic, much intrigued by the possibilities of musical symbolism, Gnosticism and theosophy, and his work is laced with these ideas throughout. His Third Symphony was said to represent *'the evolution of the human spirit from pantheism to unity with the universe'*, for example, and he also talked of an all-embracing *'Mystery'* in his grandiose orchestral works, in which music, poetry, dancing, colours and scents would apparently unite to induce in audiences a *'supreme, final ecstasy'*.

Whether or not this somewhat more gentle *Romance* for horn or cello and piano elicits such a reaction in you remains to be seen, but whatever its effect, I hope you'll agree it's a work of tender and searching beauty.

28 April

Five Songs, op. 105
1: 'Wie Melodien zieht es mir' – 'It moves like a melody'
by Johannes Brahms (1833–1897)
arr. Jascha Heifetz (1901–1987)

Written with a young singer in mind, the achingly lyrical melody of this love song by Brahms also works beautifully when transposed to the violin, courtesy of the violinist Jascha Heifetz (who apparently preferred the title *Contemplation* for his remix). Heifetz produced the solo violin version in 1933, but it was not recorded until the great Scottish violinist Nicola Benedetti (who, as it happens, was born the year Heifetz died) committed it to disc, in this orchestrated version of unabashed lushness.

Compared to some of Brahms's larger works – the magnificent symphonies, the iconic instrumental concertos and game-changing chamber music – this song in some ways is a mere bagatelle. And yet it is the sort of piece I might turn to when I need a quick sonic fix: a little over three minutes of purely lovely music. Sometimes, I find, that's enough; that's more than enough.

29 April

Black, Brown and Beige Suite
1: Introduction
by Duke Ellington (1899–1974)
arr. Nigel Kennedy (b. 1956)

I once asked my former BBC Radio 3 colleague Rob Cowan, who has possibly the most encyclopedic knowledge of classical music of anyone I know, who in his view was the greatest composer of the twentieth century. He answered: Duke Ellington. This might come as a surprise, given Ellington's reputation as the king of jazz, but Ellington himself was animated by the phrase *'beyond category'* as an organizing principle. For him there were only two types of music: 'good' and 'bad'. It goes without saying that he composed, across some two thousand pieces, a hell of a lot of good.

Edward Kennedy Ellington was born on this day in Washington, D.C. In addition to his inestimable contribution to the world of jazz he wrote symphonic music, operas, concertos, oratorios, suites for orchestra and, in 1943 became the first African-American bandleader to play Carnegie Hall with his extraordinary, symphony-like epic *Black, Brown and Beige*, which he described as *'a parallel to the history of the American Negro'*.

Yet, as his biographer explains: *'Ellington struggled to achieve acceptance in the world of classical music, beset with institutional racism and widespread disdain toward jazz and popular music. A few discerning composers seemed to "get" him, such as Percy Grainger and Constant Lambert, but in 1943 classical music critics were not kind to his magnum opus.'*

It must have been a source of great frustration not to receive the recognition he deserved. Then again, as Ellington himself quipped: *'Critics have their purposes . . . but sometimes they get a little carried away with what they think someone should have done, rather than concerning themselves with what they did.'* Touché, Duke.

30 April

Songs Without Words
2: 'Lied' – 'Song'
by Anne Cawrse (b. 1981)

To my shame, it was comparatively recently that I discovered today's composer, but what a treasure trove awaited me when I started delving into her work.

Born in rural South Australia, to a non-musical farming family, Anne Cawrse composes music with unpretentious intelligence and a beguiling directness. Very rarely programmed outside of her own country – yet! – I reckon she deserves a wider audience. (As, I hardly need to say, *so* many composers do, especially those who happen to be not white and male. Anyway! Onwards . . .)

Remembering how she started to explore her own compositional voice at school, Cawrse explains: '*It was Mr Garwood, my [school music teacher], who suggested I try my hand at the subject Composing and Arranging in Year 12 . . . What I recall most,*' she says in an interview with the Australian organization Music Trust, '*is spending hundreds of hours on [this] – far more time than I did practising piano, or studying any other subject – and it never feeling like work. It was fascinating, exciting, and intriguing; the way I could put notes down on manuscript and manipulate them to make a sound that to my (naïve) ears hadn't existed before.*'

Like many contemporary composers, Cawrse says she particularly enjoys creating music for others to play or sing – in, as it were, real time. '*That fact alone has probably influenced my writing and approach to the artform more than any other.*' She adds: '*Connection, too, is increasingly important – connection with audiences, performers, students, friends, and the wider community. There is a communion in music making that is unlike anything else; a coming together in a space that is all about communicating very real, very big feelings, but doesn't necessarily need words to do so.*'

MAY

1 May

From the Bohemian Forest, op. 68, B. 133
5: 'Waldesruhe' – 'Silent Woods'
by Antonín Dvořák (1841–1904)
arr. Lothar Niefind and Gunter Ribke

In this book, I don't generally press my readers to listen to a certain performance of a piece, let alone a certain arrangement of a piece. But today, I am making an exception.

Nineteenth-century audiences were voracious in their demand for new arrangements of 'popular' works in all imaginable combinations of instruments. The trend occasionally continues with so-called 'classical' works – this genre having lost the 'popular' moniker long ago – to this day.

This particular modern arrangement for solo cello and cello ensemble, made for the exceptional young Austrian-Iranian cellist Kian Soltani (b. 1992) and members of the Berlin Philharmonic, is, I hope you'll agree, utterly charming.

Antonín Dvořák, the son of a butcher and innkeeper, was born in a small village on the Vltava River, not far from Prague. Despite these humble beginnings, Dvořák rose to become one of the most famous Czech composers of his time (maybe *all* time) producing around 200 significant works, including fourteen string quartets, twelve operas and nine symphonies – of which the ninth, the iconic Symphony 'From the New World', is quite familiar even to non-classical audiences. (Hovis bread, anyone?)

Altogether less epic, but in its miniature way, still telling a whole story – as Kian Soltani describes it, Dvořák had *'insatiable creativity'* – this piece is five and a half minutes of romance without a cliché in sight. I find it hopelessly touching. Especially when I listen to it today, the day that Dvořák died.

2 May

Concerto for recorder and two violins in A minor
2: Largo
by Alessandro Scarlatti (1660–1725)

Today we enjoy a two-minute sliver of Baroque beauty from a composer whose achievements have often been overlooked for those of his brilliant son Domenico, who produced a breathtaking contribution to the keyboard canon. But Scarlatti *père* deserves recognition for his operas, religious works and courtly entertainment pieces, as well as instrumental works such as this one. He clearly had a great knack for a good theme, and his formal innovations and use of chromatic harmony was prescient, prefiguring much of what was to come in the future Classical and Romantic eras.

3 May

Rosary Sonata no. 16 in G Minor for solo violin
Passacaglia
by Heinrich Ignaz Franz von Biber (1644–1704)

Today we stay in the Baroque era, and mark the anniversary of the death of a composer who, in his day, single-handedly pushed the limit of what the violin – and a violinist – might be capable of.

The Rosary Sonatas – also known as the 'Mystery Sonatas' – from which this mournful, intricate, complex piece comes, were likely written around 1676, but their manuscript was lost until the late nineteenth century and they were not widely known until 1905, when they were finally published. Technically fiendish, abounding in outrageously demanding multi-string chords, this piece also requires of its player great heart, or it can come across as rather cold and mathematical. Played well, though, with the right balance of virtuosity and soul, I find its spare, clear lines have the effect of a mental detox; I listen and it's as though my brain is somehow re-wired. Incredible.

4 May

L'Ondine
by Cecile Chaminade (1857–1944)

Published in 1900, this glittering little tone-sketch for solo piano depicts a water sprite, deftly rendered with fluid arpeggios (broken chords) and rippling pianistic effects that have a pianist traversing the whole keyboard.

Born into a bourgeois Parisian family, Chaminade showed such musical promise as a little girl that the famous Georges Bizet, composer of *Carmen* and a family friend, described her as a '*little Mozart*'. Defying her father, who was appalled at her desire to forge a career in music, Chaminade went on to publish some 400 pieces, and in 1913 became the first woman admitted to the Order of the Legion of Honour, the premier order of the French Republic.

Her piano music is elegant, tuneful, vivacious and as rewarding to play, according to the concert pianist Joanne Polk, as it is to listen to. '*She writes wonderfully for the piano,*' Polk observes. '*Favourably, comfortably, and idiomatically.*' Of course, such attractive properties have proved no protection against the sexism that has long sidelined female composers, including Chaminade, but hopefully, well over a century since fellow composer Ambroise Thomas declared, '*This is not a woman who composes, but a composer who happens to be a woman,*' we're gradually moving in the right direction.

5 May

Sacred Origins
by Ola Gjeilo (b. 1978)

The Norwegian-born, New York-based composer Ola Gjeilo has an intricate working relationship with the external world. Not for him scribbling away in an ivory tower, entirely disconnected from reality: instead he takes practical inspiration from getting out and about and working with his surroundings. *'I often record my musical ideas and listen to them further in an outside element,'* he says, *'throughout the city or its parks. If the music corresponds with the beauty of the surroundings, it's a sign that the music might be on the right path.'*

Other influences on Gjeilo's ethereally beautiful music include jazz improvisation (his father was an amateur trombonist and saxophonist), film music, sacred texts, and choral music by composers such as Bach, Brahms and Handel. As a student at New York's Juilliard School he was also apparently much inspired by contemporary American figures such as Eric Whitacre (19 April), Morten Lauridsen (11 January) and John Corigliano (16 February), a professor at the school. Yet, in a pretty crowded field, Gjeilo has managed to cultivate a stunningly distinctive musical language of his own. I take great solace from the evocative and atmospheric impact of his shimmering musical lines, which often have the curious effect of both grounding and elevating me.

6 May

The Lark
by Mikhail Glinka (1804–1857)
arr. Mily Balakirev (1837–1910)

This piece was originally a song, part of a twelve-part collection called *Farewell to St Petersburg*, and although it's lovely in that version, it's the subsequent arrangement for solo piano by Glinka's young acolyte, Mily Balakirev, that I fell in love with the first time I heard it. Wistful and wandering, birdlike indeed, with a piano melody that, at times, seems to take radiant flight, it's a fine example of the ability to seamlessly fuse Russian folk and European musical traditions that has elevated Glinka to the status of fountainhead of Russian classical music.

7 May

6 Romances, op. 6
1: 'Ne ver', moy drug' – 'Do not believe, my friend'
by Pyotr Ilyich Tchaikovsky (1840–1893)

It is a relatively rare occurrence, in my game, to discover anything new. *Especially* by composers as famous as Tchaikovsky – the composer of *The Nutcracker*, *Swan Lake* and one of the most popular violin concertos ever written. Yet that's what happened not so long ago, when I happened to stumble across a recording by one of my all-time favourite violinists, the amazing Lisa Batiashvili, playing this haunting piece, barely three minutes long, from a collection of romances that Tchaikovsky apparently dashed off in a single week, in 1869.

Mournful without being remotely self-indulgent, deeply emotional without being mawkish or sentimental, it exemplifies the qualities I love most about Tchaikovsky's music. And its melancholy vibe is all the more poignant when you consider the fact that he battled, his entire life, debilitating depression and self-doubt, yet never gave up. The spring after writing this, for example, he wrote, in a letter:

> *I am sitting at the open window (at four a.m.) and breathing the lovely air of a spring morning . . . life is still good, [and] it is worth living on a May morning . . . I assert that life is beautiful in spite of everything! This 'everything' includes the following items: 1. Illness; I am getting much too stout, and my nerves are all to pieces. 2. The Conservatoire oppresses me to extinction; I am more and more convinced that I am absolutely unfitted to teach the theory of music. 3. My pecuniary situation is very bad. 4. I am very doubtful if [the opera he was working on] Undine will be performed. I have heard that they are likely to throw me over. In a word, there are many thorns, but the roses are there too . . .*

8 May

Piano Sonata no. 8 in C minor, op. 13 (Pathetique)
2: Adagio cantabile
by Ludwig van Beethoven (1770–1827)

Continuing with the subject of the elusiveness of music when it comes to being captured in mere words, for today's entry I sat staring at an empty page for the longest time. I'd start to type something, then immediately delete it. I'd type something else, then scrap that too. I came to realize there's basically nothing I could say about this piece that might begin to do justice to its perfection. I could talk about Beethoven breaking free of the Classical era's genteel shackles, bidding a metaphorical goodbye to his great inspirations, Haydn and Mozart, and striding forth into the Romantic era. I could talk about how his musical imagination in this piece led to technical innovations that pushed boundaries for the literal width and power and frame and strings of the piano itself, leading to the 'concert grand' as we know it today. I could talk about how the seemingly effortless melody of this movement, a sort of platonic ideal of phrasing, lends itself so obviously to lyrics that people have continually found themselves reaching instinctively for words to go with it, from writer John Murray Gibbon in 1933 to Billy Joel (with the song *This Night*) in 1983. I could tell you all manner of things, but I hope you'll forgive me and not take it as a cop-out if I say: just listen. *Listen to this.*

9 May

Fantasies and Delusions
Invention in C Minor
by Billy Joel (b. 1949)

As noted yesterday, Billy Joel is a fan of Beethoven. '*I listen to Beethoven . . .*', he says. '*To me, that music is as alive as it ever was.*' In fact his love of classical music more generally goes deep. '*I grew up listening to classical music,*' he has said, '*and the people I idolized when I was very young were jazz musicians and classical musicians. I read a quote from Neil Diamond: "I've forgiven myself for not being Beethoven." And I realized my issue was I haven't forgiven myself for not being Beethoven.*'

It feels only fitting, then, to wish this absolute musical legend the happiest of birthdays today by celebrating with a solo piano piece that, if you didn't know that it happened to be written by one of the biggest pop stars on the planet, I bet you wouldn't question as a work of 'classical music'. Not that the classical community has exactly embraced Joel as one of their own. '*The classical critics take you apart with a scalpel,*' he told the website Vulture after he released the album from which this Invention, with its deferent nod to Bach and Chopin, comes. '*It's a very refined ripping of the skin and bleeding of the arteries. Those guys are nasty . . .*'

Their loss, I say. Billy, you are welcome in these pages, and loved all the more for it.

10 May

Merry Christmas, Mr Lawrence
by Ryuichi Sakamoto (b. 1952)

It was on this day in 1983 that the Japanese war movie *Merry Christmas, Mr Lawrence* was premiered, at the Cannes film festival. Starring David Bowie, it also marked a major debut (as both actor and composer) for Tokyo-born Ryuichi Sakamoto, who has since gone on to win an Oscar, a BAFTA, a Grammy and two Golden Globes for his music.

Although Sakamoto is regarded chiefly as a pioneer in electronics, with his work as part of the Yellow Magic Orchestra having inspired everyone from techno to hip-hop artists, it is avant-garde classical music that Sakamoto himself cites as a great source of inspiration and influence on his musical language, including twentieth-century darlings such as Pierre Boulez, Karlheinz Stockhausen and György Ligeti (12 June). And, just as with Billy Joel's 'Invention' yesterday, I suspect that if you came at this piece from a place of total neutrality, with your ears open, you wouldn't blink at the idea that it could be included in a treasury of classical music. So there we go: yet another reason to feel frustrated by the limits of that baggage-laden term 'classical music' and to push as hard at the boundaries as we possibly can.

Anyway. The first time I ever heard this piece, I had to immediately stop what I was doing to find out what it was. And once I knew, I took it into my heart and I listened to it again and again and again. I hope you will too.

11 May

Symphony no. 1 ('Afro-American')
4: 'Aspiration': Lento, con risoluzione
by William Grant Still (1895–1978)

Today's piece has the dubious honour of being the first ever symphony written by an African-American to be performed by a major American orchestra. I say 'dubious' because that event took place in 1931, which, by any measure, is depressingly, outrageously late. (The origins of the 'symphony' itself may be nebulous, but it is beyond refute that symphonies by white people have been performed to great fanfare since at least the eighteenth century.)

One of the many cheering aspects of this work is the fact that Still, who was born on this day, did not bend his own musical language to suit the overwhelmingly white, European formalities of the time. Like other figures in the fight against systemic racism in classical music, he blended his top-notch grasp of white European music gleaned while studying at Oberlin University with popular and folk idioms that have their roots in African music. And he was overt about his mission, incorporating jazz, blues and spirituals into his work and declaring:

> I seek in the Afro-American Symphony to portray not the higher
> type of colored American, but the sons of the soil, who still retain so
> many of the traits peculiar to their African forebears; who have not
> responded completely to the transforming effect of progress.

Still's legacy is remarkable: he was also the first Black man to conduct a leading American orchestra, the first to have an opera performed by a major company, the first to have his opera performed on national television, and so on. No wonder he was nicknamed 'the Dean' by other African-American composers; his name should be known by every self-respecting classical fan.

12 May

Three Melodies, op. 7
1: 'Après un rêve' – 'After a Dream'
by Gabriel Fauré (1845–1924)

Today marks the anniversary of the birth of one of French music's great innovators and influencers, Gabriel Fauré, who represents a vital bridge between the end of the Romantic era and the advent of early-twentieth-century Modernism. Composer of orchestral works, choral music and one of the great Requiem settings of all time, he also produced miniatures such as this which are perfect little gems of the repertoire.

In the original version of this piece, he sets a poem by Romaine Bussine (based on an anonymous Italian text) that depicts two lovers taking flight from the world towards some otherworldly light. Later, around 1910, the piece was arranged for solo instruments and piano, and, although in those cases we might lose the specifics of the words, it's a fantastic example of how music can somehow, miraculously, transmit meaning anyway. Lyrical and rich, that sense of the lovers' yearning and longing pours out of every phrase. As the great pianist Graham Johnson writes of the gorgeous arrangement for cello and piano, it proved *'how easily a tune like this can become a song without words'*.

13 May

Twilight
by Arthur Sullivan (1842–1900)

Yesterday we were in Fauré's dream world, and we remain in a some-what nocturnal state today with this piece by Arthur Sullivan (as in Gilbert & Sullivan; as iconic a musical brand as, say, Simon & Garfunkel). Sullivan, who was born on this day, contributed an inestimable amount to the English musical scene, yet often infuriated classical critics for writing music that was both comic and – shock horror! – widely accessible. Without question his was music for the people, in the very best possible sense. As one critic wrote:

> There is no attempt made to force on the public the dullness of academic experience. The melodies are all as fresh as last year's wine, and as exhilarating as sparkling champagne. There is not one tune which tires the hearing . . . All through we have orchestration of infinite delicacy, tunes of alarming simplicity, but never a tinge of vulgarity.

This is precisely one of those *'tunes of alarming simplicity'*: a wistful little vignette for piano that nevertheless packs emotional sincerity and story into its three or so brief minutes.

14 May

Horseplay
2: 'Lively'
by Errollyn Wallen (b. 1958)

Belize-born British composer Errollyn Wallen has been described as a *'peerless'* figure in contemporary classical music. Over the past forty years or so she has contributed at least seventeen operas, many solo piano works, orchestral, choral and instrumental repertoire, award-winning scores for the screen and even a piece for the opening ceremony of the London 2012 Paralympic Games. She is also a generous and innovative musical collaborator, working with everyone from the groundbreaking Chineke! Orchestra, which showcases artists from minority backgrounds, to the Canadian astronaut Steve MacLean. In addition to her many other activities Wallen also co-founded Ensemble X, whose rather brilliant motto is: *'We don't break down barriers in music . . . we don't see any.'* I love that idea.

This texturally varied piece was made for the Royal Ballet and premiered in Sheffield in 1998. It's a work that energizes and delights me, and the way the bright percussive opening gives way to a melody that is at once playful and plaintive gets me every time.

15 May

Lamento della ninfa – The Nymph's Lament
from Madrigals, Book 8
4: 'Amor'
by Claudio Monteverdi (1567–1643)

This book is brimful of composers who have contributed immeasurable riches to the musical canon, but for all the diverse genius that is gathered here, there are certain figures who truly stand apart when it comes to the history and development of classical music. Monteverdi, who was baptized on this day, is one such character: it sounds so obvious now, but he was really the earliest major composer to clock that a human being singing a single vocal line could be a very, very powerful thing. From that simple revelation comes opera, comes lieder, comes bel canto concert arias, and comes, obviously, the modern pop song as we know it. He quarried the rock from which every subsequent vocal sculpture has come, and aren't we thankful for it?

As the de facto godfather of opera and songwriting, Monteverdi was also uniquely attuned, as no composer had been before him, to the possibility of creating nuanced human emotion onstage. Thus his characters move us because they feel real. In this madrigal, a lament involving a nymph and three shepherds (*pastori*) composed sometime between 1614 and 1638, he indicates that the singer of the nymph line must interpret it *'al tempo dell'affetto del animo'* – 'according to her emotions' – while the *pastori* must sing *'al tempo della mano'*, 'in regular time'. The effect of these blended voices gives it a humanity, an imperfection, that I find intoxicating.

16 May

Valse élégiaque
by Valborg Aulin (1860–1928)

I discovered this piece fairly recently on an album called *Neglected Works for Piano*. Confession time: I had never heard of today's composer. In her day, Valborg Aulin was a figure in the late-Romantic Swedish classical scene, but despite the charming immediacy of her compositions, such as this lovely lilting waltz, her work fell completely out of favour and was largely forgotten until the 1990s.

For me it's always a bittersweet feeling, a story such as this. On the one hand, it makes me happy that we're finally in the process of rediscovering a totally neglected composer; on the other hand, it only serves as a painful reminder of how many other forgotten female voices there must be, scattered throughout history.

17 May

Solfeggio no. 1 in C Minor
by Carl Philip Emanuel Bach (1714–1788)

Speaking of the 1990s, players of the vintage computer game *Treasure Mountain* may be jolted back in time by the inclusion of this piece, also known as *Solfeggietto*, which served as its theme music. (I am reliably reminded by the internet that the *Solfeggio* was also used as the music in the club house, and when you deposit your collected treasures in the chest at the top of the castle.)

It's not the only time music by a member of the Bach family has shown up in video game soundtracks, by the way. Growing up in the 1980s, with two video-game obsessed older brothers, I remember well that music by C. P. E.'s father, the great Johann Sebastian, featured in the classic Atari 2600 video game *Gyruss* (his Toccata and Fugue in D Minor). Even the most perfunctory investigation online reveals that J. S. Bach's music has actually been included on more than *forty* video-game soundtracks, the earliest one dating back to 1981 in a game called *Lock 'n' Chase*, which featured the Brandenburg Concerto no. 5.

Perhaps it's the complex mathematical underpinnings of music like this that makes it complement a video game so well; perhaps it's the inherent energy and sense of forward momentum that carries you through to the next level, and the next. Either way, whether you're an avid gamer or not, I hope you'll find something enjoyable about this sprightly and vigorous track.

18 May

España, op. 165
3: 'Malagueña'
by Isaac Albéniz (1860–1909)

Albéniz, who died on this day, was one of the greatest Spanish composers of all time, and a master when it came to incorporating into his music traditional idioms from his homeland. This piece is full of such flourishes: a Malagueña is a dance, originating from Málaga in the Andalusian region, and often associated with a particular religious celebration which takes place in May.

I listen to this piece and I am transported: for me it is a stellar example of music that allows you to travel without moving to other places, other cultures, other times. And what a gift, never to be taken for granted, that can be.

19 May

Andante for Clarinet and Orchestra
by Alice Mary Smith (1839–1884)

Happy birthday to a talented English composer who published her first song at just eighteen and went on to write one of the largest collections of sacred choral music by a woman ever. For all the challenges and prejudice she must have faced as a female composer in the Victorian era, she managed to produce prolific amounts of music, writing for many different types of ensembles and across multiple genres.

I find this piece for clarinet and orchestra utterly beguiling: elegant, graceful, redolent of some of the better-known Romantic greats – Mendelssohn, Brahms, Schumann – and yet, equally, pointing forward. (I can hear in its lyrical narrative drive elements of a lavish period drama soundtrack, and I mean that in a good way!) Ultimately, though, the musical language is delightfully Smith's own, and in my mind all the more worthy of celebration for it.

20 May

Piano Concerto in A minor, op. 7
2: Romanze: Andante non troppo con grazia
by Clara Schumann (1819–1896)

Speaking of lavishly gifted women, lest we need any further evidence of the phenomenal talent of Clara Schumann, née Wieck, it's worth pointing out that she was just thirteen years old when she started writing this, her only piano concerto; she was the grand old age of fourteen when she first performed parts of it in public. After several revisions, including by her future husband Robert, whose edits she actually then reversed, she finally performed the whole thing in 1835, just shy of her sixteenth birthday, conducted by none other than Felix Mendelssohn.

The work is magnificent by any metric, let alone when you consider that it was composed by a teenaged girl growing up in an era which did not remotely take women's achievements in classical music seriously. Today is the anniversary of Clara's death: I will be taking a moment to stop and reflect on those phenomenal achievements.

21 May

Fratres
by Arvo Pärt (b. 1935)

'*I could compare my music to white light,*' Arvo Pärt once declared, '*which contains all colours. Only a prism can divide the colours and make them appear; this prism could be the spirit of the listener.*' I love the notion that the '*spirit of the listener*' plays a critical part of the process of bringing music into life: that dialogue and connective continuum is one of the things that inspires me most about this extraordinary art form.

Pärt, whom we first encountered here back in February, is arguably one of the composers who has helped us change how we hear music: a quietly groundbreaking force who developed a distinctive and vastly influential musical language based on Medieval musical principles which he called *tintinnabuli*. This piece emerged as a direct result of that development. Composed in 1977, during a period of explosive creativity, *Fratres* (meaning 'brothers') is based around a set of variations and recurring motifs, all spinning into a mesmerizing, meditative whole.

As with many other pieces by Pärt, the seemingly simple composition is, in fact, governed by complex mathematical rules. But it's to Pärt's great credit, I think, that as a listener your primary experience is of the emotional impact and beauty of that system being delivered without the deadening effect of an overly cerebral intellectual concept, which – alas – is not something that can be said for all avant-garde, twentieth-century music.

22 May

Requiem Mass
7: Libera me
by Giuseppe Verdi (1813–1901)

It truly sends shivers down my spine to think that, on this day in 1874, at the San Marco church in Milan, a group of singers and musicians came together, under the direction of the composer himself, and out of the silence in that church, the first notes of this extraordinary piece emerged. For the *very first time*.

Maybe it sounds crazy, but this fact moves me so: that one day, this music did not exist, lay silent as black marks on a page, and that then it did. And will, now, for ever. What a brain-exploding miracle that is.

Anyway. The premiere marked exactly one year since the death of the Italian novelist and poet Alessandro Manzoni, whom Verdi much admired, and for a while it was even dubbed the 'Manzoni Requiem'. But the seventy-five-minute *Requiem* has long transcended the legacy of its dedicatee, becoming one of the most enduringly popular works in the classical canon, performed less in liturgical settings than on concert stages around the world ('*Verdi's latest opera, though in ecclesiastical robes*' was the verdict of legendary conductor Hans von Bülow at the time). As ironic as it sounds, perhaps it's because of Verdi's own religious scepticism in later life that it has always resonated so profoundly with audiences of all faiths and none.

Some of the most moving performances of Verdi's *Requiem* must surely have been those that were given, with ever-decreasing forces, by persecuted Jews at the Nazi concentration camp Terezin, as they awaited deportation to Auschwitz and other Nazi death camps. I hear this, and I cannot but think of them.

Libera me. Deliver me.

23 May

Phantasy Trio
by Joan Trimble (1915–2000)

Along with her sister Valerie, a fellow pianist with whom she put on fantastically popular duet recitals, the Irish composer Joan Trimble was practically a household name in the 1940s and 1950s. She is not someone we hear much about these days, yet she was clearly a force of nature. Much in demand as a concert pianist, she also worked full-time for the Red Cross during the World War Two, had a thirty-three-year stint as editor and proprietor of her family's successful Enniskillen newspaper *The Impartial Reporter*, was a professor of music at the esteemed Royal College of Music in London, and still managed to keep the show on the road at home as the mother of three children.

With such a busy schedule it's no wonder that she felt compelled to describe herself as an 'occasional' composer: how she found the time to write anything is impressive. What compositions she did produce, though, are beautifully crafted and reflect a distinctive talent. This piano trio was apparently brought into life thanks to the encouragement of one of Trimble's teachers, Ralph Vaughan Williams; I always find it intensely atmospheric, a sonic soundscape I can lose myself in completely.

24 May

Pour un baiser!
by Francesco Paolo Tosti (1846–1916)

Today's piece is an unabashedly sentimental song, served up with a kiss. The Italian-British composer Paolo Tosti overcame severe poverty in his early life – it is said that for a period he survived on nothing but oranges and stale bread – to become a serious mover and shaker in the highest echelons of British society; in 1908, he was even knighted by his friend, King Edward VII.

Tosti's music invariably tends to be dubbed – sometimes with a sneer – 'salon' music: it's light, expressive, unpretentious; no wrenching symphonic epics or complex contrapuntal affairs for him. Yet his knack for songwriting is evident in this, a charming 1904 setting of a French love poem by Georges Doncieux.

Pour un baiser sur ta peau parfumée,	*For a kiss on your scented skin,*
pour un baiser dans l'or de tes cheveux	*For a kiss in the gold of your hair,*
reçois mon âme toute, ô bien-aimée!	*Accept my whole soul, oh beloved one!*
Tu comblerais l'infini de mes voeux . . .	*You would fill the infinity of my wishes . . .*
Par un baiser!	*With a kiss!*

25 May

Souvenir d'un lieu cher – Memory of a Beloved Place, op.42
3: 'Mélodie'
by Pyotr Ilyich Tchaikovsky (1840–1893)

This utterly gorgeous violin melody emerged as the finale of a three-movement suite written to commemorate Tchaikovsky's stay at Braïlov, a beautiful Ukrainian estate that belonged to his extremely generous patroness, the music-loving Nadezhda von Meck. As his benefactress, von Meck enabled Tchaikovsky to have financial stability, an unimaginable luxury for most freelance creators, and the correspondence between them indicates a close, collaborative and mutually reinforcing friendship, although they never actually met.

Tchaikovsky was a creative genius riddled with insecurity; a closeted homosexual and a man who suffered crippling bouts of depression and mental illness throughout his life. His letters, especially those that are wracked with self-doubt, are deeply moving testimonies to a human being wrestling with inner darkness and overwhelming questions. It makes me very happy, then, to think of him around this period, late May of 1878, enjoying life in a beautiful part of the world, unstrained, musically inspired, capable of producing music of such unalloyed lightness. Having sent it to von Meck, the work was published the following year, featuring a dedication to Braïlov itself.

26 May

Aether
by Hildur Guðnadóttir (b. 1982)

To a contemporary musical powerhouse today, the classically-trained but genre-fluid Icelandic composer Hildur Guðnadóttir.

Previously a member of the Reykjavík-based think tank, record label and art collective Kitchen Motors – along with the likes of the late Jóhann Jóhannsson, for whom she also played cello on many of his film scores, including *Sicario* (2015) and *Arrival* (2016) Guðnadóttir has written music for the concert stage, theatre, dance, television and film. Her profoundly ruminative works often call for a wide range of textures and instrumentation: as well as vocals she uses electronics and diverse instruments, including zither, vibraphone, viola da gamba, harp and vocals, all of which she invariably plays herself. For her Emmy-winning score to the TV mini-series *Chernobyl*, she recorded in a decommissioned nuclear power plant and in the process the sonic secrets of that space become something akin to an instrument itself.

This much earlier piece, from her 2009 album *Without Sinking*, reflects a period in which, Guðnadóttir says, her solo music was '*a way to really look inwards, and to spend time completely by myself with an instrument, without any outside dialogue*'. She adds, self-reflectively: '*A lot of my music is kind of contemplative, and somehow that always tends to tilt on the darker side. My inner conversation is apparently quite dark.*' That may be true, but nevertheless I find a gleaming luminosity at the core of Guðnadóttir's music.

27 May

Caprice in E major, op. 1 no. 1
by Niccolò Paganini (1782–1840)

Today we celebrate the legacy of one of the first real superstars of the violin, Niccolò Paganini, who died on this day and who left behind a catalogue of works that really became a cornerstone of the repertoire for any serious violinist. With his formidable technique, breathtaking virtuosity and futuristic imagination, he pushed and pushed at the boundaries of the violin's technical capabilities, and went on to inspire generations of future fiddlers.

Paganini was famous in his day not only for his musical genius – he was also a talented guitarist and mandolin player – but also for his extravagant womanizing and gambling, even setting up a casino in Paris (it failed). Such peccadilloes, however, did not do much to harm his reputation: he has always been viewed as one of the all-time violinistic greats, and in his day was revered by many fellow composers, including Hector Berlioz (14 July) and Gioachino Rossini (29 February).

28 May

Homesickness
by Emahoy Tsegué-Maryam Guèbrou (b. 1923)

'We can't always choose what life brings,' says Emahoy Tsegué-Maryam Guèbrou. *'But we can choose how to respond.'*

Life has certainly 'brought' much to this remarkable Ethiopian nun, pianist and composer, and it's fair to say she has responded in pretty singular fashion. Born into one of Ethiopia's wealthiest families, Guèbrou was educated at a Swiss boarding school, became something of a high-society girl in 1960s Addis Ababa, even singing to Emperor Haile Selassie, and was all set to study at London's prestigious Royal College of Music before she switched course, becoming a nun, living a reclusive life, barefoot in a remote hilltop monastery, and remaining largely unknown for decades before word began to emerge of her stunningly distinctive and unusual compositions.

Trained in Western classical music, steeped in the chants and modalities of the Orthodox tradition, deeply inspired by Romantic heroes such as Frédéric Chopin, and yet also aligned with those compatriots of hers who exemplify what has come to be known as 'Ethio-jazz', Guèbrou produces music like no other human on this earth; this jaunty, rippling, free-flowing, wistful yet cheering piano melody might be as good a cure for homesickness as it's possible to imagine.

29 May

African Suite
5: Akinla: Allegro non troppo
by Fela Sowande (1905–1987)

Born on this day in Abeokuta, near Lagos, Nigeria, the composer, scholar, ethnomusicologist, educator and organist Fela Sowande is one of the great pioneers of modern African classical music. Raised under British colonial rule, he was educated in the European tradition but found many innovative ways to incorporate and celebrate the sounds of his homeland in a body of work that holds a singular place in twentieth-century musical history.

To those who criticized or dismissed his work as a craven homage to the European colonialists, rather than a valid African art form, Sowande responded with the sort of frank openness that characterizes his overall approach. '*We are not prepared,*' he once said, '*to submit to the doctrine of apartheid in art by which a musician is expected to work only within the limits of his traditional forms of music, [and] uncontrolled nationalism, in which case nationals of any one country may forget that they are all members of one human family.*'

Written in 1944 and originally broadcast by the BBC, this piece blends West African styles – including the popular dance form highlife and a folk melody from southern Nigeria – with European formalities. Sowande considered it a cornerstone of his argument that West African music could be heard on European terms.

30 May

Suiren
by Pauline Oliveros (1932–2016)

Modernist, avant-garde, singular, today's composer sought to create a form of sonic transcendence in which the boundary between music and listener practically dissolves. Smart and curious, the Texas-born Oliveros began playing her mother's household accordion and was proficient by the age of nine; during her schooldays she became equally accomplished on the tuba and French horn; later she would become a talented multi-instrumentalist as well as a composer who danced always at the vanguard of musical possibility.

Oliveros was one of the first members of the San Francisco Tape Music Centre and an early pioneer in electronics, avidly adopting new technologies such as magnetic tape and prototype synthesizers. A proponent of the philosophy she developed called 'Deep Listening', she produced recordings that blended seamlessly into the broader sound world of their surroundings; what she once described as the *'beautiful canopies of sound'* that emerge from the natural world yet elude formal musical notation. *'When explaining the process that informed her performances,'* notes *New York Times* journalist Clare-Louise Bennett, *'Oliveros identified two sorts of listening: focal attention and global attention. The first is when I attend to a specific local sound; the latter is when I take in all the sounds around me and those inside of me, including sounds I remember as well as ones I imagine.'* She adds, in a phrase which I think sums up this haunting, evocative, timeless-seeming soundscape perfectly, *'Oliveros's sequences of sounds and shifting tones seem to deliver the incremental comprehension of an ancient secret.'*

31 May

Meditation on Haydn's Name
by George Benjamin (b. 1960)

George Benjamin's gateway to classical music was Disney's *Fantasia*, to which his parents took him as a child. '*I was very reluctant to go,*' he once told *The New Yorker*: '*Tantrum on the way. Bliss on the way back.*' Afterwards, he began inventing songs in his head at bedtime each night, and thus one of Britain's most significant composers started to find his own creative voice.

Benjamin's prodigious talents were further honed when he became a student of the great French composer Olivier Messiaen (3 January); by the time he was twenty his music was being performed at the BBC Proms. He offers a fascinating insight into what it takes to compose: '*It is so, so difficult that it needs sort of trancelike concentration to do it, and utter commitment,*' he has said. '*Every mark you make on the musical canvas influences the memory of what has come before, and has an effect on the future as well. So not only do you write one note at a time – you're writing the whole piece in every gesture that you make. It's very, very demanding, and very strange. The world has to shut down.*'

I find that notion captivating: that one human's world shutting down enables the opening up of one for another. With this piece, I can't help but take that literally: Joseph Haydn, the great Classical-era composer on whose 'name' this composition is based, died on this day in 1809. The piece, Benjamin tells us, is '*based on the pitches derived from the letters of Haydn's name – BADDG . . . These notes sound throughout my piece as an immobile chord at the centre of the pian-istic texture. Every other melodic line and harmony that colours and surrounds this static chord is derived from Haydn's name, in inversion and transposition. At the end the basic notes BADDG flower and reson-ate over the whole keyboard.*'

JUNE

1 June

Violin Concerto no. 4 in D major, K. 218
2: Andante cantabile
by Wolfgang Amadeus Mozart (1756–1791)

'You have no idea how well you play the violin,' wrote Leopold Mozart to his son Wolfgang, *'if you would only do yourself justice and play with boldness, spirit and fire, as if you were the finest violinist in Europe.'* For all his father's criticisms, Mozart, who apparently much preferred playing the keyboard, seems to have dazzled audiences around Europe with his virtuoso violin playing; certainly in his writing for the instrument there are plenty of opportunities for boldness, spirit and fire.

Every time I play Mozart myself, I sense a profound sense of kinship with the violin. He gets it to do amazing things – not necessarily the crazy, boundary-pushing pyrotechnics of, say, Paganini (27 May) or von Biber (3 May), although you certainly need a decent technique to play his violin music. But things that feel poetic and lyrical and sweet and yearning and human and are all the more wonderful for it.

Astonishingly, or perhaps not, given it is Mozart we're talking about, his violin concertos were all dashed off in a single year, 1775. He was nineteen. This one is less technically demanding than some of the others; as such it was among the first concertos I learned when I was growing up. And it has grown alongside me, keeping me company through my life; our connection evolving and shifting and deepening over time. All five Mozart violin concertos are beautiful, but there's always been a special place in my heart for number four, and most especially this sublime slow movement.

2 June

Four Choral-Songs, op. 53
1: 'There is Sweet Music'
by Edward Elgar (1857–1934)

'*A clinker*', is how Edward Elgar described this charming 1907 setting of a poem by Alfred, Lord Tennyson – '*. . . the best I have done*'. He dedicated it to Canon Charles Vincent Gorton, who, on hearing it, responded:

> *Oh my friend, what a wonderful man you are, and with what a stupendous gift . . . it is no light thing for me to see my name on the finest part-song ever written . . . the thing unfolded itself in its consummate beauty and the audience were entranced.*

Elgar made a groundbreaking decision to write the song in two keys simultaneously, with the men singing in G and the women in A flat. It's deceptively difficult to sing, but when a choir gets it right, my goodness it is sweet, sweet music indeed . . .

> *There is sweet music here that softer falls*
> *Than petals from blown roses on the grass,*
> *Or night-dews on still waters between walls*
> *Of shadowy granite, in a gleaming pass;*
> *Music that gentlier on the spirit lies,*
> *Than tired eyelids upon tired eyes;*
> *Music that brings sweet sleep*
> *down from the blissful skies.*
> *Here are cool mosses deep,*
> *And thro' the moss the ivies creep,*
> *And in the stream the long-leaved flowers weep,*
> *And from the craggy ledge the poppy hangs in sleep.*

3 June

Blumenleben, op. 19
2: 'Veilchen' – 'Violets'
by Dora Pejačević (1885–1923)

Today we hear from a direct contemporary of Elgar, who featured yesterday: a woman breaking her own ground in a very different country and culture. Born in Budapest into a noble Croatian family, Dora Pejačević showed great musical promise as a child. She started composing seriously at the age of twelve and is often described as Croatia's first modern symphonist for her splendid 1917 symphony in F sharp minor, which she dedicated to her mother.

Despite her aristocratic background, which might have insulated her from the realities of those less fortunate than her, Pejačević became acutely aware of the gross inequities of her society. During the World War One, she volunteered as a nurse, and wrote to a friend: '*I simply cannot understand how people can live without work, and how many of them do, especially the higher aristocracy . . . I despise them because of this.*' Her ever-deepening social conscience led to a breach with those of her background – '*I cannot stick with the members of my class,*' she declared. When she died, tragically, just four weeks after giving birth, she was buried, as per her wishes, not in the opulent family crypt but in a regular grave marked by a simple tombstone that bore only her name, '*Dora*', and the words '*Rest now*'.

Although Pejačević wrote over a hundred compositions, including dozens of solo piano pieces such as this one, as well as songs, chamber music and orchestral works, very little of her music – as is so often the case with female composers – has been recorded. *Yet*, I have to hope. Yet.

4 June

Never Saw Him Again
by Mary Lattimore (b. 1980)

I first encountered the music of Mary Lattimore, an LA-based harpist, through Julianna Barwick (20 April), who remixed this track.

Harps tend to fall victim to the worst excesses of musical stereotyping, as somehow celestial things, invariably played by beautiful, young, white women with flowing locks and vaguely Pre-Raphaelite features. Pushing five thousand years old (fragments of harps have been excavated at burial grounds in the ancient Sumerian city of Ur), the instrument has long played a role in the music of many diverse cultures, serving everything from mainstream symphony orchestras to avant-garde electronic experiments. Yet I've never heard it like this.

Lattimore's sound world is spacious yet structural: '*like watching the setting sun filter through the towering trees, seeing the morning sun bathe an immense mountain range, or most anything you experience where all you have left to do is sit and wonder,*' noted critic Grayson Haver Currin.

Or as *The New Yorker*'s Amanda Petrusich puts it, Lattimore '*makes complex and expansive songs that evoke, for me, seismic emotional shifts – it's not so much music to zone out to . . . as music to self-actualize by*'. Though she uses vocals sparingly, '*her songs*', reckons Petrusich, '*still feel heavily narrative-oriented. Like all artists, she is interested in the odd and tumultuous path of a human life. Her songs track what it's like to experience something, and then to find yourself changed by it – the strange and often puzzling way our bodies and minds rearrange themselves at unforeseeable intervals.*'

I'm quoting this not just because it's a fine piece of music criticism. But also because it stirs me deeply, this idea that a person being changed by an experience in turn creates a piece of art that changes another person. And on we go. Together.

5 June

O Lord, in thy wrath
by Orlando Gibbons (1583–1625)

There is something wrenching about hearing this setting of Psalm 6, verses 1–4 on the day that the English composer Orlando Gibbons died, suddenly, at the tender age of forty-one. The words are so plaintive, so desperate, so very human in their beseeching:

> *O Lord, in thy wrath rebuke me not,*
> *neither chasten me in thy displeasure.*
> *Have mercy upon me, O Lord, for I am weak:*
> *O Lord heal me, for my bones are vexed.*
> *My soul is also sore troubled:*
> *but, Lord, how long wilt thou punish me?*
> *O save me, for thy mercy's sake.*

It's a characteristically detailed setting, showing off Gibbons' outstanding facility with counterpoint and harmony. I also love his liberal deployment of suspensions, which create such an atmosphere of tension and release – reliably so, yet never not devastatingly effective. Gibbons was one of the most gifted and versatile composers of the Elizabethan era; one can only imagine what else he might have gone on to achieve had his life not been snuffed out so early.

6 June

'Un beau baiser' – 'A Beautiful Kiss'
from *George Sand*
by Louis Andriessen (1939–2021)

It was on this day that the great Dutch composer and former musical enfant terrible Louis Andriessen was born. He was a composer of numerous stage, orchestral, chamber, vocal and piano works, as well as the 1980 opera *George Sand*, from which this haunting and rather lovely choral piece comes.

Andriessen, who from his radical student days remained a mercurial and controversial figure, had a particularly interesting take on the age-old chestnut of whether or not music can – or should – be political. '*Many composers view the act of composing as, somehow, above social conditioning,*' he said. '*I contest that. How you arrange your musical material, the techniques you use and the instruments you score for, are largely determined by your own social circumstances and listening experience . . . abstract musical material – pitch, duration and rhythm – are beyond social conditioning: it is found in nature. However, the moment the musical material is ordered it becomes culture and hence a social entity.*'

This position, coupled with a truly innovative and complex musical sensibility, helped to propel Andriessen to the status of the most important composer of his homeland, as well as a prominent figure on the European classical scene. As Tom Service puts it: '*In an inevitably reductive nutshell, Andriessen's music is the sound of the most fruitful of collisions between political radicalism, minimalist pulsation and European modernism; at its most profound, it's much more than that.*'

7 June

Guitar Quintet in D major, G. 448
3. Grave assai – 4. Fandango
by Luigi Boccherini (1743–1805)

His name may not be heard too often today, but Luigi Boccherini was one of the great composers of instrumental music in Italy during the latter half of the eighteenth century. His fame as both composer and performer spread around Europe, and he became something of a musical celebrity in Vienna, Paris and Madrid, where for fifteen years he held a lucrative court appointment to the Spanish Infante, a younger brother of King Charles III.

I first discovered this piece on an album from the Spanish string quartet Cuarteto Casals, in a fantastic arrangement entitled *Night Music from the Streets of Madrid*. I love its nocturnal, sensual vibe, in which a sultry slow movement gives way to an electrifying closing fandango, based on a popular folk dance that originated in eighteenth-century Spain. Traditionally, couples with castanets would dance a fandango to a triple-meter guitar accompaniment, and Boccherini captures that tantalizing mood with his own use of castanets and a jangling, tambourine-like rattle called a 'sistrum'.

For all its sizzling vitality, there's a note of longing laced throughout, an energy that keeps it taut and highly charged until the very final bars.

8 June

Waveland
by Noam Pikelny (b. 1981)

A recipient of the 2010 Steve Martin Prize for Excellence in Bluegrass and Banjo (yes, *that* Steve Martin), the American banjo player Noam Pikelny brings lyricism and magic to that very special little instrument. This alluring track is not, apparently, named for anything physics-related, but rather for the street behind Wrigley Field, the baseball park in Chicago (Pikelny is a lifelong Cubs fan). Nevertheless, it is built around mathematically complex patterns, redolent of the Baroque structures of, say, J. S. Bach or von Biber (3 May). But it wears its intellectualism lightly: I find the overwhelming and immediate effect is one of sheer delight.

Although Pikelny has no formal classical training, he admits to seeking *'inspiration'* from classical composers and listening, for example, *'to a lot of the solo [Debussy] piano preludes as I was working on this record, just trying to get into the spirit . . .'* I love that it's a work that pulls together such varied musical traditions into a finished result that is entirely distinctive and wholly itself. Captivating.

9 June

Sueño recurrente – Recurring Dream
by Angélica Negrón (b. 1981)

To a direct contemporary of Noam Pikelny today, and the idiosyncratic Puerto Rican composer Angélica Negrón, whom I first
encountered thanks to the visionary, exploratory spirit of American
pianist Lara Downes.

   If you thought yesterday's banjo was a wild pick, Negrón composes
music for instruments that extend even further beyond the traditional
classical canon, including accordions, electronics, whistles, toys and
robots. She also writes for more conventional forces, including chamber
ensembles, orchestras, choirs and 'regular' instruments, such as this
piece for solo piano. As the title implies, it's a dreamy work; and one
that tends to have the effect of lifting me out of wherever I am –
conferring an alternative perspective that I am always grateful for.

10 June

Sleep On: Lullaby
by Mark-Anthony Turnage (b. 1960)

Staying in a world of sleep and dreams, today we say happy birthday to the leading British composer Mark-Anthony Turnage. The *Guardian* describes Turnage as a composer willing '*to engage with the nitty gritty of contemporary life*' and his subjects are typically uncompromising and thought-provoking; he has written major operas, for example, about the former playboy model Anna Nicole Smith, and Oedipus Rex. As you do.

Turnage wrote this hypnotic suite of lullabies for his young son, but as you might expect from a composer of his depth, the approach is far from childlike: for all its lyricism and gentle drift, this movement also offers a glimpse into the spiky, dark and often jazz-infused aspects of Turnage's radically distinctive musical style.

11 June

Idyll
by Hazel Scott (1920–1981)

Born on this day in Port of Spain, Trinidad and Tobago, Hazel Scott showed such early musical promise that her musician mother took her to New York City at the age of four. By eight, she had won a scholarship to study at the Juilliard School, probably the most iconic classical music conservatoire in the world. Her music, such as this yearning free-form melody, is often improvisatory and infused with the jazz she so adored (and which she began singing professionally in New York nightclubs as a teenager). But Scott's love of classical music also ran deep, and her take on pieces by the likes of Bach, Rachmaninov, de Falla, Liszt and Chopin show an artist with profound soul and sensibility as well as terrific virtuosity and wit.

Scott's fascinating career includes being the first Black American woman to have her own TV show – cancelled one week after she voluntarily appeared before the House Un-American Activities Committee in 1950. Always hugely popular with audiences, even after that incident, she was committed to using her platform as one of the most prominent African-American entertainers of her day to advocate for civil rights and the fight for racial equity.

Hazel Scott is buried at Flushing Cemetery, in Queens, New York – not so far from where Louis Armstrong and her great friend Dizzy Gillespie are buried. Although unlike them her name is not often now heard outside of niche jazz circles, her legacy is stellar. Her taking up space (in today's parlance) *'provided'*, as historian Dr Dwayne Mack puts it, *'a glimmer of hope for African-American viewers'*. Or, as Scott's biographer Karen Chilton notes: *'Considering the times, her achievements in the music industry were noteworthy: a young Black woman with crossover appeal, sellout concerts and record-breaking album sales was rare indeed.'*

12 June

Sonatina for piano 4 hands
2: Andante
by György Ligeti (1923–2006)

A little piano music today to mark the death on this day of one of the great musical innovators of the twentieth century. Born in Transylvania, Ligeti later lived in Hungary before escaping the strictures, both personal and musical, of the Communist regime. In 1956, he managed to emigrate to Austria, where he remained and became a full citizen in 1968.

Once settled in the West, Ligeti was able to give full flight to his imagination, developing new compositional techniques such as 'micropolyphony' ('*such a beautiful word!*' he once remarked, describing its effect as '*impenetrable texture, something like a very densely woven cobweb*').

If that all sounds a touch daunting, Ligeti was also capable of transcending the world of avant-garde classical music and communing with more mainstream pursuits. In 1968, the great film-maker Stanley Kubrick drew richly from Ligeti's music in his sci-fi epic *2001: A Space Odyssey*. This piece, brief as it is, grounds me and brings me a sense of overwhelming calm.

13 June

Ten Preludes
1: Andantino espressivo
by Carlos Chávez (1899–1978)

Today we celebrate one of Mexico's musical greats, Carlos Antonio de Padua Chávez y Ramírez. Born on this day in Mexico City, Chávez came to prominence after the Mexican Revolution, and his work reflects the search for national identity that saw the flowering of an Indianist movement across the arts in general. Widely travelled, including in Europe and the USA, Chávez developed a musical language that combined the melodic patterns, rhythmic inflections and percussive tropes of indigenous Mexican folk music with the modernist revolutions that he saw emerging across Europe and America, thanks to the likes of Igor Stravinsky, Arnold Schoenberg and Aaron Copland. These angular, percussive, strangely wistful solo piano preludes are short but powerful examples of the way he synthesized those influences, and I love this opening movement in particular.

Even in the Euro-centric world of Western classical music, Chávez became a significant figure in his lifetime. He was also a respected conductor and Music Director, and in 1958–9 he had the distinction of presenting the Charles Eliot Norton lectures at Harvard University; other such honorees include Leonard Bernstein, John Cage, and Copland and Stravinsky themselves, which should give a sense of the esteem in which he is rightly held.

14 June

Movement for String Trio
by Coleridge-Taylor Perkinson (1932–2004)

Born on this day in Salem, North Carolina, today's composer was named for the earlier African-British musical pioneer Samuel Coleridge-Taylor (15 August). In twentieth-century America, riven as it was with structural racism and vast inequality of opportunity, Coleridge-Taylor Perkinson nevertheless went on to forge a ground-breaking career, collaborating with many legends in the soul, jazz, pop, film, television and ballet worlds (including with choreographers Jerome Robbins and Alvin Ailey and musicians Harry Belafonte, Max Roach and . . . er, *Marvin Gaye*!) as well as in classical music.

Perkinson was particularly gifted at synthesizing many genres and styles. Within his classical compositions, it was *just music*: he exemplified the belief that Baroque counterpoint, Elizabethan love lyrics, seventeenth-century dance forms, high Romanticism and Black folk music all rub shoulders together; all have their place in the fervent of his imagination. To say, '*Wow, you can't quite put your finger on it*' – as I have done, many times – is a simple way to sum up his complex genius.

Perkinson was a close friend of African-American classical violinist Sanford Allen, the first Black member of the New York Philharmonic – he dedicated various compositions to Allen – and it was Sanford Allen who I have to thank for introducing me to this piece. I will always be grateful!

15 June

Violin sonata no. 3 in C Minor, op. 45
2: Allegretto espressivo alla Romanza
by Edvard Grieg (1843–1907)

Although they are less frequently performed than many other famous violin sonatas, Edvard Grieg was proud and rightfully so of his three forays into the genre. The great Norwegian Romantic composer wrote to a friend that *'these three works are among my very best and represent different stages in my development: the first, naïve and rich in ideals; the second, nationalistic; and the third with a wider outlook'*.

The wide horizons of no. 3 were conjured in 1887, some two decades after Grieg had last worked in the form, by which time he had become a celebrated composer, of piano music in particular, widely lauded for his ability to draw on the potent folk traditions of his musical homeland. (Often, in fact, original melodies by Grieg were assumed to have been adapted from folk songs.)

Violinists are spoiled rotten when it comes to sonata repertoire, and the famous warhorses by the likes of Mozart, Beethoven and Brahms can sometimes get in the way of less obvious gems. But from the very first time I got to play this, having no idea what was in store, I was totally hooked. I hope you will be too.

16 June

~~~~~~~

Mazurka de salon, op. 30
by Teresa Carreño (1853–1917)

The mazurka is a sixteenth-century Polish dance form that was brought to widespread popular attention – and the ballrooms of western Europe – by the great Warsaw-born Romantic composer Frédéric Chopin. This one, composed in Paris in 1869 by a brilliant Venezuelan pianist, conductor, soprano and composer called Teresa Carreño, is a splendid example of the way music crosses national lines – and it has the delightful effect of instantly transporting me, in my mind, to some opulent ballroom on the Left Bank, ballgowns ablur and chandeliers aglitter. I love it.

17 June

Lyric for Strings
by George Walker (1922–2018)

It was this day in 1997 that former Washington, D.C. mayor Marion Barry declared to be 'George Walker Day'. Among many other distinctions, the D.C.-born composer George Walker had become, the previous year, the first African-American to win the Pulitzer Prize for Music. That such a momentous occasion occurred only in 1996 should give us all pause, but still. It's a noteworthy achievement and richly deserved.

Walker was so musically talented that whilst still a student at Dunbar High School he was simultaneously studying – and giving public recitals – at Howard University, one of the leading historically Black colleges and universities in the US. By the age of fourteen, he had been accepted to study at Oberlin, whose music programme remains one of the best in America today. He went on to attend the storied Curtis Institute of Music in Philadelphia, becoming, in 1945, one of the earliest Black students to graduate from that elite conservatoire – and with not one but two diplomas, as it happened, in both piano performance and composition.

Walker's lengthy and distinguished career reflects his singular voice, in which influences as diverse as spirituals, jazz, pop music and Romantic classical stalwarts such as Beethoven, Chopin and Brahms are all synthesized and given their own unique character.

18 June

Špalíček Suite no. 1, H.214a
V: The Wedding Dance
by Bohuslav Martinů (1890–1959)

A cheery wedding dance today from a 1930s ballet-opera by the Czech composer Bohuslav Martinů. *Špalíček* or *The Czech Year* had the sub-title '*A ballet of national games, customs and fairy tales*', and I think you can hear those roots in its spirited dance rhythms, its gutsy, hearty melodies and cheeky orchestration. The sudden and unlikely intro-duction of the piano towards the end is always a particular surprise and delight.

19 June

Fanfare on Amazing Grace
by Adolphus Hailstork (b. 1941)

Today is Juneteenth, or African-American Emancipation Day. A day to mark the ending of legal slavery in the United States. From the original Juneteenth celebration in Galveston, Texas in 1865, to President Biden signing a bill in 2021, it has been a long road to make this day become 'official', i.e. a federal holiday in the US. It's not much. But it's *something*.

Living in our post-2020 world, we are at a moment of historical inflection and a long-overdue cultural, social and racial reckoning. What, you might say, has this to do with classical music? I would say: everything.

Classical music has been, overwhelmingly, a white man's game. There are many intersectional reasons for this; this book is not the right forum to analyze them. But wherever I can, I want to celebrate those incredibly resilient and single-minded Black composers who have been kept out of the spotlight – or worse – and have overcome.

Today's composer, the New York-born Adolphus Hailstork, is one of those. Hailstork recalls watching the traumatic news of George Floyd's death in May 2020 – and soon started composing a powerful requiem cantata, *A Knee on a Neck*. Earlier in his career, he *'went to Africa, to Ghana, and saw the forts and the pens where soon-to-be slaves were held before they shipped in the Middle Passage (part of the trans-Atlantic slave trade where millions of Africans were transported to America)'*. He adds: '*That touched me.*'

It can sometimes be hard to hold on to the idea that art, that music, can play an essential role in human progress. But unless we believe in and champion that idea, then the opposite will triumph. Today's piece takes the radically positive view: a celebration through music of the victory of our common humanity.

20 June

Sonata for arpeggione and piano in A minor, D. 821
1: Allegro moderato
by Franz Schubert (1797–1828)

As unlikely as it may sound, in Schubert's day the 'arpeggione' represented the very cutting-edge of modern instrument technology: only invented in 1823, the fretted six-stringed instrument was a sort of guitar-cello-bass-viol hybrid, shaped like a medieval fiddle. It likely produced a rich and sensuous sound, but I say 'likely' because it is virtually extinct and almost impossible to hear in real life. I have never heard one played (although I have nerdily sought them out to gaze at in museums such as the Metropolitan Museum of Art in New York).

The only extant work of any significance featuring an arpeggione is this stunner by Schubert, which he composed in 1824. (Nowadays, the arpeggione line tends to be played on cello or viola.) When Schubert wrote this lyrical and intimate piece, he was already in the throes of the syphilis that would steal his life four years later. And whether you're aware of that fact or not as you're listening, I think there is something inherently tender encoded in the notes. As cellist Gautier Capuçon says: *'You can feel the fragility in the music . . . it's very touching'*.

21 June

Porcelain
by Helen Jane Long (b. 1974)

When she's not busy composing music, often for TV shows, adverts and films (including assisting the legendary Howard Shore on the score for *The Lord of the Rings* trilogy), the award-winning and versatile British composer Helen Jane Long can be found waterskiing, or perhaps training for her next triathlon, or maybe baking brownies for her colleagues. Not for her the isolated, lofty life of the mind that some composers promote, upholding the tiresome stereotype of classical musicians as some kind of elite class, superior to the rest of humankind.

That refreshing lack of pretension – which not for one minute, by the way, detracts from Long's seriousness as an artist – has helped to create music that has proved wildly popular with audiences: her second album *Embers* was once the most requested record on Classic FM; in 2011 she was the only female to be featured in that station's annual Hall of Fame. She was also the first ever pianist in the US to hit over a billion streams. If that grates on some classical purists, who'd rather keep artists such as her out of the canon, then the last laugh is surely on her.

22 June

Four Sea Interludes, from Peter Grimes, op. 33a
3: Moonlight
by Benjamin Britten (1913–1976)

Generally considered to be the most important British composer since Henry Purcell (who died in 1695!), Britten's influence is inestimable – it's no wonder he became the first composer ever to be honoured with a life peerage. The son of a dental surgeon and a housewife, his background was ordinary but his musical gifts extraordinary. When Aaron Copland, the leading American composer of the day, reviewed Britten's homage to his beloved teacher, *Variations on a Theme of Frank Bridge*, in 1937, he declared: '*The piece is what we would call a knockout.*' Britten was still in his twenties.

It was *Peter Grimes* (1945) that both marked a milestone in British opera and made its composer an international star. The tragic story of a Suffolk fisherman and his uncomfortable relations with the local townfolk, it is sometimes seen as a powerful allegory of homosexual oppression. Britten himself, in a 1948 interview for *Time* magazine, preferred to describe *Grimes* as '*a subject very close to my heart – the struggle of the individual against the masses . . . The more vicious the society, the more vicious the individual.*'

Britten lived (for almost four decades with his partner Peter Pears) on the coast in Aldeburgh, Suffolk. The sea always loomed large in his creative imagination. '*My parent's [sic] house,*' he recalled, '*directly faced the sea, and my life as a child was coloured by the fierce storms that sometimes drove ships on to our coast and ate away whole stretches of the neighbouring cliffs.*' Among the unforgettable characters in *Peter Grimes* is the North Sea itself, conveyed in all its menace and magnificence and here shrouded in moonlight.

23 June

Biafra
by Alex Baranowski (b. 1983)

Today's composer, the young and gifted Alex Baranowski, writes music for theatre, television, dance, opera, commercials and film – including *McCullin* (2012), an award-winning documentary about the iconic photojournalist Don McCullin, from which this music comes.

Baranowski is a former student of Liverpool Institute of Performing Arts, housed in Paul McCartney's old school (he says he was drawn to go there because of his love of the Beatles, especially groundbreaking albums such as *Revolver*). But it's because of his own family history that he was inspired to pursue a *'musical life'* at all: Baranowski tells a moving story about his Polish grandparents being sent to Siberia during World War Two, where they endured horrific conditions, but managed to survive. His grandfather, an architect for whom *'music was . . . life'*, bought an accordion after the Battle of Monte Cassino in 1942. *'He played it on the battlefield,'* Baranowski notes, *'and now I play it to my children.'* He adds: *'It makes me feel lucky – what hardship people had to go through. We can have the world.'*

Music, photographs, works of art in general: they are such powerful agents of empathy, aren't they? McCullin's photojournalism from Biafra is easily available if you search online; I highly recommend looking at those extraordinary images while you listen to this brief but stirring track.

24 June

Six morceaux, op. 85
3: Cavatina
by Joachim Raff (1822–1882)

An unashamedly lovely and romantic little 'morsel' today from a Swiss-German composer who is scarcely spoken of these days, but who in his own time became well known and much admired by the likes of Felix Mendelssohn and Robert Schumann. Self-taught in music, Raff initially worked as a schoolmaster, composing in his own downtime – creative side-hustles were real, even for nineteenth-century men – before eventually, after his music started being published to critical acclaim, finding a way to compose full-time.

Raff, who died overnight on 24 June, carried his pedagogical gifts into music education, working from 1878 at the Hoch Conservatory in Frankfurt where he employed (praise be!) Clara Schumann and even established a class specifically for female composers – an act of radical early feminism in classical music for which we can all be grateful today.

25 June

Argentine Dances, op. 2
2: 'La moza donosa' – 'Dance of the Beautiful Maiden'
by Alberto Ginastera (1916–1983)

Today we celebrate one of Argentina's most important composers, Alberto Ginastera, who died on this day.

Written in 1937, this is one of Ginastera's early works but it's a fantastic example of his ability to evoke the vast magnificence of his homeland through music, blending local idioms with more formal European classical norms. Right from the opening bars of the intriguing melody that floats throughout the first section, there is a sense of anticipation or tension that is gradually released – but not entirely resolved. It's one of those pieces that for me yields something new every time I hear it: whoever that beautiful maiden was, her dance is alluring indeed.

26 June

A Lover's Journey
4: 'Shall I Compare Thee to A Summer's Day?'
by Libby Larsen (b. 1950)

I hope wherever you are on this June day it is temperate and lovely, but just in case you're in need of a musical love letter or some sonic sunshine, here's American composer Libby Larsen setting the immortal words of William Shakespeare, Sonnet 18. It is part of a suite of four pieces *'which chronicle,'* as Larsen puts it, *'the extraordinarily commonplace yet supremely elegant story of love . . .'*

> *Shall I compare thee to a summer's day?*
> *Thou art more lovely and more temperate.*
> *Rough winds do shake the darling buds of May,*
> *And summer's lease hath all too short a date.*
> *Sometime too hot the eye of heaven shines,*
> *And often is his gold complexion dimmed;*
> *And every fair from fair sometime declines,*
> *By chance, or nature's changing course, untrimmed;*
> *But thy eternal summer shall not fade,*
> *Nor lose possession of that fair thou ow'st,*
> *Nor shall death brag thou wand'rest in his shade,*
> *When in eternal lines to Time thou grow'st.*
> > *So long as men can breathe, or eyes can see,*
> > *So long lives this, and this gives life to thee.*

27 June

Cello Concerto no. 1 in C major
2: Adagio
by Franz Joseph Haydn (1732–1809)

The existence of this beloved concerto reflects not just Haydn's ability to write absurdly beautiful music, but also his canny grip on the economics of what was, in 1760s Europe, a newly competitive and fast-evolving market for orchestral music – and therefore, orchestral musicians. At his court orchestra in Esterházy, Haydn kept his finest musicians sweet by composing them works which would show off their individual talents and give them a coveted moment in the solo spotlight. It was a wise move.

This was written for one such cellist, Joseph Weigl, although the score was subsequently lost and only came back to prominence in the modern era after it was rediscovered in 1961. I can't bear to imagine what other masterpieces might have been lost to us along the way – it puts me in mind of Tom Stoppard's play *Arcadia*, and the moment when Thomasina cries: '*Oh, Septimus! – can you bear it? All the lost plays of the Athenians! Two hundred at least by Aeschylus, Sophocles, Euripides – thousands of poems – Aristotle's own library . . . How can we sleep for grief?*'

How can we indeed?

And then I emit a great sigh of relief that there is this!

28 June

Two Aquarelles
I: Lento, ma non troppo
by Frederick Delius (1862–1934)

Music, today, that was first heard in London on this day in 1917, in a concert given at the very height of World War One. It is the opening movement of a two-part suite that the Bradford-born Delius had originally written for vocal ensemble; it was later arranged, in 1932, for string orchestra by his amanuensis Eric Fenby (who had volunteered to help Delius after the older composer started to go blind due to the syphilis contracted in his youth).

The piece is languid, serene and intensely nostalgia-inducing without ever being twee: I find it almost incomprehensible to imagine this being premiered against the backdrop of one of the grimmest conflicts in history. But for that fact alone, it also insists, quietly, unobtrusively, on the great solace and salvation that music can provide: how it offers a glimmer of connection and hope against unfathomable disconnection and darkness. *'There is only one real happiness in life,'* Delius once said, *'and that is the happiness of creating.'* I might add that there is much happiness to be gained from receiving such creations as this, too.

29 June

And I saw a new heaven
by Edgar Bainton (1880–1956)

A student of Charles Villiers Stanford (17 March), friend of William Henry Harris (24 July) and devotee of Ralph Vaughan Williams, Edgar Bainton is largely overlooked these days. This anthem, a soaring and glorious mainstay of English church music, is one of the few works that is still performed with any regularity.

Yet Bainton was an important figure in what is sometimes described as the English Renaissance, becoming a valiant advocate for contemporary English music, especially in the North of England, where he proved himself an inspiring community leader. And his own story is fascinating: in the summer of 1914, whilst on his way to the Bayreuth Festival, Bainton was arrested and interned for four years at a former racecourse that had been converted into a prison camp at Ruhleben, near Berlin. With six men forced to sleep in a single horse box each night, the conditions must have been tough, but again he threw himself into the role of community musical leader, organizing Sunday evening concerts of great range, forming a madrigal group ('Bainton's Magpies'), running music exams, and conducting the ad-hoc orchestra with whom, as we know from reviews in the camp magazine, he also played Mozart piano concertos.

In 1934, Bainton and his family settled in Australia. In her biography, his daughter Helen recalls the *'abiding love'* he had for his work: *'whatever he undertook was done with his whole mind and heart. His vitality was unbounded; his thoughts simple and direct.'* She notes his possession of a *'deep philosophy of life . . . From this he realized how precious were the small, simple, day to day tasks and was contented with his life. He never strove for success nor wished for power, but was deeply aware of the need for spreading the understanding and appreciation of an artistic inheritance.'* Such men, I think, are rare. And necessary.

30 June

1B
by Edgar Meyer (b. 1960)

I first discovered the intoxicating music of American composer Edgar Meyer through cellist Yo-Yo Ma, one of the most famous classical musicians of our time. I then discovered that Meyer had collaborated with many other revered classical artists, including violinists Joshua Bell and Hilary Hahn, pianist Emmanuel Ax and the Emerson String Quartet. That the multi-award-winning Meyer writes uncategorizable music that also traverses genres such as bluegrass, newgrass and jazz seems, then, beside the point.

This mesmerizing track comes from the 2000 Grammy-award-winning album *Appalachian Journey*, featuring Yo-Yo Ma as well as violinist Mark O'Connor. If it doesn't transport you somewhere else, instantly and delightfully, perhaps to a sun-drenched, corn-fed American landscape, I'll eat my hat.

JULY

1 July

Avant-dernières pensées – Penultimate Thoughts
3: 'Méditation'
by Erik Satie (1866–1925)

A shimmering, startling minute of music to open this new month from Erik Satie, who died on this day.

There is so much more to Satie than the famous *Gymnopédie no. 1* that gets rolled out so often, in TV ads, film scores, 'relaxing classical' compilations. This somewhat unsettled 'Méditation' provides the briefest of glimpses into a rare musical sensibility that, for all it both baffled contemporary detractors and bred a generation of slavish imitators, continues to evade easy categorization. Idiosyncratic (one of his works is supposedly written '*in the Shape of a Pear*'), a little obscure (at the time of his death he was barely known outside of Paris) and wildly romantic (after his death his friends discovered stacks and stacks of unsent love letters to his muse Suzanne Valadon: see tomorrow), Satie remains profoundly influential. It's impossible to imagine the twentieth-century soundscape without the hypnotic, seductive, transcendent music he pioneered – Satie-esque particles lodge, *scintillant*, in everything from John Cage (5 September) to Steve Reich (26 March, 3 October) to Aphex Twin (14 April) and, indeed, tomorrow's composer . . .

2 July

Absynthe Cocktail
by Elena Kats-Chernin (b. 1957)

'*A complicated, funny, talented man,*' is how the Uzebekistan-born Elena Kats-Chernin fondly describes yesterday's composer Erik Satie: '*I have loved him from the first note I ever heard.*' Of her 2017 album *Unsent Love Letters*, a stunning and intimate extended homage to the French composer, from which this piece comes, she adds, '*I hope there is a little bit of Satie magic sprinkled throughout . . . to remind us how wonderful his music is.*'

Taking as her starting point the dozens of unsent love letters that were discovered in Satie's Paris apartment after his death in 1925, Kats-Chernin has produced a suite of twenty-six miniatures – '*some are questions, some are feelings, many started as a one-bar meditation written down as an afterthought*'. These pieces not only riff lovingly on Satie's own music but touch directly on aspects and anecdotes from his life, including his broken heart (he loved only one woman, Suzanne Valadon, his whole life; apart from one short affair it was not requited) and his death from cirrhosis of the liver, probably caused by too much drinking (his preferred, lethal tipple was absinthe). That gives this piece, with its '*quiet, almost oriental, other-wordly quality*', as the composer describes it, a bittersweet if beautiful tinge.

3 July

'Glück das mir verblieb' – Marietta's Lied
from *Die tote Stadt* – *The Dead City*
by Erich Wolfgang Korngold (1897–1957)

This aria from Korngold's smash hit 1920 opera, premiered in Germany when he was just twenty-three, works beautifully in the many different arrangements that have been made of it – for example, for violin, cello and even the trumpet. (There is something about the sound of the trumpet reaching for Korngold's sustained, yearning notes that I find particularly wrenching.)

In its original form the aria includes lines such as '*You are my light and day. . . Hope soars heavenward . . . Death will not separate us. If you must leave me one day, trust that there is another life . . .*' and even in a version without words, that longing sentiment somehow gets conveyed; a testament to Korngold's prodigious ability to write music that powerfully evokes narrative drama.

Such gifts were later put to superb use when the Austrian-born Korngold, fleeing Nazi persecution, arrived in Hollywood in 1934, at the suggestion of his countryman and fellow Jew, the theatre director Max Reinhardt. Korngold went on to become the godfather of film music as we know it, and one of the most influential composers of screen music ever to have lived.

4 July

'America'
from *West Side Story*
by Leonard Bernstein (1918–1990)

For 4 July, I couldn't resist: let's hear it for a singular American, writing an American anthem, from a totemic work that remains as potent in contemporary America as it ever was. Bernstein – born in Massachusetts, died in New York – was among the first American-born, American-educated classical musicians to really make his mark. (Those who preceded him, such as Aaron Copland and George Gershwin, studied extensively in Europe; the outbreak of the World War Two kept Bernstein on home turf.)

And oh, what a mark 'Lenny' made. Whether in the opera house or concert hall, on Broadway, on television, in person or in print, Bernstein truly had it all. A passionate educator; a searing intellect; a beautiful writer; a superb pianist; an electrifying conductor (and as fine an interpreter of the classical greats, especially Beethoven and Mahler, as we have arguably ever had); a socially engaged humanitarian; a legit celebrity; a devoted father, if tormented husband; and perhaps that rarest of all things in classical music, an actual man of the people. (When his funeral procession moved through the streets of Manhattan towards his final resting place at Green-Wood Cemetery in Brooklyn, construction workers famously stopped, removed their hard hats, waved and cheered, 'Goodbye, Lenny!')

And then – then there is Bernstein's music, his extraordinary music. Perhaps you might think: oh yeah, *this* one. I know this. I can skip this. But please don't – listen again, listen anew. It is five minutes of pure, outrageous genius. Happy Independence Day, America!

5 July

'Kapsberger'
by Giovanni Girolamo Kapsberger (1580–1651)

After yesterday's antics, some cooling, calming, gently repetitious music today from the early Baroque era, and a German-Italian composer (sometimes known as Johann Hieronymous) about whom we know little, other than that his contribution to music for lute and theorbo (a fourteen-stringed plucked instrument with a long, extended neck) was significant.

If the name Kapsberger is relatively unfamiliar today, though, he seems to have been much admired in his time. Not only were the 'academies' he founded in Italy described as among the *wonders of Rome*', but the contemporary polymath Athanasius Kircher – the man who thought he had deciphered Egyptian hieroglyphs, no less – declared him a *'superb genius'* . . . one who had *'successfully penetrated the secrets of music'*.

Whether or not it is penetrating secrets, I could listen to music like this all day (and if you're looking for a great performance of this I would recommend Paul O'Dette's on Harmonia Mundi). If I need a mental reset of the purest sort, it delivers.

6 July

~~~~~

Plan & Elevation: The Grounds of Dumbarton Oaks
4: 'The Orangery'
by Caroline Shaw (b. 1982)

We first encountered the formidably talented American composer Caroline Shaw back in April, with the piece for which she became, in 2013, aged thirty, the youngest ever recipient of the Pulitzer Prize for Music. Today we'll hear a piece composed two years later, while she was the inaugural Music Fellow at Dumbarton Oaks, the historic estate in Georgetown, Washington, D.C. which played host to the famous 1944 conference that led eventually to the foundation of the United Nations.

The string quartet from which this comes was commissioned to mark the seventy-fifth anniversary of that momentous event, and Shaw reveals that much of her inspiration came from walking the handsome grounds of the estate itself. This mesmerizing, minimalist fourth movement evokes the orangery and *'the slim, fractured shadows in that room as the light tries to peek through the leaves of the aging fig vine'*, as she describes it. It's a beautiful instance of history, music and architecture converging in one sublime whole.

7 July

Étude in E major, op. 10 no. 3 ('*Tristesse*') by Frédéric Chopin (1810–1849)

Apparently, Chopin himself thought this was the most beautiful melody he'd ever written. Which is really saying something, because pretty much *every* melody he composed in his tragically short life is a masterpiece. I'm not even kidding (type 'Chopin' into your preferred musical search engine and you'll see what I mean). But yes, this one: it's practically perfect in every way.

The nickname '*Tristesse*' – 'Sadness' – was not given by Chopin himself, but whoever coined it was on to something. I was particularly moved to learn that sometime in 1943 or 1944, in Birkenau, this piece was arranged by Alma Rosé, niece of Gustav Mahler and leader of the Women's Orchestra of Auschwitz. It was strictly forbidden, of course, for the music of Polish composers to be performed in the Nazi death camp. But this was intended for a secret performance for the benefit, call it soul-sustenance, of the orchestra members themselves, as well as a handful of trusted prisoners.

Violinist and Birkenau inmate Helena Dunicz-Niwińska, who survived the Holocaust, clearly recalled '*preparing and playing the melody of Chopin's Tristesse I (Etude Op. 10, No. 3 in E major) as arranged for voice and orchestra by Alma*'. She wrote in her memoirs: '*We could not, of course perform that work publicly at any of the Sunday concerts, because the playing of Chopin was forbidden under the Third Reich. We played it for ourselves and for women prisoners who sneaked in to listen to something special, something that expressed through music our resistance to the German oppressors.*'

8 July

Requiem – Songs for Sue, op. 33
'W. H. Auden'
by Oliver Knussen (1952–2018)

'*Music of exceptional refinement and subtlety*', is how the British composer Colin Matthews describes his late, great colleague Oliver Knussen's output: '*a few bars of Knussen may have more impact than whole movements by lesser composers*'. The composer, conductor and artistic director who died on this day was revered by the classical community around the world, not just for his own music but for the vision and generosity with which he performed and often premiered other contemporary works. '*He was,*' notes Matthews, '*the central focus of so many activities, and an irreplaceable mentor to his fellow composers, who constantly sought and relied on his advice and encouragement.*'

Composers can often come across as a rather isolated and ego-driven breed, so to have someone of Knussen's stature extend such support to others is cheering indeed. A precocious talent who was conducting his own first symphony by fifteen (performed by the esteemed London Symphony Orchestra, no less) he was but eighteen when his second symphony was commissioned by Yehudi Menuhin, one of the greatest classical artists of all time. And he went on to have a stellar career, producing chamber works, more symphonies, and two 'fantasy operas' in collaboration with Maurice Sendak, including the much-loved *Where the Wild Things Are*.

Today's piece is on a more personal and intimate scale: a movement from a requiem he wrote in 2005–2006 in memory of his late wife, Sue. This movement sets words – '*If I could tell you I would let you know*' – by W. H. Auden, described by Knussen as '*a special favourite of Sue's and mine*'. Of the music, he says, with touching humility: '*It's not a huge work . . . but it's a big piece emotionally.*'

9 July

Let Nothing Trouble You
by Roderick Williams (b. 1965)

Another multi-talented British musician takes centre stage today: the baritone, composer and sometime BBC Radio 3 broadcaster Roderick Williams.

This ravishing choral work sets a prayer, *'Nada de turbe'*, by the Spanish mystic St Teresa of Ávila, and Williams – who was commissioned by the Genesis Foundation to write this for the leading British ensemble The Sixteen – says he was instantly drawn to the *'comforting nature'* of the words: *'Hers is a prayer of protection and consolation,'* he notes, *'but it also has a sort of loving maternal feel about it, almost like a lullaby.'* I find in both the music and the words intense solace indeed.

10 July

Piano Quartet in A Minor
by Gustav Mahler (1860–1911)

Mahler, son of a tavern proprietor and soap-maker, one of classical music's all-time greats, is known principally for his epic symphonies and his genre-defining song cycles; this is the only piece of chamber music, at least that survives, that he wrote without a vocal line. As far as I'm concerned, that only makes it more precious. Right from the opening bars, in which the instrumental lines emerge, eerily, out of the silence, he creates a certain dramatic, even filmic atmosphere and sense of foreboding. (Martin Scorsese included this work in his 2010 horror movie *Shutter Island*, starring Leonardo DiCaprio.) But it's beautiful too, *so* beautiful – with soaring melodic lines and a sweet-ness, at moments, that breaks my heart.

The work is even more impressive when you consider that Mahler was only fifteen or sixteen when he started writing it; still a student in Vienna. A single movement (most quartets have four) for piano, violin, viola and cello, it was probably intended as the opening of a full quartet which was never completed.

The premiere performance took place on this day in 1876 at the Vienna Conservatory, with Mahler himself at the piano; we know that at least two further performances took place that same year, and then . . . nothing. The manuscript was lost until his widow Alma discovered it in the 1960s, shortly before her death. It was finally published in 1970, fifty-nine years after Mahler's death, the same year that the Beatles released *Let It Be*, Simon & Garfunkel released *Bridge Over Troubled Water* and Miles Davis released *Bitches Brew*. Quite the thought . . .

11 July

An American in Paris
by George Gershwin (1898–1937)

On this day, we lost one of the most luminous musical geniuses of all time, and we lost him cruelly, tragically early: George Gershwin was just thirty-eight when he died from a malignant brain tumour. Like Mozart or Hendrix, Winehouse or Cobain, it hardly bears thinking about what he might have gone on to produce had he only lived on.

Still, we are blessed to have what we have. Masterpieces such as *Porgy and Bess* (1935), *Rhapsody in Blue* (1924), standards such as 'I Got Rhythm' (1930) or 'Summertime' (1935), and this orchestral glory from 1928, his so-called 'rhapsodic ballet', inspired by his time living and studying in the whirl and glamour of 1920s Paris (he even brought back four taxi horns from Paris for the New York premiere).

At seventeen or so minutes, this is one of the longest pieces in the book, but it's also like a mini-universe in musical narrative, so if you can settle in, I promise it will elevate and energize whatever you're up to today. In fact, I'm going to go so far as to say I'm certain there is nothing, no life circumstance, that can't be uplifted by this music.

12 July

Trio Sonata in C major, RV 82
2: Larghetto
by Antonio Vivaldi (1678–1741)

It's fair to say the mandolin doesn't get a lot of time in the classical solo spotlight. Yet the instrument, a small and unobtrusive member of the lute family, holds a certain magic: no less a figure than the mighty Beethoven both played it and composed pieces for it, and it also features in works by composers as varied as Verdi, Massenet, Mahler, Schoenberg, Webern and Stravinsky.

One of the mandolin's greatest advocates was the Baroque genius Antonio Vivaldi. Although he didn't write a *vast* quantity of mandolin music – presumably there was hardly the same market for it as for his wildly popular violin concertos – the pieces that he did write for the instrument, both solo and duo, are simply delightful. And this trio sonata, although originally written for the lute alongside violin and continuo, works an absolute treat in the version for the mandolin, especially this spellbinding slow movement, which offers a perfect opportunity for the hushed, expressive eloquence of the mandolin to shine.

13 July

Another Hike
by Volker Bertelmann, aka Hauschka (b. 1966)

It was a local church service in his German hometown that first introduced the musician known as Hauschka to the beauty of classical music: aged nine, he started to learn classical piano, which he studied for the next decade. Along the way, he also formed a rock band and later a very successful hip-hop duo with his cousin, before becoming the de facto modern master of what is known as 'prepared piano' (an instrument whose insides have been altered with, for example, mutes, tape, bottle caps and other assorted elements so its keys produce radically different timbres and effects). Much inspired by the likes of Erik Satie, John Cage and Max Richter, Hauschka has collaborated with major classical musicians such as Finnish violinist Pekka Kuusisto, ex-Kronos Quartet cellist Jeffrey Zeigler and star American violinist Hilary Hahn, to whom he is married.

This track, released in 2019, was a chance discovery for me, stumbled upon while I was searching for something else. (Sometimes I really do love the internet.) I'm grateful for that moment of serendipity: this quiet, undulating piece for solo piano from an album celebrating the profound beauty of the natural world has become something to cherish.

14 July

Les nuits d'été – Summer Nights, op. 7
1: 'Villanelle'
by Hector Berlioz (1803–1869)

For Bastille Day, *la Fête Nationale* in France, we'll hear today from one of that country's most forward-thinking, free-spirited and brilliant, if occasionally controversial, composers.

Born into the post-Revolution era, Berlioz was expected, like any good bourgeois son, to follow his father into a 'proper' career – in this case, medicine. (Berlioz *père* was at least relatively progressive: he is credited as being the first European to write about acupuncture.) The music-obsessed young Berlioz had other ideas. Ferociously, intellectually curious and bookish even as a boy, he was largely home-schooled and interested, it seems, in everything, from geography and anatomy to literature and the Classics (ever the romantic, he reportedly wept at Virgil's account of the tragic story of Dido and Aeneas.) He became crazy about Shakespeare – and about the Irish Shakespearean actress, Harriet Smithson, whom he saw play Ophelia in a fateful 1827 production of *Hamlet* and then pursued for about seven years (*'emotional derangement'*, as one of his biographers put it), until she finally capitulated. (The marriage was a disaster.)

Literature remained a major influence on Berlioz's musical output: his operas include *The Trojans*, after Virgil's *Aeneid*; *Beatrice and Benedict*, based on Shakespeare's characters from *Much Ado About Nothing*, and *The Damnation of Faust*. *Les nuits d'été*, his exquisite 1840 suite of six songs about love, desire and longing, sets poetry by his friend Théophile Gautier, who was admired by everyone from Balzac and Baudelaire to T. S. Eliot and Ezra Pound. I adore this high-spirited, ebullient opening number, which is full of the joys of spring and new love in its first flush.

15 July

Virelai (Sus une fontayne)
by Harrison Birtwistle (b. 1934)

Happy birthday to a towering figure in contemporary English music, Sir Harrison Birtwistle – or 'Harry', as he is fondly known. Prolific, provocative, a creator of everything from huge-scale operas and epic orchestral canvases to intimate chamber gems such as this one, he has been described by *The Times* as '*A great original . . . one of the most gifted composers of his generation.*'

This piece for twelve-part ensemble dates from 2008 but, as is often the case with Birtwistle, whose ultra-modernist aesthetic tends to be applied to subjects from mythology and prehistory, the inspiration goes much further back in time. A 'virelai' is a medieval poetic form; the particular one on which Birtwistle riffs here is '*Sus une fontayne en remirant*', by an obscure but at the time highly regarded fourteenth-century Flemish composer (and contemporary of Chaucer, to put him into context) called Johannes Ciconia. It was thought to have been written as a homage to his teacher Philippus de Caserta: the critic Tim Rutherford-Johnson tells us that the original virelai quotes three works by Philippus, including his '*En remirant*', which itself borrows a text from Guillaume de Machaut (21 April). '*No doubt,*' he notes, '*Birtwistle enjoyed the chance to add a link to this 700-year-old chain.*' Certainly this twenty-first-century take on ancient music is superbly crafted: full of intricate rhythms, striking melodic lines and unsettling, Birtwistle-ish contrasts.

16 July

Dixit Dominus, HWV 232
8: 'De torrente in via bibet' – 'He shall
drink of the brook in his way'
by George Frideric Handel (1685–1759)

Written while a twenty-two-year-old Handel was living in Italy and soaking up all the Italian musical influences he could get his ears on, this sublime setting of Psalm 110, *Dixit Dominus*, is his earliest surviving autograph manuscript. It was likely first performed on this day in 1707, at Santa Maria di Montesanto in the Piazza del Popolo in Rome. The whole work is magnificent: bright and virtuosic and brimful of the bold dramatic gestures that would go on to make him such a superlative opera and oratorio composer, but in this heart-stoppingly beautiful movement, time seems suddenly suspended, as two shimmering soprano lines emerge and intertwine, clash and resolve over a bed of lilting strings and male voices singing in unison, all to truly ravishing effect.

17 July

Page for Will
by Paul Paccione (b. 1952)

'*In all [my] pieces,*' reveals American composer Paul Paccione, '*I try to define what is beauty. I don't know whether this is possible or not . . . but it's a definition I work towards.*'

This short solo piano piece from 2003, not even two minutes long (just a page) and dedicated to the composer and music professor Wilbur Ogdon, is a distillation of something that feels very close to beauty for me. It's music that does so much with so little, I feel I hardly need to say more. I'll leave it at that.

18 July

Haï luli
by Pauline Viardot (1821–1910)

Described by Franz Liszt as '*a composer of genius*' (and he should know), the French-Spanish mezzo-soprano, pedagogue and composer Pauline Viardot was born on this day. Hailing from a ridiculously gifted family (her father was the celebrated tenor Manuel García, and her older sister was the diva and composer Maria Malibran – see 23 September), Pauline went on to become a stunningly accomplished musician herself, as virtuoso pianist and celebrated opera singer. As well as Liszt, she counted among her fans and admirers many other artistic superstars of the day, including Saint-Saëns, Berlioz, Fauré, Gounod and the writer Ivan Turgenev.

Viardot seemingly never intended to become a composer, yet for someone who was dabbling in it on the side, her output is impressive, including five operas, multiple choral and instrumental works, and over a dozen songs – including this one, which sets words by Xavier de Maistre to rather rhapsodic effect. It was Frédéric Chopin who once reportedly said, of Viardot's songs: '*I have always listened with rapturous pleasure*'. I'm inclined to agree.

Je suis triste, je m'inquiète,	*I am sad, I am worried*
Je ne sais plus que devenir.	*I no longer know what is to come*
Mon bon ami devait venir,	*My lover should have come*
Et je l'attends ici seulette.	*And I wait for him here alone.*
Haï luli, haï luli,	*Haï luli, haï luli,*
Qu'il fait donc triste sans mon ami.	*How sad it is without my love.*

19 July

A Little Prayer
by Evelyn Glennie (b. 1965)

Happy birthday to the ferociously brilliant Dame Evelyn Glennie. The Scottish multi-instrumental percussionist and composer is one of Britain's most prominent and high-profile musicians – and in her spare time, she is also a writer, a TED speaker, a jewellery designer, plays the Great Highland bagpipes and has her own registered tartan, known as 'The Rhythms of Evelyn'. And so on . . .

(She is also profoundly deaf, but that has never stopped her.)

Glennie composed this lyrical piece when she was, she tells us, *'still a child myself and had already lost ninety percent of my hearing . . .'* As a meditation in resilience, it takes some beating. *'As a child I would never have believed that such a short and simple piece of music, would come to grow this much. A little prayer serves to prove that one should always bet their chips on what they believe in, for nine out of ten it will be worth it!'*

20 July

Widerstehe doch der Sünde – Just resist sin, BWV 54
1: Aria: 'Widerstehe doch der Sünde'
by Johann Sebastian Bach (1685–1750)

This is Bach's first extant church cantata for voice, written for alto solo and likely to have been performed for the first time in Weimar in July 1714. Based on a text from the Epistle of St James, Bach kicks things off with an unexpected note of dissonance that immediately grabs your attention and sustains it throughout the whole gorgeous thing. The Bach musicologist and expert Alfred Dürr says that the aria *'calls for resistance'*: if so, it's possibly the most beautiful one I ever did hear.

And whatever your thoughts on the religious nature of the text, I think there's something wise and powerful about the sentiment, about resistance.

21 July

Gottes Zeit ist die allerbeste Zeit – God's time is the best of all times, **BWV 106**
by Johann Sebastian Bach (1685–1750)
and György Kurtág (b. 1926)

While we have yesterday's Bach still ringing in our ears, I wanted to offer this breathtakingly beautiful modern transcription, by the Hungarian composer György Kurtág, of a fragment from another early Bach work, the Sonatina from the *Actus tragicus*, probably written for a funeral in 1708.

Bach's original score called for two recorders, two violas da gamba, and basso continuo – a conventional collection of Baroque instruments which would have sounded pretty old-fashioned even back in 1708. Kurtág freshens it up for four hands on a single piano and brings to his spare and reverent transcription a crystalline clarity that is characteristic of his own music. ('*I keep coming back to the realization,*' he once declared, '*that one note is almost enough.*')

The result is a distillation: a work of pure musical serenity that engenders in me an inner state of peace, even resolution. I am reminded every time I hear it of the quiet but undeniable miracle that music can do this.

22 July

Italian Dance
by Madeleine Dring (1923–1977)

A quick shot of musical sunshine today, courtesy of this ebullient little dance for oboe by the British composer, actress, lyricist, cabaret performer and cartoonist Madeleine Dring. Not exactly a mainstream classical name, Dring was nevertheless a gifted and prolific composer who surely deserves recognition for managing to produce the amount of music she did in an era when women, especially mothers and home-makers, as she was, were hardly encouraged in their compositional efforts. Dring wrote solo piano works, piano duets, songs, and assorted chamber music, including pieces for oft-neglected instruments that deserve more time in the limelight, including flute, oboe, clarinet, recorder and harmonica; she also produced an opera and a dance drama. As one of just a handful of English women of the time who managed to break through as a composer at all, she should, I think, be all the more celebrated for her achievements.

Taught by leading composers, including Herbert Howells and occasionally Ralph Vaughan Williams, she nevertheless escaped their influence and managed to avoid the craze for traditional English folk-music inflections of the time, preferring to look further afield for inspiration, especially to the music of Francis Poulenc (7 January) and Rachmaninov. As we can see from her cabaret skits and West End revue lyrics, Dring was very much her own woman, and in her classical compositions she forged her own musical voice. It's a charming one, I hope you agree.

23 July

Pieces for clavecin: Book 3, 14th order
'Le rossignol-en-amour' –'The Nightingale in Love'
by François Couperin (1668-1733)

First of all, I love the idea of a nightingale in love: what an image. And from the moment I encountered it I fell hard for this music by Couperin 'the great', as the famous French Baroque harpsichordist was known in his time, to be distinguished from other members of his lavishly gifted family. (A succession of Couperins held the post of organist at the church of Saint-Gervais in Paris for 173 years!)

François, who produced some 234 surviving keyboard works, would not have been aware of it, of course, but in his graceful modalities, dance-like rhythms (seventeenth–eighteenth-century France was capital of the dance) and the agility he demands from a player, you can almost hear a sonic path being laid that will lead to the future of so much keyboard music, French in particular – to Fauré and Debussy, Ravel and Satie – and also beyond.

In fact Couperin's influence on many later composers was huge, including on Brahms (who sought to bring his music into the limelight, performing it in public concerts), Richard Strauss, who borrows a lot of Couperin's colour and shade in his own majestic chromaticism, and contemporary British composer Thomas Adès, who is a self-professed Couperin fanatic. Couperin was, as Debussy noted in 1913, *'the most poetic of our harpsichordists, whose tender melancholy is like that enchanting echo that emanates from the depths of a Watteau landscape, filled with plaintive figures'*. Beautifully said.

24 July

~~~

Faire is the Heaven
by William Henry Harris (1883–1973)

Composed in 1925, this glorious five-minute anthem by the largely neglected English composer William Henry Harris sets a verse from 'An Hymne of Heavenly Beautie' by the great Renaissance poet Edmund Spenser (c. 1552–1599). It's so beautiful, I think I'll leave it there.

> *Faire is the heav'n, where happy souls have place,*
> *In full enjoyment of felicitie,*
> *Whence they doe still behold the glorious face*
> *Of the divine, eternall Majestie . . .*

25 July

Particles
by Ólafur Arnalds (b. 1986)

Something odd happened to me when I first heard this. I had an involuntary response: I wept. I can't tell you why I was so profoundly moved, physiologically as well as emotionally; I guess it's all part of the mystery and miracle of music, why certain combinations of notes and rhythms work on us, enchant us, in the way they do.

For the 'living musical project' *Island Songs*, from which this comes, Ólafur Arnalds collaborated with local musicians across Iceland to create an extraordinary musical portrait of his homeland. '*I want[ed] to paint a picture of small town communities,*' he has said, '*because I find it to be interesting that these people don't strive to become rock stars, but to serve a role in their communities. They're organist, choirmaster, and so on . . . Even though it's my music, I feel I'm specifically making it about other people than myself . . .*'

I've never been to Iceland: there's no genetic or cultural reason why this music should sing in my blood the way it does, and yet, it does. 'Particles' was recorded on this day in 2016 in the tiny, scattered community of Garður on the isolated tip of the Reykjanes Peninsula. Two old lighthouses sit, apparently, on the wind-battered seafront, in one of which this track was recorded. Complementing Arnalds' piano playing are the ethereal vocals of his friend Nanna Bryndís Hilmarsdóttir. She grew up in Garður and says the place was formative in moulding her creativity. '*There wasn't a lot to do and plenty of time to be by yourself and your thoughts,*' she recalls. '*So I spent my time playing on the rocks by the sea . . . sometimes I would ride my bike to the lighthouse when the weather was nice . . . When I go back to Garður I get the same feeling of tranquility and vulnerability that comes with being a kid . . .*'

Tranquility and vulnerability: maybe that's it.

26 July

Inura: Teaching
by Tania León (b. 1943)

Born in Havana, now based in New York, Tania León is a celebrated composer, conductor, pianist, arts educator, founder of the Composers Now organization (*'a sonic journey through the arts landscape of our time'*) and all-round good musical egg. Resisting any pressure to write music that might force her into any single generic box, she instead draws on her *'inner curiosity'* and her mixed French, Spanish, Chinese, African and Cuban heritage to produce music that reflects her belief that *'Everything is interconnected.'* In other words, she says, *'I have been, in a sense, composing myself.'*

This vibrant and highly unusual work for voices and percussion, which was nominated for a 2009 Grammy, was created for the Dance-Brazil ensemble and is described as *'a celebration of contradictions'*. That seems a good way of encapsulating the mercurial brilliance of the composer herself, with her relentless, joyful advocacy of diversity and equality in classical music. *'All music genres,'* León reminds us, *'represent musical languages, each language generating a cultural impact in a specific segment of a society. All musical genres are therefore deserving of celebration on an equal basis.'* Word.

27 July

Piano Trio in G minor, op. 17
3: Andante
by Clara Schumann (1819–1896)

It's high summer, July 1846. Robert Schumann, the great German composer is desperately ill with the depression that will, a decade later, claim his life. He and his wife Clara travel to Norderney, an island off the North Sea coast of Germany, in a bid to try and help his mental health. (He has thus far firmly resisted the ingestion of medical substances and hypnosis or so-called 'magnetizing'.) But there are famous mineral springs at Norderney, and hydrotherapy has long been a supposed cure for 'psychic complaints'; Robert first tried the 'water cure' two years previously, with some success.

On 20 July, five days after they arrive in Norderney, Robert notes in his diary that Clara is pregnant.

A week later, presumably 27 July, he records that Clara has miscarried.

An *'illness'*, unspecified, following the miscarriage, necessitates that she is seen by a Doctor Bluhm.

And at some point around this time Clara composes this music, this astonishingly wonderful music: her only piano trio and in my opinion her masterpiece. How she manages it, I cannot imagine. (In my experience, having endured three miscarriages, the aftermath is nothing but bleak, intolerable sorrow: the purest grief, utterly physically diminishing; creativity impossible.) But she does, and it's beautiful beyond belief, and my heart breaks for all that she is going through.

28 July

~~~~~~~~~~~

Breathing Light
by Nitin Sawhney (b. 1964)

The creative collaboration between celebrated French classical pianist Hélène Grimaud and the multi-award-winning British-Indian composer, DJ and multi-instrumentalist Nitin Sawhney may sound unlikely, but it has yielded some extremely beautiful and powerful musical results. Sawhney, says Grimaud, has the ability to weave *'contrasting poetic and philosophical perspectives into a single, cogent musical ecosystem'*. The polymathic former accountant, comedian and law student, who is as well versed in Hindu philosophy and the Heisenberg principle as he is dance music, produced her 2016 album *Water,* and they worked together again on the 2018 album *Memory,* from which this track comes – and which *'serves',* Grimaud says, *'to conjure atmospheres of fragile reflection, a mirage of what was – or what could have been'*.

Grimaud is one of the most thoughtful pianists of her time and a conduit of real sensitivity and depth as well as virtuosic technique. *'Music,'* she believes, *'peels back the layers of time to reveal the essence of experience . . . [It] can help remind us that for all in our daily lives that is trivial, there's a place where meaning is stored. And . . . the capacity to reflect and remember that is the wonder of being alive.'*

29 July

Hallelujah Junction
1st movement
by John Adams (b. 1947)

Speaking of unlikely: as inspirations for contemporary classical masterpieces go, this one has to be up there. Hallelujah Junction, it turns out, is a small truck stop on Highway 49 in the High Sierras on the California–Nevada border. John Adams, one of America's greatest living composers, arguably one of the greatest composers *full stop*, happens to own a small cabin nearby. He explains, and I can hear the twinkle in his eye, '*For years I would pass through in my car, wondering what piece of music might have a title like "Hallelujah Junction". It was a case of a good title needing a piece, so I obliged by composing this work for two pianos.*'

And thus, in 2001 this piece – which for my money has one of the most thrilling openings of any piece ever written – was born. *Hallelujah*, indeed!

30 July

Lo, the full, final sacrifice, op. 26
by Gerald Finzi (1901–1956)

The British composer Gerald Finzi was a self-confessed agnostic but nevertheless found in the 'Hymn for the Blessed Sacrament' of Richard Crashaw (1612–1649) *'moments of religious emotion where he reaches an ecstasy hardly surpassed in English poetry'*. (Crashaw himself was basing his text on translations from the Latin of the *Adoro te devote* and *Lauda Sion* by St Thomas Aquinas.) I'm so intrigued by this: that we can be so moved by other people's expressions of faith even if we ourselves don't share that faith.

In any case, those ecstatic words became the basis of Finzi's extraordinary eucharistic festival anthem *Lo, the full, final sacrifice*, written in 1946 to mark an anniversary of the consecration of St Mark's Church, Northampton. It is a work which moves from brooding interiority in the opening bars into the most expansive, glorious, rapturously life-affirming and moving 'Amen' I may ever have heard.

31 July

En rêve, nocturne
by Franz Liszt (1811–1886)

The spectacle of young women shrieking, sobbing and swooning at the sight of their musical idols might seem a relatively modern phenomenon. But before there were Elvis fanatics and Beatlemania, before One Directioners and Beliebers started battling it out to be the most loyal music fans on the planet, there was so-called 'Lisztomania'. Which was an actual phenomenon, coined by Liszt's friend and contemporary, the poet Heinrich Heine.

Liszt, a Hungarian pianist, composer and pedagogue, overcame poverty and somewhat unlikely beginnings to become music's first real, bona fide 'celebrity'. (According to the *Oxford English Dictionary*, that word was first used in the way we use it now in the 1830s, just as Liszt was rising to stratospheric fame.) As Liszt's biographer Dr Oliver Hilmes describes it, his existence unleashed '*a highly infectious strain of Lisztomania that gripped Europe for years at a time*'.

And Liszt was certainly a crowd-pleaser. In a single eight-year period he performed around a thousand recitals – '*an incredible total*', Hilmes confirms. '*In the process, he effectively invented the profession of the international concert pianist. Crowned heads of state paid court to him, women threw themselves at his feet and others lost their reason. The popular press of the time reported at length on Liszt's concerts and at even greater length on the numerous escapades that fuelled their feverish interest in him.*'

For all that this is sociologically interesting, as an early instance of a phenomenon that remains entirely recognizable in our own times, I'm also moved when I think of the toll this hype must have taken on Liszt himself, on the human behind the public superstar. I've chosen a piece he wrote in old age: a contemplative and poignant nocturne.

AUGUST

1 August

Trauer – Sorrow
1: 'Vasara' – 'Summer'
by Pēteris Vasks (b. 1946)

The Latvian landscape, folklore and culture are central to the composer Pēteris Vasks' writing, and especially in his choral works. In this sublime 1978 meditation on summer in his homeland, for women's choir, he combines a modernist, contemporary sensibility with a deep reverence for ancient singing traditions. The effect is a shimmering, multi-faceted jewel.

'*Most people today,*' the composer has said, '*no longer possess beliefs, love and ideals. The spiritual dimension has been lost. My intention is to provide food for the soul . . .*'

Let us go, then, duly soul-nourished, into this new month . . .

2 August

Piano Concerto
2: Adagietto
by Arthur Bliss (1891–1975)

The English composer Arthur Bliss, who was born on this day, was commissioned by the British Council to write this piano concerto for 'Britain Week' at New York's World Fair, to be held in Flushing Meadows–Corona Park in Queens in 1939–40. Some forty-four million people attended its exhibits, and this work was given a triumphant premiere in the summer of 1939 by the New York Philharmonic at Carnegie Hall, no less.

The emphasis of the Fair was squarely on the future, with a slogan, 'Dawn of A New Day', that would prove painfully ironic, given World War Two would erupt not six months after it opened. Bliss dedicated the concerto to the people of the USA, *'so obviously,'* he noted, *'it had to be a concerto in the grand manner and what is loosely called "romantic". Surely the Americans are at heart the most romantic in the world'*. But although he indubitably pays homage to the great piano composers of the Romantic era – the influence of Liszt, Chopin and Rachmaninov is everywhere throughout the piece – Bliss also took the future-focused message of the Fair to heart. Among the concerto's lush themes and sweeping musical statements are some terrifically spiky harmonies and otherworldly effects that make sure to keep it looking forward.

3 August

Children's Suite
2: 'Cheerful Walk'
by Galina Ustvolskaya (1919–2006)

Daughter of a lawyer and a schoolteacher, Ustvolskaya, who came of age in the first generation after the Russian Revolution of 1917, was hardly destined for a career in classical music. But she beat the odds and went on to become one of very few Soviet women composers – in fact, Soviet women musicians of any kind – to gain prominence on the international scene.

Showing precocious musical talent as a child, Ustvolskaya was enrolled in 1937 as a student at the Leningrad Conservatory, where her teachers included Dmitri Shostakovich (25 September), who, just a year before, had been denounced, most likely by Joseph Stalin himself, in a famous editorial in *Pravda* for his formalist opera *Lady Macbeth of Mtsensk* (which was described as '*Muddle Not Music*', and for which a naked threat was issued, that things for Shostakovich '*may end very badly*'). To say that this was a tumultuous time in Russian musical history, is then, an understatement. With members of the arts and intelligentsia frequently disappearing overnight before ending up in labour camps and being summarily executed, the 1930s and '40s were a time to play by the rules or risk death. In art and music, that basically meant social realism: works that championed nationalist values in plain language which could be understood by everyone.

In her early career, Ustvolskaya mostly played along, composing works that were supported by the state; this piece would probably fall into that category. Later, though, and especially after Stalin's death in 1953, she was able to explore and find her own voice. It was a vivid and uncompromising one, glowing with inner fire. '*She has a hypnotic quality*,' the American conductor Leon Botstein told the *New York Times* in 2019, her centenary, '*that is not about minimalist repetition, but about sonority.*'

4 August

Azul
3: 'Transit'
by Osvaldo Golijov (b. 1960)

Premiered by the great cellist Yo-Yo Ma and Brooklyn-based ensemble The Knights on this day in 2006, this contemplative, rhythmically surprising and truly unusual cello concerto by the Argentine composer Osvaldo Golijov takes the Spanish word for 'blue' as its title. I picture a vast ocean of possibility; it's fair to say Golijov dives right in.

Ma describes Golijov, who also has operas, oratorios and song cycles to his name, as having *'an incredibly magnetic personality and a vaulting imagination'*. He adds that *'he writes music that really is of our era . . . Osvaldo composes in such a way that he allows for the introduction of new instruments and sounds.'*

This certainly sounds unlike any of the other cello music we've heard so far this year – and is all the more interesting and refreshing, I reckon, for that.

5 August

Música callada – Silent Music, Book 1
3: Placide
by Federico Mompou (1893–1987)

The Barcelona-born Catalan composer Federico Mompou so impressed the famous French composer Gabriel Fauré, who heard him perform when he was nine, that he was later invited to study at the Paris Conservatoire, where Fauré was director. Mompou was painfully shy and lacking in self-esteem, however; a career on the stage was never going to be an option. Instead, he threw himself into composing.

Much influenced by Erik Satie, by French impressionists such as Debussy, and Fauré himself, as well as by Catalan culture and the sounds and smells of his seaside hometown, Mompou became a grand success in Parisian circles – a notoriously tough crowd to please. *'The only disciple and successor to [Debussy] the composer of La Mer!'* is how the esteemed critic Émile Vuillermoz put it after hearing some of Mompou's piano music performed in 1921.

Yet these days Mompou is not so widely known. Having previously been acquainted with some of his lovely art songs, it was only relatively recently that I first heard this extraordinarily beautiful suite of twenty-eight pieces for solo piano, based on the mystical poetry of St John of the Cross. Mompou himself said that *'its mission is to reach the profound depths of our soul and the hidden domains of the vital force of our spirits. This music is silent ("callada") as if heard from within.'* Incantatory, almost bell-like (I later learned that his family owned a bell foundry and his grandfather was a bellmaker), I had to stop everything and find out what it was. This movement moves me so. I have since played it on repeat, often.

6 August

Earthly Heaven
by Rachel Grimes (b. 1970)

I first heard about the music of Kentucky-born pianist and composer Rachel Grimes through a piece of criticism, in a 2015 *New Yorker* piece by the outstanding music writer Hua Hsu. In my line of work, I am lucky enough to be sent music pretty much all day, every day, and it can be easy enough to explore only what's in front of me – often brand-new takes on hundreds-of-years-old music. (Truly, it's one of the great gifts of classical music, that every generation invariably makes and re-makes it – as Keats once wrote, '*You are always new. The last of your kisses was ever the sweetest*' – but it can also make us lazy when it comes to exploring new things.)

As much, then, as I adore reading music criticism for kicks, I confess I sometimes do it for the sheer aesthetic pleasure of the words alone. A review whose sentences make my heart sing doesn't always, inevitably, lead me to search out the music itself. There often, sadly, just isn't time. But something about what Hua Hsu said resonated so deeply that I knew I had to forage for all the Grimes I could find.

'*I always appreciate it,*' he wrote, '*when I can forget what it is I'm listening to, not because the music is easy to ignore but because I'm lost in something that sounds like so many things at once. There were moments . . . when my memories drifted toward Philip Glass and Michael Nyman, spiritual jazz and soundtrack music, Radiohead's* Amnesiac, *Ryuichi Sakamoto . . . A study in contrast – majestic and radiant one moment, ominous and weary the next. There's a feeling of presence and possibility throughout, as Grimes's sonorous piano seems to dissolve into something sublime and vaporous, a reminder that there are always greater forces at play.*'

Greater forces at play – what a way to put it! Earthly heaven, indeed.

7 August

Dum transisset Sabbatum 1
by John Taverner (c. 1490–1545)

Speaking of earthly heaven. A moment of sonic respite and repose today.

If modern life is getting you down, if it's all a bit much, as it often is for me, I would urge you to try and take a moment and just shut the door, metaphorically or literally, close your eyes, and press play on this glowing, rapturous, centuries-old sacred motet which is barely even ten minutes long but somehow remakes the world.

If none of that applies to you, then congratulations! I'm in awe. I still think and hope you'll find in this music something magical.

8 August

Rêve d'enfant – Dream of a Child, op. 14
by Eugène Ysaÿe (1858–1931)

Perhaps it's being a mother of little ones myself, but there is some-thing that always hits me hard when I learn about composers writing music for their children – for example Mark-Anthony Turnage's *Sleep On*, which we heard earlier in the year (10 June), or Debussy's *Children's Corner*, dedicated to his beloved daughter Claude-Emma ('Chou Chou'), or even Shostakovich dedicating his mighty Piano Concerto no. 2 to his son Maxim on his nineteenth birthday. I always appreciate these reminders that classical composers are not just a breed of iso-lated geniuses perched in their ivory towers doing God's work, but are, often, just like us: going through many of the same things we're all going through, including parenthood.

To that end, here is a serene and lyrical lullaby, composed in 1894 while the great Belgian violinist and composer Eugène Ysaÿe – known in his day as 'The King of the Violin' – was on a long concert tour. He dedicated it to his youngest son, Antoine. Bless.

9 August

Mattinata – Morning
by Ruggero Leoncavallo (1857–1919)

A little piece of history: in 1904, this music was the first piece ever to be written especially for the Gramophone and Typewriter Company, recorded by legendary tenor Enrico Caruso with the composer himself at the piano. Leoncavallo, who died on this day, produced many songs and operas throughout his career, but apart from this historic number, he is otherwise only really known for his one-act verismo opera *Pagliacci* ('Clowns', 1892), which remains one of the most often performed operas in the repertory, usually in a double bill with Pietro Mascagni's *Cavalleria rusticana*.

Mattinata, which has become such a popular tune in Italy it has assumed something of the status of a folk song, is not exactly a ground-breaking premise, but it does the business: a lover greets his beloved at dawn, telling her to please hurry up and wake. *'Where you are not, the light cannot shine, where you are, love is born!'*

L'Aurora, di bianco vestita,	*The dawn, dressed in white,*
Già l'uscio dischiude al gran sol,	*has already opened the door to the sun,*
Di già con le rose sue dita	
Carezza de' fiori lo stuol!	*and already caresses the flowers with its rosy fingers.*
Commosso da un fremito arcano	
Intorno il creato già par,	*A mysterious shiver seems to disturb all nature.*
E tu non ti desti, ed invano	
Mi sto qui dolente a cantar . . .	*And yet you will not get up, and vainly*
	I stand here singing sadly . . .

10 August

Studies for Player Piano
Study no. 6
by Conlon Nancarrow (1912–1997)

Music today from the fascinating and reclusive Conlon Nancarrow, an avant-garde American-born composer who later became a Mexican citizen. A Communist who fought in the Spanish Civil War, joining the Abraham Lincoln Brigade to defend the Spanish Republic against General Franco, Nancarrow was extremely reclusive and barely known outside of his own circle until the 1980s. But at that point, a certain fascination with his music – mostly, like this piece, written for the auto-playing Player Piano – started to grow among a sector of contemporary music lovers and fellow composers. '*This music is the greatest discovery since Webern and Ives,*' György Ligeti (12 June) enthused after immersing himself in Nancarrow's music: '. . . *something great and important for all music history. His music is so utterly original, enjoyable, perfectly constructed, but at the same time emotional . . . for me it's the best music of any composer living today.*'

11 August

Salve regina
by Diogo Dias Melgás (1638–1700)

Back to the Renaissance today, and this intensely sensual madrigal by the rather obscure Portuguese composer Diogo Dias Melgás, about whom we know virtually nothing.

Melgás, like so many before and since, chooses as his source material a timeless Marian hymn that was likely first written, anonymously, in the Middle Ages – but still provides succour and solace today, especially in this radiant version.

Regina, mater misericordiae:	*Hail, holy Queen, Mother of Mercy,*
Vita, dulcedo, et spes nostra,	*Hail our life, our sweetness and our*
* salve.*	* hope.*
Ad te clamamus, exsules, filii	*To thee do we cry,*
* Hevae.*	*Poor banished children of Eve;*
Ad te suspiramus, gementes et	*To thee do we send up our sighs,*
* flentes*	*Mourning and weeping in this*
in hac lacrimarum valle.	* valley of tears.*

12 August

Nyári este – Summer Evening
by Zoltán Kodály (1882–1967)

This spacious, light-filled orchestral work, written in 1906 by the Hungarian composer, ethnomusicologist, linguist, philosopher and pedagogue Zoltán Kodály, is one of the longest pieces I have included in this collection. It lasts almost eighteen minutes, which is a good amount of time, I find, in which to let it open up and expand across a pleasant evening activity – sitting with a glass of wine outside and feeling the world settle, preparing dinner *al fresco*, taking a walk in the last embers of the day's warmth (hopefully). '*The work was conceived,*' Kodály himself tells us, setting the scene, '*on summer evenings at newly cut corn fields and at the murmuring Adriatic waves . . .*' I love that image, but wherever you are, I hope this music will elevate your own summer evening.

13 August

The Darkness is No Darkness
by Judith Bingham (b. 1952)

Setting text from Psalm 139, British composer Judith Bingham described this as a *'choral fantasy on S. S. Wesley's "Thou wilt keep him in perfect peace" which should follow a performance of this work . . .'*

On that note I'll say no more: see you tomorrow.

14 August

Thou wilt keep him in perfect peace
by Samuel Sebastian Wesley (1810–1876)

Born, illegitimate, in London on this day, Samuel Sebastian Wesley supposedly got his middle name because of his composer father's obsession with Johann Sebastian Bach. (I get this. My youngest son's name is Joe.)

Despite the heavy burden of illegitimacy, which was still widely stigmatized in Wesley's lifetime, he managed to become arguably the most important composer of English church music between the era of Henry Purcell in the seventeenth century and a golden period in the later nineteenth and early twentieth centuries which included composers such as Stanford (17 March), Bainton (29 June) and Harris (24 July).

This anthem is, to me, a particularly majestic example of Wesley's talents, delivering four blissful minutes of, yes, perfect choral peace. And it's the piece that inspired yesterday's 'choral fantasy' by the contemporary composer Judith Bingham. It's worth listening to them side by side, if you can.

> *Thou wilt keep him in perfect peace,*
> *whose mind is stayed on thee.*
> *The darkness is no darkness with thee,*
> *but the night is as clear as the day.*

15 August

4 African Dances, op. 58
No. 2 in F major: Andantino molto sostenuto e dolce
by Samuel Coleridge-Taylor (1875–1912)

The Anglo-African composer Samuel Coleridge-Taylor was born in London on this day, to an English mother and a Sierra Leonean physician father who, thwarted in his professional ambitions, returned to West Africa when Samuel was a small boy, leaving the family behind. Coleridge-Taylor was accepted as a violinist into London's esteemed Royal College of Music aged just fifteen, and went on to become one of the first prominent Black British composers, as well as a political activist. He was a man who faced enormous and inevitable challenges due to the structural racism of the classical music world and society in general, but who was much admired by many leading composers, including Edward Elgar (2 June). Coleridge-Taylor was also mighty skilled at incorporating the rhythms and vibrancy of African folk music, as we can hear in this spirited dance.

Coleridge-Taylor wrote prolifically, including symphonies, choral works, a violin concerto, and a trilogy based on the poetic epic *Hiawatha* by Richard Longfellow, which was a major success and made him internationally known. Despite these triumphs, he fought in vain to get paid proper royalties, existed under permanent financial stress and died, tragically, of pneumonia aged just thirty-seven, leaving behind a wife and two children.

A lifelong resident of Croydon, just outside London, he is buried in Surrey. On his modest tombstone are inscribed words written by his friend, the poet Alfred Noyes, that choke me up:

Too young to die, his great simplicity, his happy courage in an alien world, his gentleness made all that knew him, love him.

16 August

Canzonetta, op. 19
by Gabriel Pierné (1863–1937)

Today we'll hear from a multi-talented French composer who was born on this day and is now essentially forgotten. A star student at the Paris Conservatoire, where his teachers included Jules Massenet (1 November) and César Franck (10 December), Gabriel Pierné picked up top prizes in piano, organ, counterpoint, fugue and solfège, and went on to win classical music's most eminent composition prize, the coveted Prix de Rome, in 1882. Later accomplishments included conducting the premiere of Igor Stravinsky's groundbreaking ballet *The Firebird* staged by Diaghilev's Ballets Russes in 1910.

History has not been particularly kind to Pierné, who is considered a minor composer these days, except for a few terrific organ works (he was also a prominent organist in Paris). But he sure has a knack for a delightful melody, as we can hear in this charming little morsel for clarinet and piano, composed when he was just twenty-five years old.

17 August

The Wife
by Jocelyn Pook (b. 1960)

Jocelyn Pook is an award-winning British composer and former violist and pianist who first came to prominence when she started collaborating with film-maker Stanley Kubrick, including on the erotic mystery thriller *Eyes Wide Shut* (1999) for which she was nominated for a Golden Globe. Her collaborators have since included everyone from Martin Scorsese to the Bristol-based trip-hop collective Massive Attack. She is nothing if not versatile!

Pook writes for opera, concert hall, stage and particularly screen; hers is a musical sensibility, rich in narrative eloquence, that seems particularly well placed to tell powerful stories. This soothing yet unsettling track, for example, comes from the score to *The Wife*, a 2017 film starring Glenn Close and Jonathan Pryce, and about which one critic remarked '*Jocelyn Pook's understated musical score may well be the film's true hidden genius*'.

18 August

Memories in Watercolour, op. 1
4: 'Blue'
by Tan Dun (b. 1957)

Happy birthday to the Chinese composer Tan Dun, writer of such memorable film scores as Ang Lee's *Crouching Tiger, Hidden Dragon* (2000) and winner of multiple awards, including an Oscar, a Grammy and a BAFTA. As a child growing up in Changsha, a village in the Hunan province, Dun was apparently captivated by the rituals and ceremonies of the local shaman, which would always be accompanied by music. Although his route to professional composition was not a straightforward one – during the Cultural Revolution he was discouraged if not downright forbidden from pursuing music, and was instead sent to work as a rice planter on the Huangjin commune – he managed to win a place at the Central Conservatory of Beijing in 1977, where his influences included the Japanese modernist composer Toru Takemitsu. Later, after moving to New York City, he became much influenced by the likes of Philip Glass, Steve Reich and Meredith Monk.

Dun's music often draws upon organic materials, including rock and water. Although not explicit, I can definitely hear something of that sensibility in this delicate, shimmering piano piece, written in 1978. A *'meditation and a reverie'*, is how Dun himself describes it, a *'diary of longing'* inspired by the folk songs of his culture and the meaningful recollection of his childhood.

19 August

Hora Unirii
by George Enescu (1881–1955)

I first encountered this effervescent little folk-style dance thanks to the visionary violinist, sonic explorer, curator and producer extraordinaire, Daniel Hope. For one of his zillion interesting projects, Hope was putting together a tribute album to his former teacher and mentor Yehudi Menuhin, one of the greatest violinists of all time, and wanted to find a perfect piece with which to honour Menuhin's idol, George Enescu. Since childhood, Menuhin had been inspired and profoundly shaped by his collaborations with Enescu, a Romanian violinist, pianist, composer, conductor, ethnomusicologist and pedagogue whom Menuhin believed was the greatest all-round musician of the twentieth century, yet often overlooked.

When asked how he discovered this piece, Hope revealed: '*I have someone who works for me. He is like a private detective in the libraries and archives of the world and finds me works that no one (has) ever heard of . . . generally speaking a lot of Enescu's music is still unknown . . . I think it's a pity that the world doesn't pay enough attention to (him) . . . his music is truly fabulous.*' This one is certainly like an energy shot in the arm, not even two minutes of Romanian gypsy glory.

20 August

War Song
by Phamie Gow (b. 1980)

Phamie Gow is a Scottish composer and multi-instrumentalist whose experiences run the gamut from performing at the opening of the Scottish parliament in 2011 to featuring at the closing ceremony of the London 2012 Olympics to being asked by Philip Glass (14 February) – who describes her music as *'full of melody and surprise'* – to perform in his benefit concert at Carnegie Hall. As you do.

Although Gow is also an accomplished harpist, accordion player and singer, it's the keyboard that is her first love. *'I'm so in love with the piano!'* she once said: *'. . . I feel like the piano is like the orchestra; you've got the whole orchestra in your hands. I can hear all the different notes and different sounds in my head . . .'* I love that idea.

21 August

Illogical Lullaby
by Hatis Noit (b. 1985)

'*The human voice,*' says Japanese vocalist and composer Hatis Noit, '*is our oldest, most primal yet most powerful instrument.*' Born in Shiretoko, a small town on the island of Hokkaido, and entirely self-taught as a musician, Noit's name refers to the stem of the lotus: in Japanese folklore, if the flower of the lotus represents the living realm and the root the world of the spirit, the stem is the liminal bridge between the two. And her music somehow reflects this: hard to pin down, it draws upon wide and deep influences including Japanese classical music, Bulgarian choral traditions, the ancient Western practice of Gregorian chant, ballet, opera and even some pop conventions to create a delicate, haunting and multi-layered sound world. '*I use [the voice],*' she says, '*to describe nature's many sounds, a language that isn't logical. Yet it forms a beautiful conversation that isn't restricted to words like the human language is. I want my music to remind us of that.*'

Aged sixteen, Noit underwent something of an epiphany on a pilgrimage to Lumbini, the birthplace of the Buddha, in Nepal. Whilst staying in a temple run by female monks, she woke up one morning to the sound of a lone woman chanting a mantra and was immediately awakened to what has become her own calling: using the raw power of the human voice to communicate directly, and with intense power, things that elude words. '*The sound moved me so intensely . . .*' she says. '*It was so primal. I knew then I wanted to sing and feel that visceral connection myself . . .*' She also explains, '*I didn't understand what the mantra meant, but still, I could feel the energy. Voice comes from our body . . . [and] has so much information from our body and genes . . . The sound of the voice contains this long memory of our long history.*'

22 August

Solo e pensoso – Alone and Pensive
by Luca Marenzio (1553–1599)

Arguably the finest madrigalist of his day, the Renaissance Italian composer Luca Marenzio, who died on this day, is barely mentioned outside of *extremely* niche circles these days. Yet he was prolific in his time, popping out madrigals, villanelles and motets by the dozen – many of which exhibit a distinctive gift for setting text and evoking mood. I'm also struck by the sheer daring of his harmony: such chromaticism and brazen dissonance, often left completely unresolved, would not be heard again with any degree of regularity until the late Romantic and early modern eras.

Perhaps, then, it is no wonder that Marenzio was such an influence on the boldest of his contemporary colleagues, including Claudio Monteverdi (15 May), and the Englishman John Dowland (22 December).

23 August

Disco-Toccata
by Guillaume Connesson (b. 1970)

Today's composer is one of the bright lights on France's contemporary scene; he has also been Composer-in-Residence at the Royal Scottish National Orchestra and is much in demand around the world.

Frankly, Connesson had me at the title *Disco-Toccata*, but I subsequently fell in love with the energy and vitality of his music – which takes influences as varied as François Couperin, Igor Stravinsky, Claude Debussy, John Adams and Steve Reich and turns them into something popping; something entirely his own.

24 August

Four Pieces, op. 78
2: Romance
by Jean Sibelius (1865–1957)

As you may have noticed by now, I have a real weakness for gorgeous, romantic instrumental chamber works such as this one. I know it's basic, but I always find the sheer simplicity of two melodic lines combining in a way that is so much greater than the sum of their parts quietly magical; it gets me every time. This lovely and completely unaffected piece is all the more affecting when I consider the tormented man behind its lyric poetry.

Sibelius was undoubtedly Finland's greatest composer: creator of vast symphonic masterpieces and nation-defining musical statements. But he battled with throat cancer, alcoholism and profligacy; his long-suffering wife Aino had to spend time in a sanatorium because of the mental health damage their marriage inflicted on her. He was a mess, in other words. He was human. And I find such pathos there – and such gratitude, for the toll exacted on the man as he yet gave to us, in all the generousness of any creative act, music like this.

25 August

Chroma: Transit of Venus
by Joby Talbot (b. 1971)

Happy birthday to the British composer Joby Talbot, whose wonderful scores for ballets such as *Alice's Adventures in Wonderland* (2011) and *The Winter's Tale* (2014) have electrified the Royal Opera House in recent years, and who also writes TV and film scores, instrumental concertos (including a brilliant one for guitar, premiered at the BBC Proms), choral works and much more.

It was ballet that first introduced me, inadvertently, to Talbot's music, via his 2006 collaboration with leading choreographer Wayne McGregor on *Chroma*, the multi-award-winning one-act work from which this comes. I remember going to see the ballet, not knowing what to expect, and being utterly transfixed: it was one of those rare experiences that I knew would stay imprinted on my mind for ever; much of which, I am convinced, was due to Talbot's captivating and mesmeric score. I am happy to say that it has lost none of its raw power for me in the intervening years.

26 August

Suite for Cello and Orchestra (after C. Debussy)
4: Nocturne (after Debussy's *Nuit d'étoiles*)
by Sally Beamish (b. 1956)

And happy birthday to another outstanding voice in contemporary British music today, Sally Beamish. She started her career as a viola player but has since become a respected composer of over 200 compositions, including instrumental concertos and music for dance, opera and film. Her influences include everything from jazz to the folk music of her adopted homeland, Scotland.

'*It didn't occur to me that I could earn a living by composing,*' she once confessed, '*but I had spent ten years in London playing contemporary music and working with composers.*' Oliver Knussen (8 July), as it turned out, was particularly encouraging. '*(He) gave me a series of lessons in between concerts,*' she recalls. '*I would bring a score every day and he would look at it and talk about it. Working with him was life-changing.*'

Beamish is candid when it comes to the challenges faced by her gender. '*There are all sorts of reasons why we don't know about women composers,*' she says. '*There is an issue of confidence, and I think that has affected me quite a lot, by not studying composition, never conducting – that was something that guys did. We all have impostor syndrome, but I still feel that I am not the real deal, and [I don't know] whether that's because all of my role models are males, or they were when I was a child.*' She adds: '*I knew Clara Schumann, and I decided she was going to be my kind-of patron saint, because she was the only woman I had ever heard of that wrote music.*'

As depressing as this is (no shade to Clara) it is thanks to the work of Beamish and her sisters, so to speak, that no aspiring female composer growing up today would have to settle for just one patron saint. In that sense she is a reminder of how far we've come – but also, how far we still have to go.

27 August

Lullaby
by Rebecca Clarke (1886–1979)

Another day, *another* pioneering British composer. Rebecca Clarke, who was born on this day, studied at the Royal College of Music under Stanford (17 March). She had a terrible childhood, in which she and her three siblings were reportedly badly whipped by their philandering father, who later cut her off without a penny, and suffered all her adult life with a form of severe depression and lack of confidence. Despite this, Clarke not only became one of the first professional viola soloists – previously the viola had not been considered a legitimate solo instrument – but one of the first ever female professional orchestral players too, after Sir Henry Wood, visionary founder of the Proms, invited her to join his top-notch Queen's Hall Orchestra in 1912. Clarke also founded or played in a number of all-female chamber groups, including the English Ensemble, before moving to the USA in 1916, where she remained until her death, aged ninety-three.

She was also a very fine composer – arguably the most distinguished British woman writing music between the wars – yet her work has been largely neglected or forgotten. Her output includes some fifty-two songs, eleven choral works, twenty-one chamber pieces – including this tender, lilting lullaby from 1909, a piano trio, and a viola sonata which is one of the benchmarks of the repertoire – but at least half of this music is yet to be published, far less recorded. In 2000, however, the Rebecca Clarke Society was established to champion the study and performance of her music, so we have to hope that sorry state of affairs is on its way to changing.

28 August

'Sleep'
from *Five Elizabethan Songs*
by Ivor Gurney (1890–1937)
arr. Iain Farrington (b. 1977)

To one of Rebecca Clarke's direct contemporaries today and another British composer, Ivor Gurney, who was born on this day. Like Clarke, he studied at the Royal College of Music under Charles Villiers Stanford (on a coveted scholarship); like Clarke, he suffered from crippling depression; like Clarke, his creative gifts were immense, and he deserves far greater recognition.

It's said that Stanford considered Gurney the most talented in his class, which is really saying something as his other pupils, quite apart from Clarke, included the celebrated composers Arthur Bliss (2 August), John Ireland and Ralph Vaughan Williams. Gurney was also a brilliant poet, publishing a number of collections, although this set of songs, composed in the winter of 1913–1914, sets not his own words but texts by the Jacobean playwright John Fletcher (1579–1625). There is a particularly painful irony to this one, given Gurney's tragic life. He had suffered a nervous breakdown even before he enlisted as a private in 1915, and although he survived a harrowing World War One, where he was twice wounded, once by gas, he was permanently traumatized. By 1921, his mental health had completely broken down and he spent the last fifteen years of his life in institutions, dying of tuberculosis in the City of London Mental Hospital. I find this piece, especially in this stunning arrangement for tenor and string orchestra, desperately moving. It haunts me – but in the very best possible way that wonderful art and human stories can.

29 August

Idyll
5: Adagio
by Leoš Janáček (1854–1928)

Leoš Janáček was profoundly influenced by the Moravian folk songs, rural speech patterns, scales and melodies of his homeland, as well as by Romantic musical titans of the day, including Richard Wagner and Anton Dvořák. He is now considered one of the most important Czech composers of all time and a major voice in late-Romantic/early modernist music. But he struggled for recognition throughout most of his career and only became widely known at the age of sixty.

Although Janáček was still composing well into old age, and indeed wrote all his most celebrated works in the last decade of his life, today we'll hear a piece from his youth. The *Idyll*, for string orchestra, is only the second large-scale orchestral work of Janáček's that survives. Written when he was just twenty-four and completed on this day in 1878, it had its premiere later that year, conducted by the composer himself, and must have felt like a momentous occasion: his hero Anton Dvořák, whose influence can be strongly felt and heard throughout the piece, was in the audience.

It would be at least another thirty years or so before Janáček reached the sort of critical esteem in which he is held today. As John Rockwell in the *New York Times* puts it, his lifelong struggle for recognition and eventual triumph *'should be one of the great inspirations for late bloomers everywhere'*.

30 August

The Seasons
4: 'Summer'
by Thea Musgrave (b. 1928)

As we head towards the close of summer, in the northern hemisphere at least, a last nod to the season today from one of the most formidable and prolific British composers of our time, the Scottish-born, New York-dwelling Thea Musgrave, who writes, as she puts it, in pursuit of *'vivid dramatic forms for abstract music'.*

Musgrave is a force of nature, no other phrase for it. Well into her nineties and still embracing life with gusto and vigour, she is often to be spotted around New York's concert halls and theatres. (I once bumped into her and her husband, the opera conductor Peter Mark, holding hands, on a Manhattan subway platform. I asked if they were headed home, like I was, as it was getting late; they informed me that, no, they were on their way to a party.) And she is as busy composing as ever, a living exemplar of her own advice to young aspiring composers: *'Don't do it, unless you have to. And if you do, enjoy every minute of it.'*

She truly does seem to enjoy every single minute. Musgrave has written vast amounts of music in her long career, including more than a dozen operas, many based on the lives of historical figures such as Mary, Queen of Scots and Harriet Tubman. She is also much influenced by the visual arts: *The Seasons,* from which this comes, was sourced from a fruitful visit to the Metropolitan Museum of Art. *'It is fulfilment and celebration,'* Musgrave explains. *'Inspired by Van Gogh's Le 14 Juillet à Paris, Jasper Johns' Flag, and Monet's Rue St Denis Festivities of June 30, 1878, the scene of season, place and rejoicing is reinforced in the music by the layering of the national anthems of the USA and France . . . the liberation from tyranny.'*

31 August

Ich wandle unter Blumen – I wander among flowers
by Alma Mahler (1879–1964)

An intriguing sliver of a song to end the month from the ever-enigmatic Alma Mahler, Gustav Mahler's wife, who was born on this day. Although Alma had been crazy about composing in her early years, she left behind only seventeen songs at the end of her turbulent and chequered life, giving us only the merest hint of the talent that might have been.

It's long been argued that Gustav Mahler as good as forbade Alma from continuing to compose after they were married in 1902 (he was nineteen years her senior and already a major figure in the musical establishment); whether this was true or not, we know that she did effectively stop composing at that point. When their marriage seriously hit the rocks in 1910, after they'd lost their beloved first daughter to diphtheria and Alma had begun an affair with the architect Walter Gropius (who would later become her second husband), Gustav, in despair, did seem to relent, even editing a few of her songs – including this one – and setting her up with his own publisher, Universal Edition. But it was not enough; nowhere near enough: Alma never composed again.

SEPTEMBER

1 September

'September'
From *Vier letzte Lieder – Four Last Songs*
by Richard Strauss (1864–1949)

And just like that: September has come.

Strauss was in the very autumn of his life, eighty-four years old, when he composed his *Four Last Songs*. They were never published or performed in his lifetime – he died the following year – but hold iconic status among singers. As a legacy, there's nothing else quite like them.

1948 and the world was still reeling after the horrors of World War Two, the Holocaust, the devastation of so much, so many. Strauss was not immune: he had witnessed the decimation by Allied bombs of his homeland – and had immortalized his despair in the extraordinary string piece *Metamorphosen* of 1945; he had also endured the shame of appearing before a denazification tribunal, having unwittingly become a puppet of the Nazi regime in the early 1930s, when he was appointed Director of the Reichsmusikkammer before being swiftly removed from office when he stood firmly by the Jewish librettist Stefan Zweig.

Four Last Songs look not back but forward, to death, yet they do so with tremendous peacefulness and serenity. And in the forces he chose to write for at the very end, it is almost as though Strauss is bidding farewell to his three great musical loves, with a soprano line (his beloved wife Pauline was a soprano), a solo horn part (his beloved father Franz was a horn player), and the orchestra itself – for whom he paints a canvas so vivid in colour and rich in storytelling power it takes one's breath away. Although it was later grouped as second in the set, 'September' was the last he wrote; the last time Richard Strauss ever put pen to manuscript paper. And I honestly think it's one of the most beautiful things I've ever heard.

2 September

Umbrian Scene
by Ulysses Kay (1917–1995)

Born in Tucson, Arizona, today's composer was born into a family of jazzmen, but he decided to focus his own considerable talents on classical music – and I, for one, am most grateful. Ulysses Kay's mentors or teachers included William Grant Still (11 May, 10 October), and Paul Hindemith (16 November); he went on to become a prolific classical composer as well as a highly respected music educator.

I love this piece. I mean, *I love it*. I love the chromatic colours, the unusual tonal palette – definitely of the twentieth century (he wrote it in 1963) but not so *obviously* showing itself to be of that moment. I love its timelessness. I love the lyrical, rich harmonies of his orchestration: at times, the romantic lushness; at others, the almost polyphonic sparseness. I love the sense of space and yet drama and something that all great music has: an ineffable quality, of just being *it*.

Kay won many plaudits for his music (this piece refers to an Italian sojourn following his victory in the legendary Prix de Rome competition.) Yet – sigh – his work is shamefully ignored, at least to date. Hopefully that will be redressed soon. Ponder this: if a composer with such lavish gifts just happened to be white, would it be the same scenario?

3 September

'The Flight of the Bumblebee'
from *The Tale of Tsar Sultan*
by Nikolai Rimsky-Korsakov (1844–1908)

This dizzying little interlude has become mainstream famous in its own right, and for obvious reasons, but it originally hails from an opera Rimsky-Korsakov wrote in 1899–1900 based on a poem by Aleksandr Pushkin, with the catchy title *The Tale of Tsar Sultan, of his Son the Renowned and Mighty Bogatyr Prince Gvidon Saltanovich, and of the Beautiful Princess-Swan.*

In the opera, this music takes place at the end of a tableau scene in Act 3, during which the magical Swan-Bird has transformed the Tsar's Son, Prince Gvidon, into a bumblebee, so that he can fly away to his father, who does not know that he's alive. It is characteristic of Rimsky-Korsakov, one of the architects of Russian classical music as we know it and one of the most brilliant orchestrators in musical history, that he is able to evoke this breakneck flight in a flurry of notes.

4 September

Requiem
Introitus 1: Requiem aeternam
by Cristóbal de Morales (c. 1500–1553)

Today we hear music by one of the most significant composers of the early sixteenth century: Cristóbal de Morales, memorably referred to as *'the light of Spain in music'*, as writer Juan Bermudo put it in 1555. Most music historians agree that de Morales was the first composer of international renown to hail from the Iberian peninsula. He wrote prolifically, producing music at times of fiendish technical difficulty, but invariably with great emotional and spiritual depth.

Very few biographical facts about his life have survived, but we do know that on 4 September 1553, de Morales made an active case to be re-considered for the position of *maestro de capilla* at the resplendent modern cathedral at Toledo, one of Spain's plum musical gigs, where he had worked previously. We will never know how successful he could have been, however, because unfortunately he died shortly afterwards (reasons unknown). Within a decade of his death, though, de Morales' name was famous in musical circles in Italy, France, Germany, the Low Countries and the Americas: quite the feat, given the age.

5 September

Six Melodies
1: *Rubato*
by John Cage (1912–1992)

Today's composer John Cage, who was born on this day, has been one of the most hugely influential composers of the modern era. (Max Richter once said that he most admired *'people who have really invented something – I'd count John Cage . . . among those'*.)

Cage himself, in this set of six brief and cool melodies from 1950, was much influenced by Erik Satie (1 July). He had recently spent time in Paris engaged in deep study of Satie's scores, with their own aphoristic, wandering melodies. This was also a period when Cage was exploring what would become pioneering developments around the aesthetics of silence. Within two years, he would produce *4' 33'* (pronounced 'four minutes thirty-three seconds', or just 'four-thirty-three'), his famous/infamous three-movement work that calls for the performer *not* to play their instrument for the duration of the piece. Hand in hand with this went his fascination with Zen Buddhist thought: it was around this time that he famously pronounced, *'The responsibility of the artist consists in perfecting his work so that it may become attractively disinteresting.'*

Not that the spirit that animated his work should in any way suggest dispassion on the part of Cage, who had one of the richest and most vibrant inner lives of any artist. Even the briefest glimpse of the intensely beautiful love letters he wrote to his long-term partner, choreographer Merce Cunningham, are an indication of this. I'll leave you with a fragment of one that is pertinent to the month:

> *pardon the intrusion: but when in september will you be back? i*
> *would like to measure my breath in relation to the air between us . . .*

6 September

Elegy in D flat major, op. 17
by Alexander Glazunov (1865–1936)

As a musically-inclined teenager in St Petersburg, Alexander Glazunov started studying with the leading composer of the day, Rimsky-Korsakov (3 September), whom we met earlier this month and who, in his autobiography *My Musical Life*, recalled '*a charming boy, with beautiful eyes, who played the piano very clumsily*' but who was a quick study and whose development in harmony and counterpoint '*progressed not by the day, but literally by the hour*'.

Thanks in part to that expert instruction as well as his intuitive gifts, Glazunov went on to become a significant figure in Russian music, although he was criticized in some corners for perceived conservatism. As well as taking on the directorship of the St Petersburg Conservatoire (admitting such promising students as Dmitri Shostakovich), he produced symphonies, ballets, instrumental concertos and many smaller-scale works such as this lyrical *Elegy* for cello and piano. Lush and unashamedly romantic, it wears its gigantic heart on its sleeve.

7 September

12 Sonatas, op. 16
3: Sonata terza
by Isabella Leonarda (1620–1704)

It was on this day in Novara, Italy, that a remarkable figure in the history of Western music was born: a woman named Isabella Leonarda, who managed to produce at least two hundred compositions in her lifetime while she lived as a nun at the Collegio di Sant'Orsola.

While most of Leonarda's output was, unsurprisingly, of a sacred nature – she wrote motets, psalm settings, masses and Magnificats galore, all dedicated to the Virgin Mary – perhaps her most notable achievements were her sets of instrumental sonatas, such as this one, from around 1693. In producing these, she became the first woman ever to publish violin sonatas, a fact which gives me shivers.

Even without this distinction the sonatas would be remarkable enough: full of bold harmonies, improvisatory passages that call for great virtuosity, and moments of real grace. It's no wonder Leonarda reportedly became known as the '*Muse of Novara*'.

8 September

Fragile N.4
by Dustin O'Halloran (b. 1971)

Happy birthday to the Emmy-winning American composer Dustin O'Halloran, one of a generation of composers who are gorgeously expanding the limits of what so-called 'classical music' can be understood to be. *Lumiere*, the 2010 album from which today's piece comes also features Max Richter, Jóhann Jóhansson and Nils Frahm, warriors in this revolution, all.

(Music such as this is sometimes described as 'post-classical' or 'neo-classical' but, whatever. You know, by now, how I feel about these labels: as far as I'm concerned we should push at these stupid boundaries as lovingly, respectfully and inclusively as possible.)

Recording of *Lumiere* took place in an ancient church in Berlin, a rustic Italian farmhouse and an old New York bookshop, and it was during this process that O'Halloran apparently discovered he could hear music as colours, a neurological phenomenon known as 'synaesthesia', in which one involuntarily experiences one type of sense in another cognitive pathway. O'Halloran shares this condition with other composers, including Franz Liszt (31 July), Rimsky-Korsakov (3 September) and Richard D. James of Aphex Twin (14 April). '*Somehow in composing I had always viewed the work similar to how a painter would approach it,*' he explains, '*adding colors, texture, adding space . . .*' All of these qualities are in abundance in this soulful and introspective track.

9 September

Lachrimae
by Clarice Assad (b. 1978)

Born in Rio de Janeiro, into one of Brazil's most talented musical families (her father is celebrated classical guitarist Sérgio Assad; her aunt, uncle and cousin are also famed Brazilian musicians; her grandfather was a brilliant mandolin player), the Grammy-nominated and multi-award-winning performer, vocalist, arranger, multi-instrumentalist and composer Clarice Assad writes music that is wonderfully hard to categorize.

She first came to prominence outside of Brazil thanks to the support of the pioneering American conductor and all-round advocate of forgotten voices in classical music, Marin Alsop (see e.g. 17 November). Alsop programmed Assad's violin concerto in a 2004 concert at the Cabrillo Festival of Contemporary Music, and the composer has never looked back, collaborating with such other classical luminaries as cellist Yo-Yo Ma, who has commissioned her to write music especially for him, the storied Philadelphia Orchestra, and esteemed conductor Christoph Eschenbach.

The first time I heard this, I had to double-check it wasn't by, say, Ysaÿe (8 August), riffing on J. S. Bach. But no, it was all Assad, and all the better for it.

10 September

Come, ye sons of Art, away (Birthday Ode for Queen Mary)
5: 'Strike the viol'
by Henry Purcell (1659–1695)
arr. Christina Pluhar (b. 1965)

Henry Purcell is almost universally acknowledged to have been the most important English composer of his time (if not for many more centuries after his death) and has been duly immortalized in the canon as such. But that doesn't mean his legacy has to be preserved in overly reverent aspic: like all the greatest composers, his music can withstand all sorts of imaginative reworkings, such as this playful take by the brilliant Austrian musician and arranger Christina Pluhar and her ensemble L'Arpeggiata.

Purcell's original, written to celebrate Queen Mary II's birthday in 1694, is sparkling enough, but I love what Pluhar does here, bringing the freshness and wit of her musical imagination to an already vigorous and at times ecstatic score, which praises, above all, the joys of music.

11 September

Spared
by Howard Goodall (b. 1958)

On this day in 2001, British composer Howard Goodall was in New York City to do some filming for a TV series. He was walking downtown to meet his crew when, round about Washington Square Park, in Greenwich Village, he found himself suddenly an eyewitness to one of the most horrendous events in modern history. '*With my disbelieving eyes,*' he later recalled, '*I watched the catastrophe of the terrorist attack on the World Trade Center at first hand. I stood in the street as the second tower collapsed in front of me and as the tidal wave of dust rushed towards and through me . . . That day changed all of our lives and I knew one day I would want to compose something to come to terms with my feelings about being witness to its catastrophic events.*'

The result is this piece, which he based on Wendy Cope's '*beautiful, simple*' poem on the 9/11 attacks. Goodall says he felt an affinity with its '*heart-breaking message: that all of us that survived, wherever we were, felt spared, and needed to reaffirm . . . an understanding, at the terrifying moment of crisis, of what matters most . . . love.*'

12 September

Prelude – 'Tristes apprêts' – Sad apparitions
from *Castor and Pollux*, Act 1 Scene 3 – 'Sad apparitions'
by Jean-Philippe Rameau (1683–1764)

Rameau, who died on this day, is one of the most significant figures in the history and development of opera. A composer, harpsichordist and music theorist, he succeeded Jean-Baptiste Lully as the de facto king of French opera, ushering in a new harmonic boldness and style that appalled the so-called 'Lullistes' and delighted his own ardent fans, the so-called 'Rameauners'.

Much of Rameau's work slipped into obscurity, but by the end of the nineteenth century he was being rediscovered by the likes of Claude Debussy, who was in the audience for the first modern revival of *Castor and Pollux* which took place in Paris in 1903, and Hector Berlioz, who was reportedly a particular fan of this aria. And indeed whatever your operatic taste, there is no arguing with this utterly spellbinding passage from the 1737 opera, which is based on the myth of twin brothers Castor and Pollux, one of whom is immortal, and the princess they both love, Télaire. She, however, only loves Castor; after his death, she sings, stricken with grief, this desperate lament at his funeral pyre.

Tristes apprêts, pâles flambeaux,	*Sad apparitions, pale flames,*
Jour plus affreux que les ténèbres,	*Day more dreadful than darkness,*
Astres lugubres des tombeaux,	*Dismal stars of the tombs,*
Non, je ne verrai plus que vos	*No, I shall no longer see anything*
clartés funèbres.	*other than your funereal beams.*

13 September

'Nachtwandler' – 'Sleepwalker'
from *Cabaret Songs*
by Arnold Schoenberg (1874–1951)

Arnold Schoenberg was born on this day – and with that fateful occurrence, the path of classical music changed for ever. Bam. Schoenberg is one of those composers – along with the likes of Monteverdi, Bach, Liszt, Beethoven and Wagner – who represent a metaphorical fork in the musical road after which nothing is ever quite the same again. As a composer working in his wake, you can choose to emulate Schoenberg or reject Schoenberg but you sure as hell cannot *ignore* Schoenberg.

As such, he will always be remembered as the father of so-called 'serialism', the rigorously cerebral, stripped-back and mathematically precise 'twelve-tone' system he devised that turned almost a millennium's worth of harmonic thinking on its head and was a defiant antidote to the arguably overblown excesses of high Romanticism. But before those serial revolutions and adventures in atonality with his acolytes in the so-called Second Viennese School, Anton Webern and Alban Berg, Schoenberg did actually write music that was tonal and non-theoretical. (Think of it a little like Picasso, in his early years, producing all those perfectly figurative, realistic paintings before the earth-shattering abstractions of *Les Demoiselles d'Avignon* onwards . . .)

His eight *Cabaret Songs* of 1901 are interesting examples of this pre-serialist mode, showcasing, according to one critic, *'his most basic musical instincts and responses; these eight poems – dressed, with humor and simplicity, in a tonal language that bears no special label or distinction – give us a unique and amiable glimpse of Schoenberg's muse.'*

14 September

Berceuse, P. 38
by Ottorino Respighi (1879–1936)

To a piece composed a year *after* yesterday's Schoenberg, but sounding for all the world like it might have been written anytime in the century beforehand, today we're back to the lushly orchestrated sound world of the late Romantic era. The Bolognese composer, violinist and musicologist Ottorino Respighi was passionate about music from the past, including the likes of Claudio Monteverdi and Antonio Vivaldi, whose editions he prepared, but he also studied under the great contemporary master of orchestration, Nikolai Rimsky-Korsakov (3 September), and he brings touches of that extraordinarily vivid Russian orchestral colour into his own tonal palette.

Respighi later became best known for his three enduringly orchestral popular tone-poems, especially the picturesque *The Pines of Rome* from 1924, which was a smash hit around the world. But this early piece for string orchestra, written when he was only in his early twenties, caught me off-guard the first time I heard it and I fell for it hard.

15 September

Piano Quintet no. 2 in E major, op. 31
1: Andante sostenuto – Allegro grazioso
by Louise Farrenc (1804–1875)

An absolute cracker of a piano quintet today from Louise Farrenc, the French composer, teacher and virtuoso concert pianist who won praise from many eminent nineteenth-century composers including Robert Schumann and Hector Berlioz, especially for her magnificent chamber music.

Despite her impressive achievements, Farrenc (usual story) did not receive anything like the public recognition she deserved, and after she died, on this day, in Paris, she slipped, like so many musical women throughout history, into relative oblivion. This piece, for example, was out of print for decades and only recorded in the 1990s, well over a century after her death. Which is frankly an outrage. It more than deserves its place in the golden canon of nineteenth-century chamber music.

But for all her own equity struggles, Farrenc was what we might call a good ancestor: she not only fought for her own voice to be heard, but as the only woman to be appointed a professor at the Paris Conservatoire for the entire duration of the nineteenth century, and a revered teacher there for three decades, she also advocated tirelessly and tenaciously for the rights of her fellow women; particularly around the issue of equal pay, for which she persistently battled.

16 September

3 Piano Pieces
No. 1 in D Minor
by Nadia Boulanger (1887–1979)

And while we are on the subject of tenacious and tireless female pioneers in classical music, let us raise a toast to Farrenc's formidable
successor in the next generation, Nadia Boulanger, who was born on
this day. (Although Boulanger would probably hate to be described
thus; upon being asked what it felt like to be the first woman to
conduct the Boston Symphony Orchestra in 1938 she replied: '*I've
been a woman for a little over fifty years and have got over my initial astonishment. As for conducting an orchestra, that's a job where I don't think sex
plays much part . . .*' Preach.)

Boulanger, whose younger sister Lili we met earlier this year (15
March) made an incalculable contribution to the history of twentieth-
century music – and not just classical music but jazz and tango, funk,
disco and hip-hop. Although her dream had been to become a composer, and she certainly had considerable gifts, as we'll hear today, her
real vocation was in teaching. She counted among her students Aaron
Copland, Leonard Bernstein and Philip Glass, as well as tango master
Astor Piazzolla and, wonderfully, Quincy Jones, the legendary producer of Michael Jackson, Frank Sinatra and Aretha Franklin, who
declared her the most '*astounding*' woman and teacher he'd ever met.

She was a wise old bird, too. '*. . . life is denied,*' Boulanger once
warned, '*by lack of attention, whether it be to cleaning windows or trying to
write a masterpiece.*' In other words: pay attention.

17 September

Schulwerk – Music for Children
'Gassenhauer nach Hans Neusiedler (1536)'
by Carl Orff (1895–1982)

This is a piece of forgotten Renaissance lute music by an obscure German composer, Hans Neusiedler (1508–1563), fabulously arranged by a hardly-much-less-obscure early-twentieth-century German composer, Carl Orff, who's otherwise only really known for his smash hit *Carmina Burana* (you know the one, trust me, you know the one). Orff was also a musical educator, developing an approach for children called 'Schulwerk', from which this peppy, percussive little xylophone number comes.

I first came across it when the Oscar-winning film-maker Sam Mendes revealed to me that it was *this* piece of European classical music, unlikely as it sounds, that helped him find a distinctive sound world for his American-suburbia-set masterpiece of a first movie, the multi-award-winning *American Beauty*, which came out on this day in 1999. Mendes, it turns out, used the Orff as his temporary soundtrack on the film, setting a certain tone and vibe for his composer Thomas Newman to be inspired by. (Newman duly went and composed a score that has become justifiably iconic: re-listen to the track 'Dead Already' and you'll hear, right off the bat, his debt to *'dear old Carl Orff'*, as Mendes fondly calls him.)

18 September

Ciaccona
by Francesca Caccini (1587–1641)

Born in Florence on this day, the early Baroque composer Francesca Caccini, who enjoyed some support from the powerful Medici family, is generally thought to be the first woman ever to write an opera – at least, an opera that survives – when she produced *La liberazione di Ruggiero*, based on the *Orlando Furioso* story, in 1625. Well-educated and accomplished, also as a singer, lutenist and poet, Caccini was described as *'always gracious and generous'* and a woman of refinement and wit. I think those qualities are evident in her music.

As well as her groundbreaking opera, Caccini also wrote music for at least fifteen other stage works, most of which are lost. Today, we'll hear a rare Caccini work that survives for instrumental forces alone: her take on the chaconne, or *'ciaccona'*, which was one of the hottest dance forms of the day. It's a real foot-tapper.

19 September

Ave Maria 1
by Rihards Dubra (b. 1964)

A luminous and calming choral interlude today from the contemporary Latvian composer Rihards Dubra, this setting of the thirteenth-century anonymous Ave Maria text was written in 1989, shortly before the end of the Soviet occupation of Dubra's homeland.

It's composed in E major. I wouldn't normally think to burden you with key signatures, but as the conductor Rupert Gough, whose breathtakingly lovely recording of this was the first I heard, reminds us (quoting the eighteenth-century musical theorist Christian Schubart), *'full delight lies in E major'*. There certainly is an aura of delight here, a *'beautiful and understated expression of joy'*, as Gough puts it, *'with the main theme always resolving upwards into the tonic key of E.'* Coming home, if you like . . .

20 September

The Unquestioned Answer
by Laurie Spiegel (b. 1945)

Happy birthday to Laurie Spiegel, the American composer and computing expert who has been a tireless explorer at the intersection of music, electronics, computers, technology and ideas. In the 1970s, Spiegel worked at the legendary Bell Labs in New Jersey and made, as *Pitchfork* puts it, the so-called GROOVE system (Generating Real-time Operations On Voltage-controlled Equipment) *'sing, applying the inspiration of Bach ... Appalachian folk, and the cosmos itself to room-sized computers'*.

In 1977, the legendary astronomer Carl Sagan selected one of Spiegel's works (a computerized realization of Johannes Kepler's 1619 *Harmony of the World*) for the Golden Record which was to go on board the Voyager 1 and 2 spacecrafts; Spiegel keeps good company out there in interstellar space, alongside the likes of J. S. Bach, Mozart, Beethoven and Stravinsky.

This piece, from her 1980 album *The Expanding Universe*, is a gorgeous example of the way her music still resonates on multiple levels. It sounds, according to critic Andy Beta, writing after the reissue of the album in 2012, *'strangely contemporary. That her work can be simultaneously dystopian and luminous speaks to Spiegel's talents. She can evoke the chilling cosmos while also crafting something small-scale and warm ...'*

21 September

Introit and Blessing (*O come, let us sing unto the Lord*) by Cheryl Frances-Hoad (b. 1980)

The award-winning Essex-born composer Cheryl Frances-Hoad dedicates this lovely little setting of Psalm 91 '*to the memory of Ken Hutchinson (1920–2006) of Leigh-on-Sea, Essex*'. A respected local headteacher, he apparently '*loved the English choral tradition*'.

Frances-Hoad loves it too. Premiered in 2012 by the Choir of Gonville & Caius College, Cambridge, where she herself was a student, it proudly takes its place in that glorious tradition, I think.

22 September

'Entry of the Gods into Valhalla'
from *Das Rheingold*
by Richard Wagner (1813–1883)

It was on this day in 1869 that Wagner's *Das Rheingold* had its premiere, at the National Theatre Munich, marking a historic milestone in the history of opera. (It would be another seven years before *Das Rheingold* received its first performance as the opening instalment of the sixteen-hour, four-opera box-set *The Ring of the Nibelung*, or *Ring Cycle* as it is commonly known, at Wagner's own Bayreuth Festival.)

Wagner's *Ring* is based on ancient Norse/High Germanic myths, similar to the ones that inspired J. R. R. Tolkien's *The Lord of the Rings*, and it's fair to say things get pretty complicated pretty quickly. *Das Rheingold* not only sets the scene for the rest of the *Ring Cycle*, establishing characters, recounting key events and revealing plot devices, including musical 'leitmotifs' which will become critical throughout the rest of the series. It also served as the first major canvas upon which Wagner could expand many of the principles he had set out in his groundbreaking 1851 essay *Opera and Drama*. This essentially boiled down to a rejection of the standard conventions of opera, with their formalized arias, ensembles and choruses, arguing for a more radical approach that imagined the music could vividly embody the true *emotional* core of the characters and text through said 'leitmotifs', sort of recurring signature theme tunes which represent people, ideas and circumstances.

And for the most part, it actually works: whatever you think of Wagner the man (and by most sane assessments, he was pretty vile) the music is divine, and powerful, and among the most influential there has ever been.

23 September

Prendi per me sei libero – Take it, because of me you are free
by Maria Malibran (1808–1836)

Before there was Maria *Callas*, there was Maria *Malibran*, the original diva and operatic superstar.

Earlier this year we met Pauline Viardot (18 July); Maria was her older sister, and she was at the height of her fame and powers when she died on this day, following a freak riding accident, pregnant, aged just twenty-eight. '*The queen of Europe. What a marvel,*' is how Frédéric Chopin described her; other musical giants of the day, including Rossini, Bellini and Donizetti, were also ardent admirers.

This aria, in fact, was written by Malibran herself when she sang the role of Adina in Donizetti's opera *L'elisir d'amore*. Critic Patrick Dillon notes: '*when the formidable Maria Malibran took on Adina at La Scala in 1835, she deemed the original aria unflattering; hence, she cleverly composed a "Prendi" of her own and added to it a breezy allegro, "Oh dolce incanto," that sounds very little like the Donizetti of 1832. (The piece is often attributed to her husband, Charles de Bériot, but Malibran's latter-day champion Cecilia Bartoli has claimed it definitively as the lady's.)*' For such a short life, Malibran's legacy is remarkable.

24 September

Across the Stars (Love Theme from Star Wars Episode II: Attack of the Clones) by John Williams (b. 1932)

Lest anyone raise an eyebrow about the inclusion of *Star Wars* in a compendium of classical music, I'm just going to state that John Williams is simply one of the greatest composers of the past century, end of story.

Juilliard-trained, influenced by the likes of Wagner, Korngold, Tchaikovsky, Elgar, Holst, Mahler and any number of other classical greats we have already encountered on these pages, Williams more than holds his own against them all. Superstar classical violinist Anne-Sophie Mutter, who has her pick when it comes to performing and recording any composer she likes, roundly agrees. In 2019 she collaborated with Williams on an album of arrangements of his music for violin, many written especially for her. '*There is only one John Williams,*' she says, fondly. '*What he writes is just extraordinary. Every time I go to one of his films and there is a violin or cello, I think, I would like to play that!*'

I must confess that *Attack of the Clones* (2002) is not my favourite *Star Wars* movie, but the theme that charts the burgeoning romance between Anakin Skywalker and Padmé Amidala really got under my skin, right from the mournful opening refrain in the oboe to the lush, sweeping strings and the spectacular brass. It's classic Williams, and therefore magnificent.

25 September

Impromptu, op. 33
by Dmitri Shostakovich (1906–1975)

Dmitri Shostakovich, who was born on this day, was quite frankly a colossus of twentieth-century music. Born and living through a tempestuous and critical juncture in Russian history, he was persecuted for his musical instincts yet managed to survive thanks to his genius, in part by skillful manipulation of the expectations placed upon him and by riding the Stalinist wave until he was able to give full expression to his musical truth after Stalin's death. Arguably no other twentieth-century figure occupies such a freighted but fascinating place in the classical imagination.

It was cause for some celebration, then, on 25 September 2017, when to coincide with his birthday it was announced that a previously unknown piece from 1931 had been discovered in Moscow's state archives. *New Shostakovich!* Sadly the new discovery was not an epic symphony, *à la* his no. 7, the so-called 'Leningrad' (which has come to be seen as a major musical statement that pays testament to the twenty-seven million Soviet people who lost their lives during the World War Two); or even another provocative, political opera like *Lady Macbeth of Mtsensk*, which had so enraged Stalin in 1934. It was just a little vignette for viola and piano – but an intensely poignant and moving one, a little blues-inflected, a little folksy, at that.

Most likely written for his friend, Alexander Ryvkin, the viola player of the Glazunov Quartet, this appears to have been dashed off in one sitting, but the piece is no less affecting for it. And as far as I'm concerned, all new Shostakovich is a cause for celebration.

26 September

Time on Our Hands
by Delia Derbyshire (1937–2001)

Having heard from Laurie Spiegel earlier this month (20 September), it's time today to celebrate one of Britain's own heroines working at the frontier of music and technology.

Back in the early days of the BBC, sound effects, sound design and compositions for in-house productions were created in a now-legendary department known as the Radiophonic Workshop which was founded in 1958. In 1962, the Workshop was joined by a particularly bright, Coventry-born young woman, Delia Derbyshire. She was working as a BBC trainee, having previously been turned away for jobs (including as a Decca recording engineer) due solely to her gender. Derbyshire was brilliant at mathematics as well as music, and had always been fascinated by sound, as well as by composers such as Bach, Beethoven and Mozart.

The following year, she produced an electronic realization of a score by Ron Grainer which became the theme tune to *Doctor Who*. It was one of the first ever television themes to be created using only electronic means and it remains iconic. (When Grainer first heard it, he was reportedly so struck by how she had rendered his theme that he asked, '*Did I really write this?*', to which she pithily replied, '*Most of it*'.)

I discovered this particular track on an album charting the history of the Radiophonic Workshop (radio nerd, *moi?*) and was instantly struck by the atmosphere and sense of story that she manages to create in an electronic track that is barely more than a minute long.

27 September

In manus tuas
by John Sheppard (c. 1515–1558)

Today we will journey back through the centuries for a spot of sumptu-
ous Renaissance polyphony from the English composer John Sheppard.

Sheppard gets a lot less airtime than his more famous contemporaries, including Thomas Tallis (23 November) and John Taverner (7
August), possibly because so much of his output has been lost. If this
four minutes of music is anything to go by, that represents an unbearable loss. But at least there's this; there's this.

In manus tuas, Domine,	*Into thy hands, O Lord,*
commendo spiritum meum.	*I commend my spirit.*

28 September

Overture
from *The Bartered Bride*
by Bedřich Smetana (1824–1884)

One to blast away the cobwebs today.

Consider this a six-ish-minute energy shot courtesy of Bedřich Smetana, who was one of the great founding fathers of Czech classical music. Set in a country village with realistic characters who feel, unlike most operatic figures, as though they could be actual people, *The Bartered Bride*, which premiered in 1866, celebrates the prevailing of true love over those who would wish to manipulate matters for their own ends (in this case, a scheming marriage broker and some blindly ambitious parents: you get the picture).

It's generally considered the first great Czech opera; as Smetana's biographer Vladimir Helfert notes, he '*is more than a mere musician: he is one of the chief builders of modern Czech civilization, one of the chief creators of Czech culture*'.

29 September

Un Regalo – A Gift
by Mark Simpson (b. 1988)

'*I'm convinced,*' the British composer Mark Simpson once said, '*that if there was some kind of neurological study into the part of the brain that makes a person spiritual and the part that makes them musical, there would be similar things going on. If a concert really grabs me, the hair on the back of my neck stands up and I have chills down my body. It's a physical experience. I can feel the part of my brain that's on fire. There have been moments when I've stopped breathing in concerts . . .*'

I love the way he puts this, encapsulating so many of my own thoughts about music and spirituality. But Simpson is nothing if not thoughtful. A visceral, virtuosic composer who is also an outstanding clarinettist with a major solo career, the young Liverpudlian has been lighting up the classical music scene since he won both the coveted BBC Young Musician of the Year and BBC Young Composer of the Year awards as a teenager (he is still the only person to win both). Simpson, who wrote this piece for his friend, cellist Guy Johnston, is also an ardent advocate for the benefits of music education and opening up a world that can be hideously elitist. He speaks passionately, for example, about the opportunities that came his way growing up in working-class Liverpool thanks to visionary community music education initiatives, including a contemporary music ensemble run by the Royal Liverpool Philharmonic Orchestra that changed his life. '*I became obsessed with the idea of the "new" in classical music after hearing* The Rite of Spring *aged twelve,*' he recalls. '*To hear music written by composers who sat just a few seats away from me, to meet and talk with them, to discover music that I had no idea existed, presented in varied, exciting concerts, was a revelation . . .*'

30 September

Bagatelle III
by Valentin Silvestrov (b. 1937)

Music should be so transparent that one can see the bottom and that poetry shimmers through this transparency.

I was about to start writing more, but I think the Ukrainian composer Silvestrov, who celebrates his birthday today, has captured the essence of his ravishing music here with such perfect clarity that I'll let the Bagatelle itself do the talking.

See you next month!

OCTOBER

1 October

A Downland Suite
3: Minuet
by John Ireland (1879–1962)

What on earth has a truck manufacturer from Cheshire got to do with one of the most popular pieces of English music from the twentieth century? You may well ask, but it was the Foden's Motor Works Band who won the National Brass Band Championship of Great Britain, which took place in London's Crystal Palace on this day in 1932. And they were performing this piece, which Cheshire-born John Ireland had written especially for the competition.

Inspired by composers such as Debussy and Ravel, Stravinsky and Bartók, Ireland is sometimes described as an English 'impressionist'. This work can be read as a kind of musical love-letter to the English landscape, about which he was passionate (and in particular the Sussex Downs, where he later retired and lived, in a converted windmill, for the rest of his life). With its air of bucolic pastoral, the music exhibits a note of English nostalgia. That said, it manages to avoid straight-up cliché and I think it endures because the music itself is authentic, unfussy and true. Also, fact: there's nothing like the sound of a good brass band, and this, in my opinion, is an ideal piece to show that sound off in all its glory.

2 October

Viderunt omnes – All have seen
by Pérotin (*fl.* 1180–1225)

To one of the very earliest surviving examples of polyphony today, from arguably the most important member of the Notre Dame school, a group of composers who were likely living and working in and around Notre-Dame Cathedral in Paris from about 1150 to about 1250. We have precious little biographical information about Pérotin except from one extant treatise by someone self-styling themselves as 'Anonymous IV'. The fragments of salient information Anonymous IV thinks to include are that Pérotin had a Master of Arts degree, and that he bore the title 'Magister', which apparently also gave him a licence to teach.

That's a small but significant detail, as Pérotin's extraordinary, otherworldly, spiritually grounding (and yet elevating) music has been a blueprint not only for much of the sacred choral tradition that followed, but also the non-sacred too. It's with Pérotin, and to a degree his predecessor Léonin, that we can begin to trace the roots of Western music as we know it today: these composers ushered in the first new style of musical notation since the ancient Greeks, and wrote in modes that would eventually pave the way for what would become modern harmony. Consider the minimalist revolutions of the twentieth and twenty-first centuries, many of whose greatest exponents have featured on these pages. As tomorrow's composer, Steve Reich, points out: '*Pérotin is the master of slow, elongated harmonic rhythm, and it's markedly contemporary sounding.*' Speaking of the '*emotional magnetism*' he experienced when he first heard this, as a student in college, Reich adds: '*Viderunt omnes has had an enormous effect on me . . .*'

3 October

Music for 18 Musicians
'Pulses'
by Steve Reich (b. 1936)

The happiest of birthdays to one of the all-time musical greats, Steve Reich, who is, according to critic Andrew Clements (and I agree) one of *'a handful of living composers who can legitimately claim to have altered the direction of musical history'*. Born in New York City on this day, Reich was a pioneer in the development of the twentieth-century musical style known as 'minimalism' and has been inestimably influential on the music of multiple genres as a result.

This piece (especially after a landmark recording on ECM from 1978) was one of the works that cemented minimalism as a serious musical movement, proving that it could be more than just mindlessly repeating phrases and patterns without an emotional core. I will never, ever, forget the first time I heard it, and the immediate, life-changing, mind-altering thrill it gave me. Even today, many years after my first time, *Music for 18 Musicians* has lost none of its power: I find it beautiful and reverberant, mathematically precise yet somehow organic, warm, life-giving, oxygenating, pulsating, magical. As we heard yesterday, Reich likes to describe the instantaneous connection one can have with certain pieces of music as *'emotional magnetism'*; that's a perfect description of how I feel about this one.

4 October

Melodia en La menor [Canto de Octubre]
by Astor Piazzolla (1921–1992)

I realize it's never a good idea to try and connect too bluntly the details of a composer's biography to their musical output, but this dark and pensive piece does seem to reflect a particular moment in Piazzolla's life. *Song of October* was written in 1965 when the great Argentine tango master was on the brink of divorce from his wife Dedé Wolff, after twenty-five years together; at least one performer reckons it could have been intended *'as an elegy to the dying marriage'*. (*'I am madly in love with you, and everyone knows it,'* he had written to Dedé in happier times. *'God! The only things I think about are you and my music, which are things I most love.'*)

Either way, in its blend of classical music, jazz and old Buenos Aires street tango, it is a fine example of the 'nueva tango' style that Piazzolla – who studied with Nadia Boulanger in Paris (16 September) and had always been omnivorously curious about other types of music – pioneered. And it is an excellent piece, I find, to enjoy on an autumnal October evening – preferably with a nice glass of Argentinian red in hand . . .

5 October

Autumn Gardens
3: Giocoso e leggiero
by Einojuhani Rautavaara (1928–2016)

A track today from the late Finnish composer Einojuhani Rautavaara, who, unlike many Finnish composers of the past century, has managed *not* to be completely eclipsed by the long and formidable shadow cast by the great Jean Sibelius (24 August). Rautavaara was arguably more influenced by the twelve-tone music of Arnold Schoenberg or the holy Baltic mysticism of Arvo Pärt. Fascinated by metaphysics, he argued that there are *'other realities, other existences, other forms of consciousness . . . Those exist, I am sure,'* he once declared. *'I have experienced them myself very clearly. And music is one way to find and see a glimpse of these other realities . . .'*

This piece, written in 1999, towards the end of Rautavaara's own life, is a good example of the way he foregrounds a mystical and evocative atmosphere over other potential considerations. Music, for obvious reasons of structure and form, is often compared to architecture, but Rautavaara finds a garden to be the more appropriate metaphor for his work. He once compared composing to gardening: *'In both processes one observes and controls organic growth rather than constructing or assembling existing components and elements.'* (He was also quick to add that his compositions were more *'like "English gardens", freely growing and organic, as opposed to those that are pruned to geometric precision and severity.'*)

This final movement – 'joyful and playful' – starts off, as the composer described it, *'vivacious and brisk, but autumn is a time of leaves falling, of colours, and death, and so soon becomes a solemn dance, perhaps a sarabande in honour of the dying splendour of summer, or as T. S. Eliot said, "late roses filled with early snow".'*

6 October

If the silver bird could speak
by Eleanor Alberga (b. 1949)

Despite the intersectional odds stacked against a Black woman of her generation making her way in this industry – *'it seems to be* still *quite a leap for people'*, she muses, *'to think of a Black person writing classical music'* – the redoubtable Eleanor Alberga has never let either race or gender stand in her way. She says she always knew she wanted to be a musician: at five, she was asking her mother for piano lessons; by eight she knew there *'was something in me that wanted to express something'*, leading to her putting pen to manuscript paper. (The first piece she composed, around this time, was a portrait of her beloved golden retriever, Andy.)

Alberga was born and raised in Kingston, Jamaica – where *'as soon as you learned to walk you learned to dance'* – and she absorbed her culture's intoxicating rhythms and folk culture like oxygen. But along with African and Caribbean music she also started listening to European classical works from an early age, and in 1970 won the biennial West Indian Associated Board Scholarship, which allowed her to study at the Royal Academy of Music in London. She has lived in the UK ever since, and her vivid, candid music, which includes orchestral, vocal and chamber music as well as opera, is a distinctive blend of both sides of her heritage – *'and every mix,'* she adds with a smile, *'in between'*.

7 October

Hear Us
by Anna Thorvaldsdóttir (b. 1977)

Today we hear an ancient Icelandic hymn, or prayer, given a sublime modern treatment.

I don't know how Anna Thorvaldsdóttir does it (and even if I could explain, I would prefer to preserve the mystery!) but in her hands, notes that should be, by rights, low, in terms of their location on a scale or vocal register, become somehow soaring, high. The effect is not to be wrong-footed, but to be mesmerized.

I don't really want to say more, only to give you space to receive this music, wherever you are at. But my gosh, what a simple, and powerful, human entreaty: *hear us*.

Hear us.

8 October

Canzoni overo sonate concertate per chiesa e camera, a 2–3, libro terzo, op. 12
20: Ciaccona
by Tarquinio Merula (c. 1595–1665)

Not a name we hear too often these days, the Italian composer Tarquinio Merula was nevertheless a notable musical figure in the early Baroque period. Cosmopolitan in outlook (we know he travelled at least as far as Warsaw, Poland) and progressive in style, Merula played a key role in the development of many musical forms and innovations that are still in use across multiple musical genres today – especially, as you can hear in this vibrant *ciaccona* from 1637, '*basso ostinato*' or 'ground bass', in which musical patterns are written over a repeating bassline.

Although ground bass was certainly not invented in the Baroque era – you can hear examples of it in some thirteenth-century French vocal motets and European dances ever after – Merula's era was a golden time for the cultivation of a simple but devastatingly effective idea that would become one of the mainstays of music, in everything from classical to pop, funk, hip-hop and beyond.

9 October

Ave maris stella
by Cecilia McDowall (b. 1951)

The British composer Cecilia McDowall always loved singing choral music whilst at school: educated in London, just around the corner from Westminster Abbey, she recalls that *'wonderful building in which to sing, with its gloomy cloisters and dark shadowy corners'*. Composing, she says, *'was always my first love, my first real interest . . . but . . . being a composer didn't seem a realistic way of earning a living'*. After university she followed a much more *'realistic'* path, becoming a teacher, and it was only much later, once her children were teenagers and she was into her forties, that she returned to her original dream. *'I came late to composing,'* she notes. *'I realised I couldn't leave things much later if I wanted to pursue a career in composing otherwise that would be it!'*

As this exquisite and moving 2008 setting of the *Ave maris stella* shows, McDowall has gone on to become a distinctive musical voice, winning, in 2014, the prestigious British Composer Award for choral writing. I love her story and hope it might provide hope and inspiration for anyone who still dreams of pursuing a creative path, whoever they are and whatever stage they are at in life.

10 October

⌒

Suite for violin and piano
2I: 'Mother and Child'
by William Grant Still (1895–1978)

We first met William Grant Still back in the spring, with his epic *Afro-American Symphony* (11 May). Today we'll hear him working on a much more intimate canvas. For this three-part suite, composed in 1943, Still took as his inspiration works of 1930s visual art associated with the cultural movement known as the Harlem Renaissance, that tremendous social and artistic flowering that emerged out of the Black mecca of Harlem between the 1910s and 1930s.

This middle part of Still's musical triptych was based on work by the African-American sculptor and painter Sargent Johnson (1887–1967), who died on this day. Orphaned at fifteen, Johnson went on to produce a number of sculptures and paintings entitled *Mother and Child*, including a beautiful, dignified bronze from 1930.

11 October

Os justi – The Mouth of the Righteous
by Anton Bruckner (1824–1896)

The Austrian composer Anton Bruckner, who died on this day, is best known for his extraordinary, epic, throw-everything-but-the-kitchen-sink-at-them symphonies, but as a writer of smaller-scale church music, including this sacred motet, he's also hard to beat.

Bruckner was part of Franz Xaver Witt's 'Cecilian' movement of church music reform – so named for the patron saint of music, Cecilia – which sought to restore purist elements of Gregorian chant and Renaissance polyphony to contemporary Austrian choral music. Written in 1879, this celebratory setting of words from Psalm 37 derives its serene and spare power in part from his decision, in that 'Cecilian' spirit, to compose it in one of the ancient Gregorian chant modes: the old church Lydian mode, essentially a white-note scale based on F. This restricted his use of sharps, flats and certain other chordal combinations, theoretically limiting his options. And yet Bruckner's genius was not to be limited: for all the crystal-clear purity of its contrapuntal lines, the motet reverberates with sensibility, with Bruckner's inherently Romantic heart and soul. I find it beautiful beyond belief.

Os justi meditabitur sapientiam,	*The mouth of the righteous utters wisdom,*
et lingua ejus loquetur judicium.	*and his tongue speaks what is just.*
Lex Dei ejus in corde ipsius:	*The law of his God is in his heart:*
et non supplantabuntur gressus ejus.	*and his feet do not falter.*

12 October

Main theme from *Colette*
by Thomas Adès (b. 1971)

I honestly can't remember the last time I heard a soundtrack before I saw the movie from which it came and decided *on the strength of the music alone* that I simply had to see the film. A longtime fan of the extraordinary British composer Thomas Adès (15 November), I'd been playing this track practically on repeat before I finally got around to seeing the film in question, *Colette*, starring Keira Knightley as the eponymous French writer.

In his already long and distinguished classical career, Adès, a former wunderkind, had written for virtually every other form: his much-acclaimed operas include *The Exterminating Angel* (2016) and a scintillating take on Shakespeare's *The Tempest* (2004); his techno-inflected orchestral piece *Asyla* (1997) won the Grawemeyer, the biggest composition prize going; his violin concerto (2005) has been described as '*magical . . . a piece whose detail is endlessly absorbing but whose emotional impact is immediate and impossible to resist*'.

Colette, though, was Adès' first venture into film, and it's fair to say he didn't let us down. 1890s Paris is one of the golden moments in musical history, and he embraced it in his fabulous score. '*I'm at home with the period*,' he told *Variety* magazine. '*The material I'm using, the tunes and the harmony, would be possible in an 1890s context. Once I found a style and some material, we started talking about how it could reflect the drama. You can follow the emotional contours of the story, and each of the characters' development, through the music.*' That being said, this is one of those stellar movie themes when you don't even need to know the story or the characters: the music more than stands alone.

13 October

Haven
by Bryce Dessner (b. 1976)

Better known as a member of American rock band The National, when he's not being a legit rock star, Dessner enjoys a busy alternative life as a prolific classical composer (as well as visionary curator, festival director and producer). He has collaborated with many of the luminaries from these pages, including Caroline Shaw, Steve Reich, Philip Glass and Jonny Greenwood, as well as with such prestigious classical outfits as the New York Philharmonic, Los Angeles Philharmonic and Kronos Quartet.

In his music, Dessner appears omnivorously sonically curious, drawing on influences from the Baroque era, folk music, Romanticism and modernist aesthetics, especially minimalism, as is evident in this enthralling and mesmeric track (which is actually part of an ongoing project called *Minimalist Dream House*). Written for two pianos and two electric guitars, the track, Dessner explains, is '*woven out of very simple fragmented melodic ideas that are played on each instrument and offset, just slightly, to create a kaleidoscopic effect of rhythm and harmony.*' He adds: '*The piece, while deceptively simple sounding, is extremely virtuosic to perform and an exciting challenge . . .*'

14 October

'Das Agnus Dei'
from *8 Sacred Songs*, op. 138
by Max Reger (1873–1916)

We will take a moment of exquisite choral respite today courtesy of the Bavarian composer Max Reger, who here sets a paraphrase of the Latin *Agnus Dei* in a Lutheran chorale text that would have been used in the vernacular mass in his native Germany.

It's not even two minutes long, this music, but somehow has the power to reset the world in its simplicity and beauty. The last few seconds, for example, are among the loveliest I've ever heard. I hope wherever you are you can turn up the volume and simply relish them.

15 October

Nachtstück, op. 29
by Gottfried von Einem (1918–1996)

Today we'll hear from a twentieth-century composer who is barely known outside his native Austria. Eclectic and theatrical, much influenced by the likes of Stravinsky, Prokofiev and Janáček, Gottfried von Einem roundly embraced musicians such as Duke Ellington and Leonard Bernstein at a moment when any serious classical composer was expected to embrace Schoenberg and Webern. In other words, he was an avowed anti-modernist and his defiantly tonal (and therefore hopelessly unfashionable) idiom – on splendid display here in this mellow orchestral nocturne from 2006 – simply could not hold its own against the rise of the avant-garde. '. . . *possibly the most conservative composer in Europe'*, is how one of his former students, the American composer Martin Bresnick, described him. '*He wrote tonal, melodious, rhythmically pulsate music without the slightest regard for the prevailing atonal, a-rhythmic fashion at the time.*'

'*I was always eager to be a communicative composer,*' von Einem conceded in his autobiography, *I've Experienced an Infinite Amount.* '*For me it is about dialogue with the audience.*' For what it's worth, I have never seen a work by von Einem performed live; in fact, I don't think I have ever, in an entire lifetime of concert-going on many continents, spotted von Einem's name on a single programme. And that to me is a real shame, because I'm pretty certain there's more of an audience out there for him to be in dialogue with.

16 October

Sonata in D major
7: Passacaille
by Sylvius Leopold Weiss (1686–1750)

To another largely forgotten ghost of classical music today, Sylvius Leopold Weiss, who was once arguably the most important lute composer of his day (and apparently incited such envy among his peers that one jealous violinist reportedly attempted to bite off his thumb!). Well-travelled and able to absorb and synthesize emerging musical styles from Germany, France and Italy, Weiss produced an astonishing amount of music, something like a thousand pieces, for his instrument, and by 1744 had become the highest-paid musician at the court of Dresden Hofkapelle. Now, his name is barely heard outside the nichest of niche, lute-loving circles.

Weiss was a direct contemporary of J. S. Bach, who admired his music so much he even arranged some of it. He died on this day, so it seems a fitting moment to celebrate his legacy with this beautiful and mellifluous take on the ultra-fashionable dance form, the passacaglia.

17 October

Adagio in C minor
by Nicholas Britell (b. 1980)

Happy birthday to Nicholas Britell, one of the most gifted and brilliant minds on the musical scene today. At school in New York City, Britell was part of a hip-hop collective called The Witness Protection Program, but his classical influences include Rachmaninov, Gershwin and Philip Glass. He has twice been nominated at the Academy Awards, for his scores to Barry Jenkins' films *Moonlight* (2016) and *If Beale Street Could Talk* (2018); he has also won an Emmy and many other awards for his breathtakingly beautiful, surprising and invariably deeply moving scores.

Britell is something of a polymath: he's also a film producer – his credits include Damien Chazelle's Oscar-winning movie *Whiplash* (2014) – and he co-founded, with star choreographer Benjamin Millepied, the artists' collective The Amoveo Company, which works across digital media, film, TV, music and dance.

This brief but devastating interlude from the hit HBO TV series *Succession* gives me shivers every time I hear it.

18 October

My Heart is a Holy Place
by Patricia Van Ness (b. 1951)

The contemporary American composer Patricia Van Ness has a particular interest in the ways choral music and poetry can intersect with the mystical and divine; as such she sees herself as part of a long and reverberant tradition that stretches right back to the likes of Hildegard of Bingen (30 March). Van Ness's ethereal and atmospheric choral writing draws richly from the Medieval and Renaissance eras to explore what might be called an aesthetic of musical ecstasy.

I first came across her unique compositional voice through the esteemed British vocal ensemble The King's Singers, who have performed Van Ness's compositions in different countries and cultures all over the globe. And *wherever we perform it around the world,'* notes Christopher Gabbitas, a member of the ensemble, *'it is universally well-received . . . as with all good music it breaks down the barriers of language and culture, communicating on a higher level.'*

19 October

Symphony no. 2 in C major, op. 61
3: Adagio espressivo
by Robert Schumann (1810–1856)

Emerging out of the silence, shrouded in mystery, laying a path for an oboe solo of breathtaking beauty and wistfulness, the opening music of this movement is one of the most gut-wrenching moments in any symphonic writing ever. It breaks my heart, every time, but in that simultaneously putting-you-back-together and redemptive way that only the very greatest music can.

Listening to music by Robert Schumann, it's hard not to hear it through the lens of knowing what he went through in life: that he suffered from decimating depression and mental health issues; attempted suicide; was committed to an asylum; threw himself in desperation into the Rhine; was dead by forty-six. Schumann was also a luminous musical communicator; a passionate advocate for literature and criticism and the arts in general; a loving husband to Clara; a loyal friend and mentor to many other composers, including Brahms; in short, a figure as vital and energizing in music as there has ever been.

And is it all there, I wonder, in the taut, shimmering, high strings of this movement? In the yearning plaintiveness of those woodwind lines? In the ultimately uplifting sense of triumph that prevails?

This marks a new direction in Schumann's output, and it was on this day in 1846 that he finally completed it, having been thwarted by depressive episodes and related symptoms, including incessant ringing in his ears, throughout the entire compositional process. Thinking of what this music took out of him, I am, once again, wonderstruck by the sheer *generosity* of a creative act such as this. In dark times in my own life, when I have battled my own demons, I have returned to it and have been, in some small way, saved.

329

20 October

The Unanswered Question
by Charles Ives (1874–1954)

Last month, we had electronic pioneer Laurie Spiegel and her 'Unquestioned Answer'; today we have an enigmatic 'Unanswered Question' posed by another true American original, Charles Ives, who was born on this day. Not that Ives was always recognized as such. The Connecticut-born modernist, who experimented with such ground-breaking techniques as polytonality, polyrhythms, tone clusters and so-called 'aleatory' elements (a rather surreal approach in which things are essentially left to chance by the composer) mostly worked as an insurance salesman during his early career. Lots of his music was not appreciated until much later in his life, or even after his death.

This piece, for example, was composed in 1908 but not performed for almost four decades, when its premiere was finally given by a group of Juilliard School students in New York after World War Two. It's what we would call 'programme music': Ives wrote a detailed text explaining, essentially, what was going on in the metaphysics of his *cosmic land-scape*. To wit: the slow sustained strings represent *'The Silence of the Druids – who Know, See and Hear Nothing'*. Against this mysterious background then appears a trumpet who poses and repeats an atonal phrase, seven times. This is apparently *'The Perennial Question of Existence'*, to which the woodwinds – or *'Fighting Answerers'* – subsequently offer an answer six times, each time becoming more and more erratic in their musical approach. After a while, seemingly grasping the futility of the exercise, they *'begin'*, according to Ives, *'to mock "The Question" before finally disappearing, leaving "The Question" to be asked once more before "The Silences" are left to their "Undisturbed Solitude" . . .'*

In other words, what I think Ives is getting at, is that the perennial question of existence cannot, ultimately, be answered. Fair?

21 October

24 Preludes for violin and piano, op. 46
15: Adagio sognando
by Lera Auerbach (b. 1973)

Happy birthday to the composer, pianist, sculptor and poet Lera Auerbach, born on this day in Chelyabinsk, a town in the Ural Mountains which borders Siberia. A town to which, when Auerbach was growing up, no foreigners were allowed entry, for Chelyabinsk was one of the main centres for nuclear experimentation in the Soviet Union. If that doesn't sound like the *most* auspicious beginnings for a major career in Western classical music, her story is certainly a moving testament to the power and universality of the arts. '*I was born to do this, to work in art,*' she once told an interviewer. '*I had this feeling when I was four and I had it when I came to New York . . .*'

The New York trip to which she alludes was a fateful one. In 1991, by which time she was already a promising pianist, Auerbach received permission to visit the United States on a concert tour. Despite speaking no English, and having no friends or family there, let alone any luggage – '*only her carry-on*' – she decided to defect. She was seventeen. Later, having won a place at the Manhattan School of Music, she would walk more than a hundred blocks a day to attend classes, unable to afford the Subway fare.

Auerbach subsequently went on to take degrees in both piano and composition from the Juilliard School and to make her debut at Carnegie Hall in 2002. As you do. She is now one of the most prolific and oft-performed composers in the US and beyond.

22 October

~~~~~~

Autumn Leaves
by Craig Urquhart (b. 1963)

Bach, Mendelssohn, Debussy, Chopin, Schumann . . . they've all played their part when it comes to inspiring and influencing Craig Urquhart, who worked for many years as one of Leonard Bernstein's most closely trusted personal assistants and is now, in addition to overseeing certain matters of the Bernstein estate, a composer in his own right, mostly of serene piano miniatures such as this one.

It was Bernstein himself who talked about the *'deceptive simplicity'* and *'private beauty'* of Urquhart's writing, warning purist critics not to write it off as merely *'new age'* music. Pieces such as this, an ode to the season for solo piano, may be less about showing off flashy intellectual ideas than about rendering pure and sincere emotion, but they have an *'honesty'*, as Bernstein declared, *'that is rarely to be heard in contemporary writing . . .'*

23 October

Canon (Improvisation after Pachelbel's Canon and Gigue in D major, P. 37) by Gabriela Montero (b. 1970)

The famous canon by Johann Pachelbel is one of the few pieces that has managed to transcend the narrow confines of the classical world and find a truly mainstream audience. Like Vivaldi's *Four Seasons* and the opening of Beethoven's Fifth Symphony, it has become something of a cliché: you may have heard it in all manner of contexts, from a dentist's waiting-room, to a TV advert, to your local Italian, to say nothing of practically every wedding you've ever attended. In the parlance of today, it's about as 'basic' as classical music can get.

Yet this is to do a disservice to the original brilliance of the music itself, which was possibly written (ironically) for a wedding – that of J. S. Bach's older brother, a student of Pachelbel – which took place on this day in 1694. There's a reason the music, which builds so compellingly over one of the greatest ground basses of all time, has been adopted by generation after generation. But sometimes, what we need in order to hear precious but hackneyed things anew is to literally *hear them anew*.

Enter Venezuelan pianist and composer Gabriela Montero. Using arguably the most well-known theme in all of music as a springboard for her own capacious imagination, her virtuosic flights of fancy remain rooted in superb keyboard improvisation technique and a super-tight grasp of what makes the music great in the first place. As far as I'm concerned, her efforts should be viewed in the same proud tradition of, say, Bach, Beethoven and Liszt, all of whom, like Montero, considered keyboard improvisation a serious art. '*It is music,*' as critic Charlotte Gardner once remarked, '*to let your hair down to, without discarding your brain along the way . . .*'

24 October

~◦~

An English Day-Book
9: 'Evening Song'
by Elizabeth Poston (1905–1987)

A friend to many of the leading cultural and literary lights of her time, including E. M. Forster, C. S. Lewis and Dylan Thomas, Elizabeth Poston, who was born on this day, was a respected academic, writer and pianist as well as a fine composer. She had a colourful life (which may or may not have involved her becoming a spy during World War Two) and as a composer was taken seriously enough that the BBC broadcast some of her music as early as 1928, just six years after the corporation was founded. Yet, as is so often the case, Poston is also a woman whose name has largely slipped from history and whose musical output has been largely neglected in the years since.

This piece comes from her *English Day-Book*, a sort of musical diary or journal in which she links together both sacred and secular poetry. The result, as critic John Gardner puts it, is something quite unique: *'the small-scale happenings of the day are symbolically identified with the procession of the seasons of the year, and . . . with the span of life itself. The contrasting conceptions of faith and superstition, of birth and death, of dawn and dusk, contribute alike to a serene, philosophical interpretation of our earthly destiny in terms of lyrical song . . .'*

25 October

Concerto Grosso in D Major, op. 6 no. 4
3: Adagio
by Arcangelo Corelli (1653–1713)

The Baroque composer Arcangelo Corelli was the grand master of the so-called 'concerto grosso', a super-fashionable new musical form involving small but potent ensembles of instruments, which would go on to be hugely influential in the next generation, including for composers as prominent as Handel and J. S. Bach.

We know very little else about Corelli's life, other than that his mother, one Santa Raffini, named him after his father, who had died five weeks before he was born. We know, too, that he was also a professional violinist and a skilled conductor who can be considered one of the pioneers of modern orchestral direction: during the time of the coronation of Pope Innocent XII, for example, Corelli once oversaw an orchestra of some 150 players for a special state concert welcoming the British ambassador to Rome on behalf of King James II. That's no mean feat (even the biggest modern symphony orchestras of today are nowhere near as big).

Corelli never lived to see published the set of concerti grossi from which this two-minute sliver of thoughtful and uplifting music comes, but every piece in the collection is an outright gem, a veritable grab bag of delights. I often stick on the entire album of Corelli's opus 6 if I need to focus, and invariably find it a deeply clarifying and fortifying listen.

26 October

The Seasons, op. 37b
10: 'October: Autumn Song'
by Pyotr Ilyich Tchaikovsky (1840–1893)

A nice reminder, today, that even classical geniuses sometimes just need to do bits and bobs to pay the rent. *The Seasons* was a relatively easy way for Tchaikovsky to earn some extra cash, by dashing off a short new piece for each month of 1876 as part of an ongoing feature in the St Petersburg music magazine *Nouvellist* (lucky readers!).

The idea for the series was suggested by the magazine's editor, one Nikolay Matveyevich Bernard; it was also he who chose poetic epigraphs to go alongside each month's entry. October's is a timely fragment by A. K. Tolstoy (a second cousin to *War and Peace's* Leo):

> *Autumn, our poor garden is all falling down,*
> *The yellowed leaves are flying in the wind.*

27 October

Heartbreaker
by Missy Mazzoli (b. 1980)

Happy birthday to the American composer Missy Mazzoli, who hails from that thrilling generation who are really shaking the tree when it comes to classical music in our time (see also: Caroline Shaw, Nico Muhly, Bryce Dessner, Paola Prestini *et al*). In 2018, the Grammy-nominated Mazzoli became one of the first women ever to receive a commission from New York's Metropolitan Opera; she has also held illustrious residencies at the Chicago Symphony Orchestra, the Opera Company of Philadelphia and Gotham Chamber Orchestra.

A student of David Lang (8 January) and Louis Andriessen (6 June), Mazzoli writes chamber, opera and orchestral works as well as instrumental pieces on a smaller scale, such as this dazzling little solo piano number. Mazzoli started her musical life as a pianist, but, she reveals, it was 'unexpectedly difficult' to write this, which was commissioned for the American Pianists Association competition in 2013. '*I wanted to write something virtuosic but something that stood out from the traditionally showy "competitive" pieces,*' she notes. *Heartbreaker*, then, is '*virtuosic in subtle, unusual ways. It starts out deceptively simple, and quickly spirals into something that is just within the limits of the pianist's control. It requires a virtuosity that is not about playing faster than everyone else, or even about playing more accurately than everyone else, but more about striking a balance between rhythmic precision and the free-wheeling abandon the piece requires.*'

28 October

The Seasons
Part 4: 'Autumn', no. 15: Petit Adagio
by Alexander Glazunov (1865–1936)

'*What, then,*' asks the writer Maria Popova, '*of autumn – that liminal space between beauty and bleakness, foreboding and bittersweet, yet lovely in its own way?*' Perhaps, Popova argues in her inimitably soulful way, this most wistful of seasons, '*Wedged between an equinox and a solstice, mooring us to cosmic rhythms of deep time*', is neither beginning nor ending; perhaps, rather, '*between its falling leaves and fading light, it is not a movement toward gain or loss but an invitation to attentive stillness and absolute presence, reminding us to cherish the beauty of life not despite its perishability but precisely because of it; because the impermanence of things – of seasons and lifetimes and galaxies and loves – is what confers preciousness and sweetness upon them . . .*'

Such writing stills my restless heart. And such music, too: nothing quite evokes the exquisite poignancy of this time of year for me like this piece by Glazunov. *The Seasons* was an allegorical ballet which premiered in 1900 at the Imperial Ballet in St Petersburg, choreographed by the legendary Marius Petipa, who also created definitive versions of *The Sleeping Beauty*, *Coppélia* and *Giselle*. Much of Glazunov's 'Autumn' writing takes the form of a wild and swirling 'Bacchanal', but in this section, just a few minutes long, he conjures a deeply contemplative if ephemeral musical tribute to an extraordinary season. Before long, at least in the northern hemisphere where I live, it will be winter: we must relish the dying embers of beautiful autumn while she lasts . . .

29 October

Locus iste
by Paul Mealor (b. 1975)

A moment of sonic sanctuary – literally – today. '*Locus iste a Deo factus est*' (meaning 'this place was made by God') is the Latin gradual or hymn, based on the biblical story of Jacob's ladder, which has been used to commemorate the dedication of a church for many, many centuries.

In today's case, it's Welsh composer Paul Mealor's glowing setting of the text, commissioned in 2009 by the University of Aberdeen in Scotland to celebrate the 500th anniversary of the dedication of King's College Chapel. Layering vocal line over vocal line in his own vaultingly beautiful structure, Mealor adds a final, glorious 'Sanctuary!'

Locus iste a Deo factus est,	*This place was made by God,*
inaestimabile sacramentum,	*a priceless sacrament,*
irreprehensibilis est.	*beyond reproof.*

30 October

Violin Sonata no. 1 in D minor
4: Presto
by Elisabeth-Claude Jacquet de la Guerre (1665–1729)

Last month (18 September), we met Francesca Caccini, who is generally regarded as the first woman ever to compose an opera. Today, we meet one of her successors of the next generation, Elisabeth-Claude Jacquet de la Guerre, who has the distinction of being the first ever French-woman to produce an opera: her *Céphale et Procris* from 1694, a take on the myth of Cephalus and Procris from Ovid's *Metamorphosen*.

Perhaps it's not surprising that Jacquet de la Guerre, despite the challenges faced by any woman trying to make a name for herself in classical music, would go on to achieve great things: she was a prodigy and made her debut at the court of King Louis XIV when she was still a child. As well as her historic contribution to the world of opera, she wrote cantatas, songs, a lot of harpsichord pieces, and various instrumental works such as this spirited violin sonata.

After her death, the French critic Evrard Titon du Tillet included her in his famous *Parnasse françois* of 1732, which compiled biographical vignettes about eminent French musicians and other cultural figures. *'One might say,'* he wrote, *'that never has a person of her sex had such great talent for the composition of music'* . . . As regrettable as it may be that he had to bother with including the caveat *'of her sex'*, we should still acknowledge this for the milestone it is. Onwards!

31 October

from *All-Night Vigil*, op. 37
6: 'Bogoroditse Devo – Rejoice, O Virgin'
by Sergei Rachmaninov (1873–1943)

Today is All Hallows' Eve, a holiday incorporated into the Christian tradition by Pope Gregory IV in the ninth century as the eve of the Feast of All Saints. Traditionally, the church would hold an all-night vigil in order that worshippers could prepare themselves with prayers and fasting prior to the important feast day on 1 November.

The name, which derives from the Old English 'hallowed', meaning holy or sanctified, is what gives us, of course, 'Hallowe'en'. I have resisted the urge to play spooky classical music today and have instead opted for a spine-tinglingly beautiful moment from a timeless all-night vigil from Sergei Rachmaninov. You're welcome.

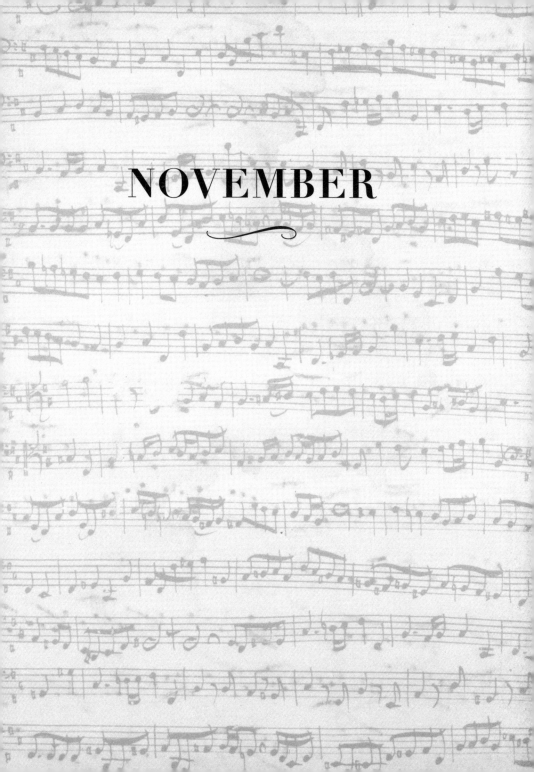

NOVEMBER

1 November

From *Manon* Ballet
Act 3, scene 2 – 'The gaoler's rooms in New Orleans'
by Jules Massanet (1842–1912)
arr. Leighton Lucas (1903–1982)

It was in 1973 that leading British choreographer Kenneth MacMillan took *Manon Lescaut*, the powerful 1731 novel of poverty, love, greed and betrayal by the Abbé Prevost, and started to turn it into a full-scale ballet. *Manon* was premiered by the Royal Ballet at Covent Garden the following year. Interestingly, for his score MacMillan decided not to use any of the music from Jules Massanet's already-popular opera *Manon*, which had premiered in 1884 and quickly gained popularity around the world (Puccini also wrote an opera, *Manon Lescaut*, based on the same rich material, in 1893). Instead, he worked with British dancer and composer Leighton Lucas to put together what we might now think of as a Massanet 'jukebox' score, showcasing much of the music of the French composer in a glorious sonic patchwork that draws on thirteen operas, two oratorios, orchestral suites, piano music and intense, soaring melodies, such as the ones included in this beautiful sequence which takes place in Act 3.

2 November

The Souls of the Righteous
by Geraint Lewis (b. 1958)

Music for All Souls' Day today, from the Welsh composer Geraint Lewis. Cardiff-born, Cambridge-educated, Lewis became an expert in the music of his countryman William Mathias, who was one of the most prominent Welsh composers of the twentieth century.

The genesis of this piece is deeply personal. Lewis had originally been tasked to write a choral anthem for All Souls' and set to work on it during the Christmas of 1991. Shortly after, during one of his regular visits with Mathias, who lived in Anglesey, he showed the beginnings of the manuscript to the older composer, who was, he remembers, warm and encouraging. Soon after, with Mathias having been diagnosed as having terminal cancer, Lewis put his own manuscript to one side and focused on helping Mathias get his papers and personal affairs in order in the final few months of his life.

After Mathias's death in the summer of 1992, Lewis was asked to write something for the Service of Thanksgiving that would be held in St Paul's Cathedral. '*I went back to my setting of "The souls of the righteous",*' he recalls, '*and completed it as a tribute to my closest friend and colleague. The text is from Wisdom and is variously a collect for All Saints – eve of All Souls.*' (Mathias had been born on 1 November, All Saints' Day, in 1945, so there was an especial poignancy in that coincidence.)

The moving result has found a wide audience not just in Wales but around the world, and has been performed everywhere from Norway to South Africa.

3 November

Notturno
by Blagoje Bersa (1873–1934)

Today we'll hear music by a largely forgotten Croatian composer who is sometimes credited with writing the first ever Croatian opera, a piece called *Oganj* from 1911. Set in a factory, it is now rarely performed but in its time it was a significant work in the post-Wagnerian mould.

Opera aside, it's Bersa's beautiful music for piano that really took my breath away once I started crate-digging. This charming and serene piece, very much in the style of the Romantic nocturne as exemplified by Chopin, is, I think, a particular neglected gem.

4 November

'Se mai senti spirarti sul volto' –
'If ever you feel a breath on your cheek'
from *La clemenza di Tito*
by Christoph Willibald von Gluck (1714–1787)

Mozart is just one of the many producers of opera who owe a considerable debt to the German composer Christoph Willibald von Gluck. Mozart's take on the Titus story (a devastatingly brilliant *La clemenza di Tito* that premiered in Prague in September 1791, less than two months before he died) is, unsurprisingly, by far the better known. But Gluck's own version, which premiered in Naples on this day in 1752, certainly paves the way.

Gluck, as Mozart would do forty years later, bases his opera on the great Italian poet Pietro Metastasio's somewhat idealized take on Roman history. (Fun fact: Metastasio's libretti have reportedly been set to music more than any other writer.) This aria from Act 2, sung as the character Sextus/Sesto is being taken away to be questioned by the senate, is particularly ravishing. Turning to his beloved Vitellia, Sesto – invariably sung by a female mezzo-soprano in a so-called 'trouser role' – tells her that if she ever feels a breeze blowing on her cheek, it is the death of her dying lover. What an image! What a song . . .

5 November

'House of Woodcock'
by Jonny Greenwood (b. 1971)

Happy birthday to the genius that is Jonny Greenwood, widely known as the lead guitarist and keyboardist from Radiohead and now an Oscar-nominated composer in his own right. This piece comes from his score to Paul Thomas Anderson's film *Phantom Thread* (2017), starring Daniel Day-Lewis, which was praised for its *'insinuating and expressive . . . blend of Minimalist-like riffs, eerie harmonies, alluring melodic lines you don't quite trust, and piercing chords that leap about aimlessly'*.

It's certainly been an impressive journey for Greenwood. He learned the recorder at school, then later joined a local ensemble (he apparently still plays in a little recorder group). It was aged fifteen that his great musical revelation came, when he heard the *Turangalîla-Symphonie* of Olivier Messiaen (3 January) and became *'round-the-bend-obsessed with it'*, even learning the ondes martenot, an early electronic instrument that Messiaen features. *'[Messiaen] was still alive when I was fifteen,'* Greenwood recalls, *'and for whatever reason I felt I could equate him with my other favourite bands – there was no big posthumous reputation to put me off.'*

Greenwood, who in 2019 launched his own contemporary classical label, Octatonic, and says he stands *'in awe'* of classically trained musicians, still cites Messiaen as a major influence (*'I'm still very fond of writing things in the same modes of limited transposition that he used'*). His other classical inspirations include Polish composer Krzysztof Penderecki and Baroque giants J. S. Bach and Vivaldi. *'I feel like I'm enthralled to [them] all the time,'* he admits. *'I love Baroque stuff.'*

Like the greatest composers, Greenwood pays tribute to his musical heroes in subtle and loving yet distinctive ways. It's hard to describe the effect of his music, but it invariably, for me, goes deep. *'The principal thing,'* he says, is *'to make sure the emotion is sincere.'*

6 November

When David heard
by Thomas Tomkins (1572–1656)

Born in Pembrokeshire, Wales, Thomas Tomkins became one of the last members of the so-called English Virginalist school, a late Tudor/early Jacobean movement that wrote not only for the 'virginals', a very early keyboard instrument, but also for harpsichord, clavichord, chamber organ and the human voice. Other members of the group include Orlando Gibbons (5 June) and William Byrd, with whom Tomkins almost certainly studied. (One of his songs bears the inscription: '*To my ancient, and much reverenced Master, William Byrd*'.)

Musically speaking, Tomkins appears to be looking back not forward, and is most inspired by the spare and radiant polyphony of the Renaissance rather than the Italianate complexity of the nascent early Baroque. This anguished choral work, which describes King David stricken with grief at the death of his son Absalom, was probably composed as a lament for Henry, the young Prince of Wales, who died on this day in 1612.

7 November

Sonata for solo harp
1: Allegretto
by Germaine Tailleferre (1892–1983)

When Germaine Tailleferre died, aged ninety-one, on this day, most of her music remained unpublished. That's despite the fact that she had been a prolific and dynamic figure in twentieth-century French music who wrote vast amounts of music for opera, ballet, film and theatre, as well as for choral, instrumental and orchestral forces. Tailleferre was also, I will never grow tired of repeating, the only female member of Les Six, the group of Erik Satie-inspired Parisian composers that also included Francis Poulenc (7 January) and who, I'll never grow tired of dreaming about, used to frequent a bar called La Gaya, which later became the great cabaret spot Le Boeuf sur le Toit at 28, rue Boissy d'Anglas in the eighth *arondissement*. (Oh, to have been a fly on those walls!)

We first encountered Tailleferre earlier this year (10 January) writing for violin, but her instrumental imagination was broad and unconstrained. She also composed for instruments that are far less well represented in the solo canon, including saxophone, guitar, and – as in today's graceful, languid sonata from 1953 – the harp.

8 November

All Shall Be Well
by Roxanna Panufnik (b. 1968)

This uplifting choral work was commissioned by Bristol-based vocal ensemble the Exultate Singers for a concert celebrating twenty years since the fall of the Berlin Wall. It was first performed on this day in 2009 at Clifton Cathedral.

Panufnik, whose father was the leading Polish composer Andrzej Panufnik, is one of Britain's most prolific and popular contemporary-music writers. Her oeuvre includes opera, ballet, musicals, choral and chamber compositions as well as film soundtracks. This piece show-cases her trademark fascination with the way different faiths, cultures and eras can all be in dialogue with each other through music. She often describes her music as a '*conversation*'; here she has combined two texts, a medieval plainchant hymn sung by Polish knights as they went into battle and those well-known and oft-quoted lines by the female English mystic, Julian of Norwich (1342–c. 1416):

> *All shall be well, and all shall be well, and all manner of things*
> *shall be well.*

As usual, Panufnik weaves powerful emotion through simple, elegant harmonies – in a piece that not only makes us think, but feel. Or not only makes us feel, but think . . .

9 November

'Soave sia il vento' – 'May the seas be calm
and the winds gentle'
from *Così fan tutte*
by Wolfgang Amadeus Mozart (1756–1791)

On this day in 1989, the Berlin Wall fell. It was a day that, says Daniel Barenboim, *'changed the whole world'*. The legendary pianist and conductor happened to be in Berlin recording Mozart's opera *Così fan tutte* with the famed Berlin Philharmonic. *'The day after the Wall fell, the orchestra asked if I would do a concert with them,'* he recalls. *'I said yes, on two conditions: it must be free and only for citizens of [former] East Germany.'*

The programme was decided upon immediately, and it included music from *Così*. The picture that Barenboim paints is evocative. *'When I arrived at the hall for a short rehearsal, thousands of people were queueing. Some had arrived at 4am . . .'* He says: *'The joy and energy of those people and the orchestra was unforgettable.'*

The 1790 opera is undoubtedly a masterpiece, yet it wasn't always so popular: Beethoven and Wagner were fierce critics, and its subject, infidelity, was considered so scandalous in the nineteenth century that productions tended either to be accompanied by an apology or rewritten.

The two main male characters, Ferrando and Guglielmo, are betrothed to sisters Dorabella and Fiordiligi. A meddling old cynic called Don Alfonso argues that all women are fickle and bets the boys that their own fiancées are no different. Certain of their women's unwavering fidelity, the two men agree to go away, disguise themselves, and return on a mission to seduce the other's girl. As a pretext for them leaving they are hastily called to war – and it is at this moment, in Act 1, that they exit to the sublime strains of the two girls and Don Alfonso singing them off.

10 November

Piano Sonatina
2: Molto adagio
by Doreen Carwithen (1922–2003)

'To recent generations,' wrote obituary writer Martin Anderson in the *Independent* in 2003, on the occasion of Doreen Carwithen's death, '*Mary Alwyn was known as the devoted wife of the composer William Alwyn. When, in 1997, Chandos Records brought out the first of two CDs of the music of Doreen Carwithen, younger listeners sat up with astonishment: the woman whose life seemed to have been devoted to easing that of her husband was revealed to be a substantial creative personality in her own right.*'

Carwithen, who also scored over thirty-five films, was once the only woman to have music featured in a Proms season (in 1952) and was sufficiently gifted that both her string quartets won prominent composition prizes. (Even the great Ralph Vaughan Williams declared himself an admirer.) Yet, writes Anderson, '*she found it next to impossible to interest a publisher in music composed by a woman, and when, in 1961, she set up house with William Alwyn ... Doreen Carwithen went into retirement, and Mary Alwyn (Mary was her middle name, and she hated "Doreen" anyway) became the public persona the world saw. She worked tirelessly on behalf of her husband, acting as his secretary and amanuensis, and generally keeping an importunate world at bay.*'

Sigh.

11 November

~~~~~~

Elegy – In memoriam Rupert Brooke
by Frederick Septimus Kelly (1881–1916)

The Irish-Australian composer and Olympic rower Frederick Septimus Kelly was killed in action in the last days of the Battle of the Somme.

In 1915 Kelly survived the slaughter at Gallipoli, only to be killed the following year. At Gallipoli, Kelly would apparently compose music in his tent, and that was where he started to write this grief-stricken elegy for his friend, the poet Rupert Brooke, who had died from sepsis en route to the Gallipoli landing. Kelly was one of the group that helped bury Brooke on the Greek island of Skyros, and he methodically copied out Brooke's notebooks to ensure the contents would get safely back to England. There are many references in Kelly's diary to the two men spending time together before Brooke's death, including accounts of idyllic evenings spent reading poems and discussing literature. The emotion that seeps from this restrained but aching elegy about Brooke's grave is deeply felt, then, and intensely personal.

'*The body lies looking down the valley towards the harbor,*' Kelly recorded, '*and, from behind, an olive tree bends itself over the grave as though sheltering it from the sun and rain. No more fitting resting place for a poet could be found than this small grove, and it seems as though the gods had jealously snatched him away to enrich this scented island.*'

Before he sacrificed his life in the grim trenches of the Somme, Kelly had exhibited wide musical curiosity: we know he'd attended performances of Wagner operas and Scriabin recitals and heard Schoenberg conduct. He was a glittering talent, extinguished too early in a senseless war. Some twelve or so composers were killed at the Somme, but Kelly is the only one to have a marked grave, at the British cemetery in Martinsart, his men having lovingly retrieved his body and carried it back through No Man's Land.

12 November

'The Dormition of the Mother of God' from *The Protecting Veil* by John Tavener (1944–2013)

It was on this day in 2013 that classical music, especially in the English sacred tradition, lost one of its most singular voices. Being a composer of deep Russian Orthodox religious faith, John Tavener was something of an anomaly in the largely secular post-war century into which he emerged, yet he was able to connect, through his profoundly affecting music, to wide audiences of all faiths and none. Perhaps it's because there seems to be something essential about Tavener's music that goes beyond theology. His *Song for Athene* was played at the end of the funeral of Diana, Princess of Wales in 1997. His exquisite setting of William Blake's poetry in *The Lamb* is an eternal favourite at Christmastime. And he even composed a song for Icelandic pop superstar Björk (*Prayer of the Heart*, written in 2000).

The title of this piece, an *'icon in sound'* composed for cellist Steven Isserlis for the 1989 BBC Proms, is a reference to the Christian Orthodox feast, commemorating a tenth-century vision of the Virgin Mary which apparently inspired the people of Constantinople to drive off Saracen besiegers. Critic Robert Maycock reveals that Tavener had told him it was not necessary to explain the theological significance. *'When I asked him whether he thought that knowledge of the metaphysical underpinning would have affected the audience's reception of the piece,'* Maycock recalls, *'he said, "No, but I think they may subconsciously have reacted to the feminine element in it, which is very strong and may have subliminally communicated itself. We live in an aggressively masculine culture. I've no idea why* The Protecing Veil *communicated so deeply, but it did so, and it may well be something to do with that feminine dimension."'*

13 November

Ceffylau – Horses
by Catrin Finch (b. 1980) & Seckou Keita (b. 1978)

Unfortunately, the harp – while a properly ancient instrument, incredibly rich in tradition – is somewhat dogged by cliché (see 4 June). Go on: if I say the word *harp*, what springs to mind? Vaguely 'Celtic' sounds as you wait on hold to speak to someone frustratingly administrative, like, your internet provider? Christmas? A Botticelli-esque cherub, maybe?

Turns out, just like so many apparently 'clichéd' things, context is everything.

I was positively *thunderstruck* when I first heard the unique partnership between celebrated Welsh harpist Catrin Finch and Senegalese *kora* virtuoso Seckou Keita. Combine the harp with a kora, the traditional West African twenty-two-stringed instrument and bam: a kind of enchantment happens! An effusive joy! The sound of two spectacularly musical cultures, separated by about 3,000 miles, a few countries and *lots* of ocean, coming together to produce something impossible to pigeonhole, boundary-hopping, relevant and dare I say it, totally new.

Or . . . not?! Which is even more delicious!

'*When we first started playing,*' explains Keita, '*Catrin was trying to write things down and score them, but eventually she just had to throw the rule book out of the window. That was when things started getting really interesting.*' Finch adds: '*I'd be playing one of my pieces, and Seckou would say – "I know that one"! It made us question whether in fact there was a deeper history there.*'

Magic. Absolutely magic.

14 November

Andante Cantabile
by Fanny Mendelssohn (1805–1847)

'*She plays like a man*' is how Fanny Mendelssohn, who was born on this day, was once described. Hmm. One imagines that the critic in question, the German composer and teacher Carl Friedrich Zelter, meant that as the highest possible praise (he also, in a letter to his pal Goethe, compared Fanny's lavish musical gifts to those of J. S. Bach).

For all her sensational talents, though, as both pianist and composer, Fanny was not exactly encouraged in her efforts. In 1820, her father wrote to her: '*Music will perhaps become [Felix's] profession, while for you it can and must only be an ornament*'. As for Felix: while he clearly respected and adored his older sister, he was equally unhelpful. Although he was instrumental in getting a few of her (460-odd) compositions published, he invariably gave them his own name, or left it vague at 'F. Mendelssohn'. In a letter to their mother, Felix wrote:

> *From my knowledge of Fanny I should say that she has neither inclination nor vocation for authorship. She is too much all that a woman ought to be for this. She regulates her house, and neither thinks of the public nor of the musical world, nor even of music at all, until her first duties are fulfilled. Publishing would only disturb her in these, and I cannot say that I approve of it.*

Thankfully, heroic work is now being undertaken by music historians and musicologists to try and unpick what might actually be by Fanny that we've long assumed to be by Felix. Her beautiful compositions, like this lovely lyrical piano work, sure don't sound like the music of a woman who would really rather be at home '*regulating her house*' . . .

15 November

Arcadiana, op. 12
6: 'O Albion'
by Thomas Adès (b. 1971)

One of the best descriptions I ever read of Thomas Adès and his music comes from critic Guy Dammann, who paints the composer as a *'figure who is constantly travelling'* and his eclectic musical language as one that is *'endlessly mining the musical subjunctive for a glimpse of something truly unspoiled'*. I find that a particularly apt characterization of this utterly spellbinding work for string quartet. Written in 1994 when the genius Adès was but twenty-three, it is music that is evocative and transporting, laced with nostalgia without ever lapsing into cliché. To me, 'O Albion' somehow feels like an extended musical sigh, an exhalation, a reset, a rest. I return to it again and again and again; it never lets me down.

16 November

Sonata for harp
2: Lebhaft – Lively
by Paul Hindemith (1895–1963)

'Remove the keyboard from a piano,' Paul Hindemith once declared, *'and what remains is basically a harp. The simpleton who took the harp for a nude piano did not know how in his innocence he touched one of the mysteries of musical genetics!'*

(Isn't that a brilliant phrase: the *'mysteries of musical genetics'*?)

Hindemith, who was born on this day, wrote this sonata in 1939, not long after he'd arrived in the USA, having fled persecution by the Nazis. (He wasn't Jewish, but his 'degenerate' music had been banned under Hitler since 1934). Although he was one of the most talented all-round musicians of the twentieth century, he didn't actually play the harp (he played viola, and was also a conductor, writer and teacher). Which makes his assured instrumentation and imaginative approach to the harmonic possibilities of the instrument, including some complex pedalling, even more impressive. I'm reliably informed, by harpist friends, that this sonata is a joy to play. Fresh and idiomatic, it's certainly a great pleasure to listen to.

17 November

Victory Stride
by James P. Johnson (1894–1955)

If you were living in America in the 1920s, the chances are you'd be familiar with a tune called 'Charleston'. It was written by James P. Johnson, who died on this day, and who invented an influential style of pianistic antics known as 'stride piano', in which the left hand leaps athletically around the keyboard.

While Johnson was alive, and for many decades after he died, the idea that this supreme jazz cat might also be considered a legit classical composer would have been roundly dismissed. But enter Marin Alsop, a bold and brilliant conductor who happens to have a *'passion'* (her word) about that *'unique period in America's musical history, when popular music and "serious" music collided and cross-pollinated to create a whole new art form'*. When Alsop discovered that Johnson had actually written reams of symphonic music, she became a woman on a mission, determined to unearth the classical output of one of America's most interesting musical minds. It was no easy feat, especially in the days before the internet, but having won over Johnson's daughter, she was given access to a treasure trove of memorabilia that had been languishing in the family attic. *'While the music clearly needed attention – and some was obviously missing – we could see its greatness and understood even more profoundly the enormous talent of this great American creator.'*

Cases like this often make me ponder how many other extraordinary musical treasures have been lost to us through straight-up prejudice, closed-mindedness and ignorance. Let the fizzing exuberance of this victorious piece be a cause for celebration that Johnson is finally, just about, getting the recognition in the classical world that he has long deserved.

18 November

Stars
by Ēriks Ešenvalds (b. 1977)

Choral music today from an award-winning contemporary Latvian composer. *Stars* is based on a poem by the Pulitzer Prize-winning American lyric poet Sara Teasdale (1884–1933), and the luminous simplicity and quiet intensity of her vision of a *'heaven full of stars'*, those *'beating hearts of fire'* seen above on a still, dark night, are, I think, matched to perfection in Ešenvalds' sublime setting.

By the way, if you're wondering what that ethereal sonic glisten is throughout: it's tuned wine glasses. For real. I could listen to this for ever . . .

Alone in the night	*That aeons*
On a dark hill	*Cannot vex or tire;*
With pines around me	*Up the dome of heaven*
Spicy and still,	*Like a great hill,*
And a heaven full of stars	*I watch them marching*
Over my head,	*Stately and still,*
White and topaz	*And I know that I*
And misty red;	*Am honored to be*
Myriads with beating	*Witness*
Hearts of fire	*Of so much majesty.*

19 November

Tres Romances Argentinos – Three Argentine Romances
1: 'Las niñas de Santa Fe' - 'The schoolgirls of Santa Fe'
by Carlos Guastavino (1912–2000)

One of the greatest gifts of having been immersed in classical music, one way or another, for pretty much my entire life, is having a deep treasure trove into which I can always delve. Whatever the occasion, whatever my mood or need, I'm rarely at a loss for what to listen to (and sharing that great good fortune is, in part, the animating spirit of this book). That said, little gives me more joy than the revelation of a completely new musical discovery, and the Argentine classical composer Carlos Guastavino was a recent one of those for me.

Although Guastavino was one of the most celebrated Latin American composers of his time – so successful that he toured Britain, China and the former Soviet Union and was in the extremely rare position of being able to live off his earnings and royalties – his music is not really considered part of the standard classical repertoire. Many of the 500 or so pieces we know he wrote remain, as yet, unrecorded. I discovered him thanks to the brilliance of Buenos Aires-born pianist Martha Argerich, whose performance of this gorgeous, sensual and unashamedly romantic dance is an absolute gift.

20 November

Part 3: 'Invisible Light: Earth Seen from Above'
from *Atlas*
by Meredith Monk (b. 1942)

Happy birthday to a singular American composer (and multi-platform, interdisciplinary artist) who has, in the sixty-odd years she has been at work, altered and expanded, in the most thought-provoking and beautiful way, what vocal music can be. Not only has Meredith Monk produced distinctive, visceral operas, music-theatre works, films and installations, but she is a pioneer of so-called *'extended vocal technique'*. Treating the human voice as an instrument to be explored, with its own eloquent language and *'primordial utterance'*, she has pushed and pushed again at the boundaries of what a voice can do; questioning what place there might be in classical composition for non-verbal sounds and in the process *'creating landscapes of sound that unearth feelings, energies, and memories for which there are no words'*.

This ethereal track, composed in 1987, is a rapturous seven or so minutes, elevating us, as the title promises, to another plane – one of sublime perspective.

21 November

momentary (choir version)
by Ólafur Arnalds (b. 1986)

Speaking of sublime perspective . . . a word of wisdom today from Icelandic composer Ólafur Arnalds.

'*We're all here,*' he says. '*We're all living in this unique moment in time, which will never happen again.*'

From my heart to yours then: this shimmering choral fragment; and the sheer marvellous miracle, frankly, of this, of this just being here, momentarily.

I have no further words.

'*We're all here.*'

22 November

Evensong
by Liza Lehmann (1862–1918)

Let us raise a toast, today, to the first president of the Society of Women Musicians and an indomitable force in the music of her time, much admired by the great Clara Schumann, although these days she is inevitably mostly dismissed by classical purists as a mere composer of 'light' music.

Liza Lehmann started her career as a celebrated operatic soprano, but after her retirement from the stage in 1894 decided to focus on composing, mostly for the voice. She was extremely successful, too, and frequently had her music performed at the Proms. (Ironically, during the early part of the twentieth century, women were much better represented on Proms programmes than they would go on to be later; this quirk reflects the fact that before 1927, financial support for the music festival came from the music publishers Chappell & Co. – who happened to publish a lot of highly popular so-called 'parlour songs' by women, just like this one, and who sold the sheet music at the concerts.)

Lehmann had a fantastic gift for text-setting and a knack for appealing melodies, as we can hear in her divine 1916 setting of Constance Morgan's poem 'Evensong'.

Fold your white wings, dear angels . . .

23 November

Spem in alium – 'Hope in another'
by Thomas Tallis (1505–1585)

'*Renaissance polyphony,*' says the great *New Yorker* critic Alex Ross, '*. . . does for the ears what the Sistine Chapel does for the eyes, giving lyric shape to divine power.*' Oof. Thomas Tallis, who died on this day, is a towering figure in that golden age of shape-giving. He was also clearly a canny operator: he managed to survive the transition from state Catholicism through the turbulence of the English Reformation and end up as a revered musician of the Chapel Royal, under Queen Elizabeth, despite possibly having never renounced his own Catholic faith.

We can only be grateful for the fact that Tallis managed, against extreme odds, to keep his head – because, what a head! Capable of producing music such as *this*: a ten-minute unaccompanied choral work in which Tallis intertwines forty separate voices in a tapestry of supreme complexity yet absolute radiance. *Spem in alium* is often held up as a sort of visionary pinnacle of the genre, and rightly so.

It's fair to say that, with the exception of an earlier Italian mass by one Alessandro Striggio (whose other music is now almost entirely forgotten), forty-part vocal works were not exactly standard. (Four parts is sort of more the norm.) We don't know why Tallis wrote it – possibly to celebrate the fortieth birthday of either Queen Mary I or that of Queen Elizabeth I – but whatever the reason, it's a masterpiece.

24 November

Magnetic Rag – Synchopations Classiques
by Scott Joplin (c. 1868–1917)

It always twists my heart a little, to think that this was the last rag that Scott Joplin would ever write. By the time he produced it he was already ravaged by the latter stages of the syphilis that would kill him three years later. As such, it exhibits characteristics that distinguish it from many of his previous rags such as *The Entertainer* and *Maple Leaf Rag* – a much darker, more melancholic middle section, for example, and a nod, in the markings and time signature, to the European classical tradition to which he desperately fought – and failed – to belong during his lifetime.

And yet, because it's Joplin, and because he was a genius, it's also infectiously wonderful, full of sincerest feeling and joy.

25 November

Symphony no. 3 in G major ('Great National Symphony') 4: Finale by Muzio Clementi (1752–1832)

If he was around today, the Italian-born musician Muzio Clementi would no doubt be described as a 'multi-hyphenate'. Pianist, conductor, editor, publisher, piano manufacturer, pedagogue, he also somehow found time to write a vast amount of music which served as a direct inspiration to many of the next generation of composers (including Beethoven, no less). While much of Clementi's output focuses on his own instrument, the piano, today we experience him in expansive symphonic mode, and paying tribute to his new home, the United Kingdom, where he had recently moved. Like an expert baker nimbly folding ingredients into the mix, you'll hear him seamlessly incorporating the theme to 'God Save the Queen' at around two minutes into this final movement.

A note for my American readers, by the way: it was Clementi's use of the British National Anthem that caught Samuel Francis Smith's ear, inspiring him to use the exact phrase for 'My Country, 'Tis of Thee'. As far as I'm concerned, this is a cheering little example of a shared musical treasure, evidence of our common creative currency. This is an idea I take great comfort in as the world hurtles towards an ever more febrile and divisive future. Time and again, I find myself having to cling to the belief that what unites us as human beings across space and time is infinitely stronger than what divides us. Music, I would argue, is the ultimate expression of this: it is perhaps the greatest connective agent we have.

26 November

Three Études for Viola
Étude 3
by Nico Muhly (b. 1981)

I love this startling and spirited étude, written, Muhly tells us, *'for my friend Nadia Sirota'*. Muhly and viola-player Sirota are not just long-time pals and collaborators; they are two of the brightest lights in the American contemporary classical scene. New York-based, they are composer and performer, respectively, yes, but also producers, curators, writers, podcasters, commissioners and all-round musical forces of nature who do brilliant work in dispelling some of the most pervasive and frankly unhelpful myths around classical music.

'*I want people to understand,*' Sirota has said, for example, '*that [composers] are human people who are alive and fallible and occasionally brilliant. And they have moments of genius and moments of total dorkdom.*' She adds: '*For me, this world has always been so incredibly vibrant and alive and exciting . . . but people do need a way in.*'

Although 'études' appear as far back as the Baroque era, with composers such as Scarlatti and Bach producing books of functional, methodical works specifically designed for aspects of technical practice, it wasn't really until the nineteenth century, and the rapid explosion in amateur keyboard playing, that the form came into its own. Notable concert étude-writers in the Romantic era include Chopin, Lizst and Debussy; in the twentieth century, radical musical minds such as György Ligeti and John Cage applied themselves to the task; and now the brilliant young American Muhly falls nicely into that same tradition.

The set of études from which this little sparkler comes '*are designed,*' Muhly explains, '*as performance pieces as well as practice études for dealing with the messy fifth-based string crossings my harmonic language sometimes outlines.*' So there you have it!

27 November

L'amante segreto – The Secret Lover
'Voglio, voglio morire' – 'I want to die'
by Barbara Strozzi (1619–1677)

There's not a huge amount of biographical information to be found about the prolific Venetian singer, composer and poet Barbara Strozzi, but according to critic Kate Hearne at least, she *'broke all the strict social rules and expectations of women in the seventeenth century. Her mother was a courtesan, her official description being that of a servant in the household of Giulio Strozzi, who was the adoptive and probably the biological father of Barbara . . . She was also a single mother with four children, a free spirit, producing an extensive array of high-quality works with a clear personal signature designed to show off her extraordinary voice.'*

In the two decades between 1644 and 1664, we know that Strozzi published hundreds of songs, often more than her male counterparts. And they invariably ring true, underpinned by sincere emotion in the text as well as exquisite musical writing: this 1651 song nails a situation that I suspect many of us have probably been through (as teenagers if not since!). Namely: when you're in love with the wrong person, and would frankly rather *die* than have the object of your affection ever find out how you feel . . . Yup. You too?

Voglio, voglio morire,	*I want, I want to die*
piuttosto ch'il mio mal venga a scoprire.	*Rather than have my woes discovered.*
Oh, disgrazia fatale!	*Oh, fatal misfortune!*
Quanto più miran gl'occhi il suo bel volto	*The more my eyes gaze at that beautiful face*
più tien la bocca il mio desir sepolto;	*the more my mouth keeps my desire hidden;*
chi rimedio non ha taccia il suo male.	*He who has no cure, should keep his illness quiet.*

28 November

~~~~~~~~~~~

Some
by Nils Frahm (b. 1982)

'*I like to treat the establishment like a cushion,*' says Nils Frahm, the German composer, producer and former DJ who is playing such a vital and thrilling role in re-energizing and redefining classical music for our times. '*I don't throw it out of the window, but I like to shake the dust off it. I want to expand what it can be.*'

I love this sentiment almost as much as I love Frahm's music – and that's really saying something, because I love, love, *love* the music. I often find myself sending Frahm tracks to friends and loved ones and colleagues, or even just to people I meet who ask me for a certain piece of music to match a certain need or manage a certain mood. There is something not only incredibly sonically diverse about his music, but emotive and empathic too. In other words, it connects.

I was intrigued to read Frahm discuss the ways he thinks he differs from other modern composers who have promoted, either directly or indirectly, the idea that classical music must necessarily be cerebral, intellectual, abstruse (and therefore, by extension, elitist). For Frahm, there's nothing wrong with a beautiful melody, an alluring rhythm, an entertaining break. '*I feel like [those composers, such as Arnold Schoenberg] wanted to tell people what was best for them,*' he says. '*I only can say what I feel and offer to share it with others. I don't want to be exclusive.*'

And a hearty Amen to that!

29 November

Eve
by Amelia Warner (b. 1982)

To one of Frahm's direct contemporaries today, another immensely warm-hearted as well as gifted composer. Amelia Warner started her professional life as an actor starring in a number of high-profile TV dramas and films, but has, in the past few years, returned to her first love: music. (She also found some success as a singer-songwriter under the name 'Slow Moving Millie', providing, for example, the music for an iconic John Lewis TV advert in 2011.)

Warner's years spent storytelling on-screen were certainly a fruitful background to her composing career: in recent years she has really found her niche in TV and film composing, including *Mary Shelley* (2017) and *Mum's List* (2016). In 2019 she was named Breakthrough Composer of the Year at the International Film Music Critics Association Awards, seen by many in the industry as a gold standard and often a precursor to the Academy Awards. 2019 was also the year Warner signed to Decca Publishing, joining a stellar roster of fellow composers.

The atmospheric track I've chosen for this late-November day comes from Warner's 2017 EP *Visitors*, each track of which is based on a fictional female character. She plays piano and organ on the record, which is also scored for violin, viola, cello, and double bass. 'Visitors *is about an imaginary house where all these women once lived,*' she explains. '*The energy left there after they have gone. I wanted it to sound like music upstairs floating down a stairwell.*'

373

30 November

Maria Magdalena
by Francisco Guerrero (1528–1599)

When wintry nights are drawing in, I find there's nothing like a spot of sublime Renaissance polyphony to warm the soul and for me, today's composer invariably hits the spot.

Francisco Guerrero was a Spanish Catholic priest and published author as well as a composer of vast popularity and influence. A student of Cristóbal de Morales, his career was based at the Cathedral in his hometown of Seville, but he was also well-travelled for the time; not just in Spain, Italy and Portugal but as far away as the Holy Land, where we know he visited Damascus, Bethlehem and Jerusalem. (On the return trip, his ship was twice attacked by pirates, who stole his money and held him for ransom. He managed to make it back to Spain but, with no money, ended up in debtors' prison. Still, it all made for good copy: his memoir of his trip to the Holy Land was published as *Journey to Jerusalem* in 1590 and was a popular success; apparently even Cervantes read it!)

Guerrero eventually succumbed not to pirates or jail but the plague. In his lifetime, he managed to find a remarkably wide audience: his music was printed in Seville, Paris, Venice, Rome and Louvain, reprinted as far away as Nuremberg and the New World, and his compositions continued to be performed and emulated around the world for the next two centuries. A significant achievement for the time – for any time.

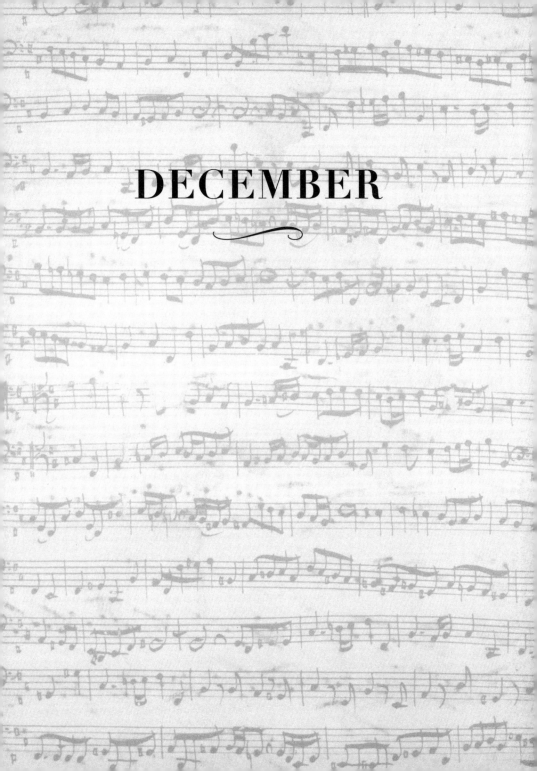

DECEMBER

1 December

Violin concerto no. 2 in G minor, op. 63
2: Andante assai
by Sergei Prokofiev (1891–1953)

Sometimes, in music as in life, things are a slow-burn. Tastes develop, change, evolve (which is obviously great). But *very* occasionally, the opposite is true. The love affair is instantaneous, total, possibly eternal.

In 1935, a very homesick Sergei Prokofiev was soon to return to Russia, having lived in exile in the West – on a League of Nations passport – since 1918. But there was to be one final European hurrah. On this very day, his second violin concerto was premiered in the Teatro Monumental in Madrid – the orchestration specifies casta-nets! – featuring the French soloist Robert Soetens and conducted by the Spaniard Enrique Fernández Arbós.

When I first heard this music – exactly fifty years since Prokofiev died, which was in *the same hour, on the same day* as Josef Stalin, as it happened – I was instantly undone. In all the good ways. I felt Prokofiev had delivered me one of those rare before-and-after pieces, the phenomenon of which I am utterly convinced by: don't ask me to explain it – there is no rhyme nor reason – but it is *real*. Once heard, never forgotten; *everything is changed*. (See 21 February for another example.) On this occasion, I felt that – metaphorically – I started holding my breath as soon as the music started, and that I could only exhale once it stopped. And afterward I was different. I have listened to this movement, which is about ten minutes or so, countless times since, and it is always a kind of magic. Radiant, dark, electric, mystical, almost improvised, always improbable – magic.

So I really hope you enjoy this, even love it. Of course, you might listen to it and be left cold or utterly indifferent. You might actively dislike it. And that is absolutely fine.

Isn't music wonderful?

2 December

In Paradisum
by Galina Grigorjeva (b.1962)

In Paradisum. What an evocative concept. And I say that as a confused agnostic at best.

> *In Paradisum deducant te Angeli*
> *May the angels lead you into paradise . . .*

No wonder that many composers – including Gabriel Fauré, Maurice Duruflé and the originators of the Gospel classic 'When the Saints Go Marching In' – have been drawn to write music for these sacred words. I particularly love this treatment by the Ukraine-born Estonian composer Galina Grigorjeva, whose birthday it is today. The In Paradisum is a part of the Latin Western liturgical Requiem Mass (an 'Antiphon' if you want to get technical). So it's inevitably religiously inflected, yes, but in her hands never dogmatic: full of subtle sonorities and richness, deeply felt yet somehow light of touch.

No disrespect to the male composers who have been justly feted for their interpretations. I believe there's room for *anyone* who is moved to create music, for whatever reason. But I find profound, idiosyncratic beauty in Grigorjeva's version.

Chorus Angelorum te suscipiant	*May the choir of Angels greet you*
et cum Lazaro quondam	*and like Lazarus, who once was a*
* paupere*	* poor man,*
aeternam habeas requiem.	*may you have eternal rest.*

3 December

Sonata for violin and continuo
3: *Imitazione delle campane*
by Johann Paul von Westhoff (1656–1705)
arr. Christian Badzura (b. 1977)

Today we hear from a bit of an outlier in the history of classical music. Despite the fact that Johann Paul von Westhoff was considered a leading violinist in his time, and even wrote the earliest known published music for solo violin, a set of partitas that very likely inspired (praise be!) J. S. Bach's own, he has since fallen into relative obscurity.

Which is a pity, because I think he's the real deal. For my money, this piece is one of the most stunning works to emerge from the Baroque era – which is really saying something, given the embarrassment of riches yielded by that period in musical history. With its eerie opening, hypnotic bassline and crunchy dissonances, this movement stopped me in my tracks when I first encountered it, and no matter how many times I hear it, I am never not mesmerized. In this haunting contemporary arrangement, it manages to sound both ancient and box-fresh all at once: a highly effective mind-re-tuner, a focuser, I find myself returning to it again and again.

4 December

Come, Holy Ghost
by Jonathan Harvey (1939–2012)

Today's music, a beautiful Pentecostal hymn written by the British composer Jonathan Harvey in 1984, is a timeless distillation of the mystery that animates all life. It distils the way music can provide *'routes to the beyond'*, as my brilliant Radio 3 colleague Tom Service has put it, regardless of your personal belief system. Yet this is also unabashedly – air-quotes klaxon – 'modern music', whatever that means.

Harvey, who died on this day, was a rare, inquiring spirit. Particularly influenced in his early composing life by the music of Britten (22 June), Bartók (25 March) and Messiaen (3 January), his life changed in the early 1980s when he received an invitation from legendary French conductor-composer Pierre Boulez to join him at IRCAM in Paris, a new institute dedicated to avant-garde music and sound, located near to Centre Pompidou, and closely allied with it. Hungry to exercise his great intellectual and musical curiosity, Harvey relished the opportunity to explore the new frontiers of electro-acoustic art music. Yet he never ever lost sight of the overwhelming questions of life and death that had always preoccupied him. How to fuse, musically, an experience of the outer physical world with an inward spiritual experience? How to reach for, and express, the – for want of a better word – *numinous*? Harvey's work was undertaken with the utmost integrity, and utmost sincerity; perhaps that is why I find his music so affecting.

5 December

Music for Strings
2: 'The Last Words of M'
by Isobel Waller-Bridge (b. 1984)

Waller-Bridge, an award-winning young British composer, writes beautifully crafted and narratively potent music, often for film and television (including her sister Phoebe's now-iconic series *Fleabag*) but also for live events, fashion shows and even an ambitious collaboration with Durham Cathedral exploring the birth of modern cosmology.

She studied with the great George Benjamin (31 May) and has, I think, a particular gift for employing ancient classical language in a modern and unexpected way. (I refer you to her brilliant take on the English sacred choral tradition that animates the world of *Fleabag*, Series 2). She writes for many types of instruments, but says her beloved baby grand piano – currently in storage, as her North London flat is too small – *'is such a friend'*.

Today she is very much tapping into the British tradition of writing expansive, filmic, emotionally searing music for strings – which is, as it happens, the name of the splendid 2015 album from which this track comes.

6 December

~~~~~~~~~

8 pieces for clarinet, viola and piano, op. 83
6: 'Nachtgesang': Andante con moto
by Max Bruch (1838–1920)

Another offering from the German composer Max Bruch, whose reputation has suffered, in a way, from the overwhelming success of one piece at the expense of almost everything else he wrote. While his Violin Concerto in G minor, arguably one of the greatest and most famous pieces of instrumental music ever written, is certainly a masterpiece, there was so much more to Bruch than just that one hit.

A supremely gifted boy, Bruch wrote his first piece aged eleven, and by fourteen had completed a symphony and a prize-winning string quartet. He went on to have a major career as a conductor, composer and pedagogue, holding posts everywhere from Berlin to Liverpool. The suite of pieces from which this profoundly expressive nocturne comes was written in 1909 as a gift for his son Max Felix, who was a talented clarinettist. I find the combination of instruments deliciously sensuous and mellow, and the pleasure I take in listening to it is only deepened by the tender thought that it was created by a father, lovingly, for a son.

7 December

Shelter Island
by Xavier Dubois Foley (b. 1994)

When, in the summer of 2021, a young American violinist called Randall Goosby released his debut album *Roots*, it was a landmark event in classical circles. Not because the launch was celebrated with, say, a concert or even a party (this was the second year of the COVID pandemic, after all), but because Goosby chose to take a stand – a musical, social, cultural stand – and it paid off. And how.

Most young classical artists, just like their pop counterparts, if they are lucky enough to get a record deal at all, have to play a game. Take the advice of – invariably older, white, male – record executives; play it safe; earn your chops; don't rock the boat. Know your place.

Not so the fantastic Goosby, who was born in 1996 to an African-American father and Korean mother. Passionate about making classical music more inclusive and socially just, and mindful of the *'pivotal'*, as he describes, *'moment in history'* we are in, post-2020, he crafted an impeccable debut which – excuse the expression – blew my mind.

Goosby's playing exudes intelligence, maturity, empathy and joy – as well as a showstopping technical mastery, as you can hear in this new work by his friend, double bassist and composer Xavier Dubois Foley. (The title pays tribute to the secluded, sylvan island on the eastern end of Long Island, New York, where they spent time at the famed Perlman Music Program as – even younger! – string players.)

'It has been a year,' Goosby observes, *'of division and isolation for so many – I hope this music will inspire not only the kind of curiosity and creativity that brings people together, but also the reflection, understanding and compassion we so desperately need moving forward.'*

Magnificent.

8 December

From *Sleep*
'Dream 3 (in the midst of my life)'
by Max Richter (b. 1966)

After yesterday, another game-changer.

When, in 2015, Max Richter's *Sleep* was released into the world, it was a real moment for classical music. A concept album that explores the neuroscience of sleep and extends, in its full version, across more than eight hours of continuous music, Richter's *'lullaby for a frenetic world'* or *'manifesto for a slower pace of existence'*, as he describes it, reached the top of the Billboard US classical chart. It has since been performed live from Sydney to Berlin to London to New York to the Great Wall of China.

I wish I could find a way to explain what happened when I first experienced Richter's extraordinary music live, but it's impossible. Words elude me. The best I can say is that I seemed to transcend my standard plane of existence and was transported into another dimension. It felt like ecstasy. It felt like a miracle. It felt like everything.

9 December

Oboe Concerto in B flat major, Wq. 164
1: Allegretto
by Carl Philip Emanuel Bach (1714–1788)

The fifth child and second surviving son of Johann Sebastian Bach, 'C. P. E.', as he tends to be known, was once more famous and more revered even than his genius of a father. His fans included the likes of Mozart – who once memorably declared, '*(He) is the father. We are all the children!*' – and his influence extended not just across different musical formats, especially instrumental sonatas and concertos such as this one, but in theory and analysis: I am not kidding when I tell you that his 'Essay on the True Art of Playing Keyboard Instruments' was a smash hit of its day. Haydn called it '*the school of schools*'; Beethoven told at least one of his students to '*be sure of procuring Emanuel Bach's treatise*'; and it is *still* widely regarded as one of the definitive works on keyboard technique.

Leaving behind the contrapuntal complexities of the high Baroque, C. P. E. Bach strode forward into the Classical era. His lyrical, melodic and expressive music made him a leading exponent of what became known as the 'sensitive style'. I love that.

10 December

Prelude, Fugue and Variation in B minor, FWV 30, op. 18
1. Prelude – Andantino cantabile
by César Franck (1822–1890)
transcribed for piano by Harold Bauer (1873–1951)

The astonishing musical gifts of César Franck, born on this day in Liège, which was then part of the Netherlands and later Belgium, were evident at an early age. Reading between the lines, young César's father was a classic 'pushy parent', if not *actually* exploitative, moving the family to Paris (where César became an exceptional student at the famed Conservatoire) and later controlling his talented son's life and fortune. Despite certain domestic challenges – Franck *père* forbade his marriage, and so on – Franck went on to become a highly respected organist, composer and teacher: a significant player in the late-Romantic French musical scene.

Franck – and his devoted disciples – really wanted to champion a new type of French music: less mawkish sentimentality, more genuine heart. The aspiration was to transmit real emotion, but building upon formidable technique and structure. Franck's musical aspirations certainly sometimes fall short, but my goodness, when he gets it right, he *really* gets it right. In these moments, for example in his celebrated Violin Sonata in A major, he is able to create soaring, almost improvisational flights of melody, underpinned by intellectual rigour yet wholly devoid of pretension.

If the biographies and contemporary character reports are to be believed, Franck was a particularly kindhearted soul. His great friend, the fellow composer Camille Saint-Saëns (3 February), was the dedicatee of today's piece. I love its gentle opening movement, especially as transcribed for the piano: its tinges of melancholy, and its pathos.

11 December

Anthology of Fantastic Zoology
'Nymphs'
by Mason Bates (b. 1977)

Today we hear from one of contemporary music's most multi-faceted and imaginative figures. Philadelphia-born Mason Bates is a Grammy-award-winner, a recipient of the prestigious Guggenheim Fellowship, winner of the Rome and Berlin Prizes for composition, and the inaugural composer-in-residence at the Kennedy Center in Washington, D.C. Cerebral without being intellectually snooty, Bates counts among his many accolades a joint BA in English Literature from Columbia University and in music composition from Juilliard, a PhD from the University of California, Berkeley, and a successful side-hustle as a San Francisco techno DJ and producer. As you do. Meanwhile, he co-founded the forward-thinking collective Mercury Soul, which mounts shows presenting classical music in nightclubs for packed crowds (no mean feat, let me tell you!); elsewhere he has collaborated with iconic film-maker Gus Van Sant as well as major classical composers including John Corigliano (16 February) and Anna Clyne (27 January). Phew!

When I interviewed Bates in 2019, he seemed lit up with the potential for classical music to be transposed into a modern, non-'expert' sphere. His mission, his sense of purpose, his lack of cynicism, was infectious. We need creators with minds and hearts like his! Bates has spoken about his orchestral music as 'a revival of the narrative symphonies of the nineteenth century using twenty-first-century sounds'; it's very hard to encapsulate his work, obviously, but I have chosen a magical, ambitious, Borges-inspired piece which was composed in 2018 for the Chicago Symphony Orchestra under legendary maestro Riccardo Muti.

12 December

'Torbido intorno al core' – 'My blood, stirred up, now races around my heart' from *Meride e Selinunte* by Nicola Porpora (1686–1768)

Poor Nicola Porpora. Despite the Neapolitan composer's prolific career, especially in the field of operas; despite becoming a stellar teacher, training many of the operatic stars of the day including the famed Farinelli and a young Josef Haydn; despite collaborating with the likes of the so-called 'poet of the eighteenth century', Metastasio (whose verses were set more than 800 times!) – Porpora never gained the recognition he felt he deserved. In 1733, for example, he moved to London, where he tried, and utterly failed, to establish an opera company to rival Handel's, and his final years were spent in abject poverty.

Yet – this music!

I have the sensational contralto and conductor Nathalie Stutzmann to thank for introducing me to this aria. *'People need beauty,'* said Stutzmann in December 2020, amid a pandemic and various worldly horrors. *'[Artists] are there to share those emotions and bring those genius scores into reality, and this beauty is even more in the light in this moment. Just imagine that you had no more concerts, no more books, no art – how can you survive such a moment?'*

Just imagine.

13 December

Well, well, Cornelius
by Howard Skempton (b. 1947)

Today's piece is a quietly moving tribute to composer Cornelius
Cardew, Skempton's teacher and later musical collaborator who died
on this day in 1981. Cardew, a fascinating, radical and not uncontro-
versial figure, was a victim of a hit-and-run accident near his home in
Leyton, east London.

The driver was never found.

14 December

Upon Your Heart
by Eleanor Daley (b. 1955)

Sometimes, the best things in life are just simple truths.

Not that Canadian composer Eleanor Daley's beautiful choral composition is in any way *simplistic*. Lovingly commissioned for a forty-fifth wedding anniversary present, this is a setting of two relatively well-known biblical texts (the Song of Songs 8:6–7, and John 15:9–12) and the sense of big, deep emotions are self-evident. But for me, this setting is so profoundly moving *because* of its simplicity. Don't get me wrong, I obviously appreciate huge, spectacular, all-the-bells-and-whistles-plus-voices kind of music too; in fact, some of my most cherished life memories involve, say, playing in Beethoven's 9th, or Mahler's so-called *Symphony of a Thousand* (so named because he calls for so many players and singers) and there is no beating the sheer exultation, adrenaline and teamwork involved.

But we need a balanced sonic diet, as in other walks of life. And there is something so incredibly restorative and quietly comforting in the sound of unadorned human voices singing together; the way it re-establishes a connection with a part of your inner interior landscape.

I think this is a perfect example.

> *Set me as a seal upon thine heart,*
> *as a seal upon thine arm,*
> *for love is strong as death . . .*

15 December

The Heaven Ladder, Book 7
'Simone's Lullaby'
by Terry Riley (b. 1935), arr. E. M. Zimmerman
for piano four hands

The Simone in question here is one of Riley's twin grandchildren; this tender musical love letter rounds out a pianistic *tour-de-force* completed in 1994 by the American composer, who grew up steeped in classical music but has since persistently defied boundaries to synthesize influences as wide as jazz, contemporary, North African and Indian classical music. One of the pianists who commissioned this beautiful, filmic work, Gloria Cheng, describes Riley's imagination as *'global, kaleidoscopic, consciousness-expanding'*, which I think is a wonderful way of putting it. *'A lot of intersections between these musics occur in my mind,'* Riley confirms. *'As I'm writing or playing something like a raga, suddenly a kind of ragtime motive might come into it . . .'*

Even now, long after the 1960s heyday when his works such as *In C* or *A Rainbow in Curved Air* pioneered genuine new directions in sound, Terry Riley's influence on contemporary classical soundscapes goes deep, and far beyond the so-called 'minimalism' with which he is perpetually associated. Well into his eighties now, he continues to inspire a new generation of artists. *'Terry Riley opened a world of infinite sound in which I could submerge myself for days,'* enthuses Los Angeles-based musician Angel Deradoorian. *'In that realm, I felt the purest inspiration to explore the meaning of music, the power of repetition and variation on a theme, and its meditative, transcendent effects.'* Another collaborator, Greg Fox, says that Riley's music, among many other things, has taught him about patience – a quality I feel we're all in short supply of these days. *'How even small things, repeating, twirling, can be extremely familiar,'* he notes, *'and also energizing, every time they reappear . . .'*

16 December

Noël
by Augusta Holmès (1847–1903)

I know, I know, it is *quite* early to break out the Christmas-themed music. But given the shops have probably been festooned with tinsel for weeks, and given you're probably already being subjected to the annual Band-Aid/Bing-Crosby/Slade/Pogues/Mariah-Carey-fest anyway (no judgement here!) I couldn't resist . . .

For it was on this day that the composer of this particular festive song, Augusta Holmès, was born, to Irish parents, in Paris. In her early career, like so many female artists, Holmès struggled to be taken seriously. (Rumour has it that the composer's mother expressly forbade her passion for music, and that, despairing, the young Augusta tried to kill herself.) Either way, we do know that she chose to employ the pseudonym 'Hermann Zenta' for her earliest compositions, presumably for its Mitteleuropean air of 'seriousness'.

But Holmès persisted; forging her own way, using her own, distinctive gifts to be noticed – and *really noticed* – to live out a vivid, creative, and full life. She went on to occupy a prominent role in Paris's high artistic circles, closely associated with the likes of Rodin and Renoir; her long-time partner (and father of her children) was the poet Catulle Mendes. Meanwhile, in her beloved field of music, she impressed many of the greatest composers of the day, including Rossini (29 February), Liszt (31 July) and Franck (10 December). And Camille Saint-Saëns (3 February), who apparently declared that Holmès was no less than France's 'muse'.

17 December

The Three Kings
by Jonathan Dove (b. 1959)

A setting of a seasonal poem written in 1916 by the fascinating English crime novelist – oh, and short story writer, playwright, essayist, linguist, translator of Dante, good friend of C. S. Lewis, early advertising maven, and so on – Dorothy L. Sayers, who died on this day in 1957.

As was her wont, Sayers cleverly inverts expectation in her poem, imagining her royal visitors as running the full gamut of ages, from a very young child, downcast of eye and doleful, who bears bitter gall (after all, Herod was in the business of infant-slaying), to a very old man, who counterintuitively brings handful upon handful of glittering gold. The masterly British composer Jonathan Dove brings something equally distinctive – haunting, layered, new – to complement the text.

I was lucky enough to be present during the Nine Lessons and Carols ceremony in the chapel of King's College, Cambridge on Christmas Eve in the year this piece was premiered. It was the year 2000. I still get goosebumps thinking about it.

18 December

Il neige – It is Snowing
by Henrique Oswald (1852–1931)

Maybe, depending which country, continent, or hemisphere you are reading this in, or depending on the vicissitudes of climate change *anywhere* (the anxious mind boggles), there is a chance of snow today . . . Either way, I sincerely hope you can enjoy this musical sketch of the white stuff, by a regrettably sidelined but very important Brazilian composer.

Henrique Oswald was born in Rio de Janeiro, to parents hailing from Switzerland and Italy. Given his familial roots, and the dominance of a long Western European tradition in classical music, it is not particularly surprising that his work gives a nod to his own heritage and to the contemporary French Romantic composers he particularly admired – e.g. Fauré (6 February, 12 May), Debussy (13 January, 28 December), Saint-Saëns (3 February).

In 1902 Oswald submitted this sparkling sliver of a solo piano piece for a major competition organized by the Parisian newspaper *Le Figaro* – and won. The judging panel included Saint-Saëns and Fauré. (Different times, indeed . . .) But what is most interesting, to me, is that in Oswald's music, these evident influences are intertwined and infused with his own Brazilian sensibilities. The mix is really exciting.

After long periods studying and working in Europe, Oswald returned to his beloved Brazil intent on educating and nurturing a new generation of younger Brazilian classical pianists and composers. He worked tirelessly at the National Institute of Music until his death, at almost eighty.

As I was reading more about Oswald, I was struck by something anew. Classical music is not the preserve of anyone from any culture. Music is a common good. We lose sight of this at our peril.

19 December

La Fiesta de la Posada
by Dave Brubeck (1920–2012)

Dave Brubeck was a genius, but his astonishing legacy in jazz history means we rarely hear his ventures into classical.

Brubeck's mother Elizabeth trained as a classical concert pianist in England (under the legendary Dame Myra Hess), and she gave him piano lessons early. He showed an intuitive grasp of complex things like counterpoint, sophisticated time signatures, and contrasting rhythms, meter and tonalities (if not sightreading). But Brubeck was 'supposed' to be a cattle rancher, like his father. So he went to college to study veterinary science. That was the plan . . . until it wasn't. According to Brubeck's biographer, his zoology professor eventually announced, *'Brubeck, your mind's not here. It's across the lawn in the (music) conservatory. Please go there. Stop wasting my time and yours.'* Harsh, but maybe fair. Brubeck changed course, and the rest was history. His subsequent classical teachers included the composer Darius Milhaud and, briefly, the massively influential Arnold Schoenberg (13 September).

For today, a seasonal piece, *The Posada*, a traditional Mexican re-enactment of Mary and Joseph's search for lodgings in Bethlehem. *'I was born in a California town founded by the Spanish, raised on a cattle ranch that had been a Mexican land grant, and have absorbed and observed Mexican folk music all my life,'* Brubeck says. Mexican music, he adds, *'reflects those qualities I most admire . . . dignity in moments of tragedy, infectious high spirits in moments of joy . . . deep respect for the shared values of one's own group – family, church, village. These qualities, I think, are universal to people with a strong communal sense – an increasingly rare attribute in urban culture. It is this sense of sharing in an event which I have tried to capture in the simple retelling of the Christmas story.'*

20 December

Nocturne in A Minor
by Chad Lawson (b. 1975)

The phenomenally successful – and disarmingly humble – pianist and composer Chad Lawson has a straightforward approach to the question about how to make classical music less forbidding: '*don't make it classical*'.

It helps that Lawson seems like a 'regular' guy (albeit a white, middle-aged one, with all the privilege that denotes). He talks about regular things: how much he loves a great cup of coffee, or the benefits of meditation and running – which he describes as '*a mental shower*'. He sends postcards to his fans whilst he travels around the world – could be a historic landmark in a city; could be a restaurant recommendation. He once shrewdly observed that the piano '*could be an adversary. Or the piano can be your therapist*'.

Lawson counts jazz, Max Richter, J. S. Bach and Frédéric Chopin as major influences. This 'nocturne' is a twenty-first-century homage to Chopin – the Polish master wrote twenty-one of the things! – lovingly translating the melody to the right hand and painting in his serene, minimalist brushstrokes. I find it quite dreamy.

21 December

Outrage at Valdez
by Frank Zappa (1940–1993)

In 1989, legendary French aquatic explorer, scientist, diver and innovator Jacques Cousteau made a documentary, *Outrage at Valdez*, about the recent environmental disaster caused when an Exxon tanker hit a reef in Prince William Sound, Alaska, pouring 11 million gallons of crude oil into the sea. And the equally legendary experimental, beyond-genre, creative artist Frank Zappa, born on this day, was tasked to provide some music for the soundtrack. The result is quite something.

By the way, although the Deepwater Horizon 'oil spill' of 2010 trumped it in terms of oil released, the Exxon Valdez disaster – or outrage – is still considered the worst oil spill ever, in terms of damage to the environment.

Also quite something.

22 December

~~~

Lachrimae
by John Dowland (1563–1626)

Today we travel to a completely different sound world, as we are transported back through the centuries to one of the most acclaimed musical figures of the Renaissance era.

The English composer, lutenist and singer John Dowland was that rarest of classical musicians: a composer who was actually paid handsomely for his work in his own lifetime. Employed for a time at the court of Christian IV of Denmark, his salary was reportedly a whopping 500 daler per year. He was also a sometime spy, engaged in acts of espionage for the legendary statesman Sir Robert Cecil (the man who first uncovered Guy Fawkes' Gunpowder Plot), and he later became embroiled in a treasonous Catholic intrigue whilst in Italy, ironically on a trip to try and meet one of his musical heroes, the celebrated madrigalist Luca Marenzio (22 August).

For all that Dowland's letters and contemporary accounts indicate a cheery chap, in his music he was a high priest of melancholy, writing works, mostly for the lute, that tug persistently on the heartstrings. Like all the very best sad music, though, it invariably has the effect of lifting the spirits and I – along with the likes of Sting, who has recorded a whole album in homage to Dowland – can't get enough of it.

23 December

'Little Serenade'
by Peter Sculthorpe (1929–2014)

Honoured in his lifetime as an 'Australian Living Treasure' by the National Trust of Australia and sometimes dubbed the 'spiritual father' of Australian classical music – he was the first composer whose music was performed at the now-iconic Sydney Opera House – the Tasmanian-born Peter Sculthorpe was a man whose ears were open to influences from all over the globe. His prolific and original musical output has made him one of the most successful composers from that region.

As well as a large body of work for string quartet that often incorporates local instruments and timbral effects, such as the didjeridu, Sculthorpe wrote large-scale orchestral works that evoke the atmosphere of the outback and bushland of Australia. He roundly embraced the idea that his music could be political, whether by addressing previous wrongs against the indigenous peoples of Tasmania, climate change or the refugee crisis.

Above all, though, Sculthorpe said his music was about his *'own experience as a human being'* and stated that he wanted his music to make people feel better and happier for having listened to it.

That's certainly the effect on me of this lovely little serenade, originally written in 1978 for string quartet, but orchestrated wonderfully in alternative versions. By the way, when I found out Sculthorpe had spent time living in a Zen Buddhist monastery in Japan, it all made sense.

24 December

Missa De Apostolis
Agnus Dei
by Heinrich Isaac (c. 1450/55–1517)

It cannot be overstated how rare it must have been to enjoy a multi-decade-long, internationally acclaimed, not to mention seriously influential career as a living composer . . . in the fifteenth century! I mean, it is pretty rare now, but imagine five-hundred-plus years ago! But that is what Heinrich Isaac managed to achieve.

In a career spanning well over thirty years, before the European Renaissance, the highly productive Isaac was able to travel far from his native Flanders into Germany, Austria, Italy, and beyond. A letter of 1514, for example, states retrospectively that the wealthy (and powerful) Medici family *'had sent for him as far as Flanders'* after the family was restored to power in 1512. Thus favoured, Isaac might have taught various Medici children, but either way, we *do* know that the Medici brothers Piero and Giovanni (later Pope Leo X) became his patrons, paving the way to various prestigious positions (including becoming provost of Florence Cathedral, a cushy-sounding sinecure, or what we might call 'money for old rope').

It must have helped that he wrote music of spine-tingling emotional power, like this.

25 December

Dormi, Jesu
by John Rutter (b. 1945)

John Rutter is associated with Christmas. Although the London-born composer can write in almost any other musical genre too, Rutter has composed or arranged dozens of carols and other seasonal fare. It is over sixty years since he wrote his first carol, and his carols have been translated into many languages. Including Tibetan.

For today, I have chosen one that was written in 1999 for the choir of King's College, Cambridge for performance during the college's Festival of Nine Lessons and Carols. Also known as the *Virgin's Cradle Hymn*, the words of *Dormi, Jesu* come from a German print depicting the Virgin Mary which was discovered by the great Romantic poet Samuel Taylor Coleridge.

Like all Rutter's finest work, this is deceptively simple, belying the exceptional craft and mastery that goes into it.

To all of you celebrating today, let your day be wonder-filled.

Happy Christmas.

26 December

Siete canciones populares españolas
5: 'Nana'
by Manuel de Falla (1876–1946)

Our human instinct to transmit solace in a melody, to soothe through music, goes very, very deep; parents from all cultures have been singing lullabies to their babies for ever, often, seemingly instinctively, using the same sorts of rocking rhythms and gentle vocal inflections no matter where they come from or what age they live in. A mother's voice, familiar from the twenty-fourth week of pregnancy, has been described as *'an acoustic bridge'*, a notion that moves me profoundly.

One of the earliest lullabies on record dates back to 2,000 BC and features words etched in cuneiform script onto a Babylonian clay tablet. Today's is based on an Andalusian cradle song that possibly has its origin in India. The Spanish composer Manuel de Falla said he heard it from *'his mother's lips before he was old enough to think'*.

Sometimes, with these great composers, I think we run the risk of forgetting that they are just like us – children, parents, people. An acoustic bridge indeed.

27 December

Negro Folk Symphony
3: 'O, le' me shine'
by William L. Dawson (1899–1990)

Dr William Levi Dawson was an extraordinary musician: distinguished as a performer, educator, choral director, administrator, musicologist and composer.

Born in Anniston, Alabama, Dawson first heard African-American folk songs, as well as jazz and contemporary concert music, as a young child. Before too long he was displaying his own unmistakable musical talent and by his early teens he had left home to study piano, trombone and composition.

As the visionary director of the choir at Tuskegee Institute (now University), Dawson presided over a golden era. The choir was even invited to perform in the grand opening of New York's Radio City Music Hall. The builder of the hall, Samuel Lionel Rothafel, reported that *'seven thousand people heard and saw the first program at Radio City on December 27, 1932'*. Even by New York's standards, that was no mean feat.

As a composer, it looked like Dawson had hit the big time when, aged thirty-five, his *Negro Folk Symphony* was rapturously received at Carnegie Hall in 1934. Olin Downes, writing in *The New York Times*, noted: *'This music has dramatic feeling . . . sensuousness and directness of melodic speech'*. Dawson said that he wasn't out to imitate Beethoven or Brahms, those titans of the symphony, but wanted those who heard it to know that it was *'unmistakably not the work of a white man'*.

But despite four back-to-back performances at Carnegie and a CBS radio broadcast, only a handful of performances were given in the months that followed. It marked both the zenith and the culmination of Dawson's symphonic career.

28 December

La plus que lente
by Claude Debussy (1862–1918)

From innovative works such as the opera *Pelléas et Mélisande* (1902) or the symphonic tone poem *Prélude à l'après-midi d'un faune* (1894) to ambitious and atmospheric soundscapes such as *La Mer* and timeless piano vignettes such as *Clair de lune* (both published in 1905), Debussy's music seems to encapsulate the musical ferment of the early-modernist Paris of which he played a central role. He is one of those rare composers of whom it is possible to say, after he died, 'nothing was ever quite the same again'. With his fondness for syncopation, blue notes and melodic abstraction, Debussy paved the way for jazz and other later musical innovations; he was also a wry and witty commentator on the music of his time. (This piece, for example, gently mocks the vogue for a 'slow waltz' – its title literally means 'The More Than Slow'.)

Although written for solo piano, it was later orchestrated, and Debussy's views on how this version should sound are revealing: he advocated for a simplicity and grace that would appeal, as he put it in a letter to his publisher, to the *'numberless five-o'-clock teas where assemble the beautiful audiences I've dreamed of'*. I think this point is key: for all Debussy was constantly pushing at the boundaries of sonic expectations and writing music that must have sounded thrillingly daring at the time, he always keeps his audience in mind, offering us musical treasures that invariably, to this day, delight.

29 December

In the Bleak Midwinter
by Gustav Holst (1874–1934)
arr. Sheku Kanneh-Mason (b. 1999)

Today's piece was already something of a beloved wintry fixture – with its stirringly evocative words by the Pre-Raphaelite British poet Christina Rossetti, who died on this day, and music by illustrious British composer and educationalist Gustav Holst, who, amongst other things, also wrote the iconic orchestral suite *The Planets*.

Then, in 2018, the British musician Sheku Kanneh-Mason arranged this for cello and piano. Given what the teenager from Mapperley Park, Nottingham had achieved already in that year – for example, oh, playing at the wedding of the Duke and Duchess of Sussex, watched by a cool twenty-nine million TV viewers in the US alone; releasing such a stupendous account of Shostakovich's Cello Concerto that he knocked the rapper Lil Baby off the US Billboard Emerging Artists Chart; all while keeping his degree going as an undergrad at the Royal Academy of Music in central London – you can only shake your head in amazement!

Kanneh-Mason's short arrangement is by turns spare, emotionally charged, technically breathtaking, playful, mournful. One minute you want to laugh with glee at its sheer brilliance; the next your heartstrings are being properly tugged. Quite wonderful.

30 December

Blue Curve of the Earth
by Tina Davidson (b. 1952)

I have to thank the incredible violinist Hilary Hahn for introducing me to the music of the American composer Tina Davidson, whose birthday it is today. Davidson was among the twenty-seven contemporary composers commissioned by Hahn to write a new piece for an ambitious and imaginative 2013 album, which extended the available repertoire of 'encores', the short but not insignificant concert pieces that soloists offer up to an audience if the main performance has been particularly well received.

And I love Davidson's contribution; every time I listen, I discover something new. Proudly cosmopolitan and curious in outlook, the composer has lived in many countries – including Sweden, Turkey, Israel and Germany – and I think you can hear that in her work. Whether deliberate or subconscious, her music bears the traces of those diverse cultural influences: a Middle Eastern flavour here, a jazzy inflection there; a sort of sonic seasoning, if you like. As she has said, with a wry smile: '*How could it have not?*'

She talks intriguingly, too, of layers in her composition, with sounds '*seep(ing) out of the violin*' and '*organic shapes of the rhythms, very intuitive, not based on mathematical schemes*' – (Davidson's father was a celebrated scientist) – but more as if she '*dreams music*'. I love that idea.

31 December

Trumpet Voluntary, op. 6, no. 5
by John Stanley (1712–1786)

Whatever your New Year's Eve celebrations look like this year, or any year hence: I am here to remind you that you are . . . alive. You made it. And that alone is cause for celebration.

This may sound like a platitude, but I *really mean it*. No matter how privileged or fortunate you might be compared to some other people, life is hard. Recently, as the world has confronted unprecedented loss and grief on a epic scale – *especially* hard. Socially, culturally, personally – I don't believe any thinking, feeling, empathetic human has been unaffected by the pandemic and ongoing aftermath.

So on this New Year's Eve, let the sheer resilience of musician John Stanley inspire you. The composer, blinded when he was involved in a terrible childhood accident, went on to become the youngest person to gain a BMus degree at Oxford University, befriend no less a celebrity musical figure than Handel, direct many landmark musical entertainments in London, including many for charitable causes – and oh, just casually compose one of *the* most famous pieces of music, ever.

Deep breath. Raise your glass. Humans are incredible.

Happy new year.

Acknowledgements

I am indebted to my mother, Gillian Hawser, for many things, including (obviously, but crucially) taking seriously the whims of a music-loving toddler, despite the lack of classical music in her own life. Mum, I owe you so much, thank you. And Dad, and my wider family, Perry and Elliot and your families: these times, wow, I hope you know how much I miss and love you all.

I am beyond grateful to my dear friends Eddie Redmayne and Elizabeth Day, for their incredible support and generosity in recording the audio book and writing the foreword so beautifully when I couldn't speak or write myself. I am also very grateful to Tara Hacking and Sophie Elmhirst, for never stopping believing in me, or this book, even when it was frankly laughable (read: grievously unlikely) that I could finish it, or anything, after 20 January 2020. Thank you to all my life-sustaining friends, in particular Andrew Staples for *Morgen!* (and much else besides). Thank you to Nicky and Wynton for that afternoon in June 2020 when you helped me to know – and really *know*: emotionally, neurologically, physically – the miracle of 'a brain on music'. And heartfelt thanks to Ursula Macfarlane and Sophie Vickers for investing in my recovery on a level that is frankly humbling. Gwendoline Bradley, Victoria Parker, Daisy Robinton, Adam Cobb, Jess Shadbolt, Hannah Young, Ameer Youssef, Simon Schama, Neil Westreich and Maria Popova you are saints, and various selfless others including Kate Crane and Belinda Hanson, you have been so generous with your time, and it is so appreciated. Ledilyn Monte, we literally could not do this without you. Alison Balsom, Sam Mendes: no words could express our gratitude for your incredible largesse with Rocky Lane. Thank you.

Huge heartfelt thanks to my amazing publisher, Lindsey Evans, and agent, Rosemary Scoular, and my ever-supportive Headline and United Agents families. And thank you – again! – to Katie Green, a brilliant, empathetic and sensitive copy-editor.

I owe so much to my extended, international music 'family': my BBC teammates, especially Matthew Dover and Emma Barnett and those at WQXR and WNYC Studios in New York. Also the many incredible instrumentalists, singers, conductors, teachers, producers, presenters and broadcasters, hailing from all corners of the globe: wow. What a joy and rich education – musically, socially, culturally, politically – it has been all these years.

Words cannot describe my eternal gratitude to the wonderful Dr Heidi Fusco and her brain rehabilitation team at NYU hospitals, especially Teresa Kiernan, Teresa Iodice-Dadin, Liat Robinowitz and Amanda Haddad; also Michelle Rodriguez at MPG (via Christopher Wheeldon, fellow lover of the Prokofiev – see 1 December); and many other doctors, therapists, nurses and stellar healthcare professionals besides. I know how wildly fortunate I have been. I don't take it for granted.

To the loves of my life: James, Tom and Joe Roscoe. Thank you for everything, but particularly for making it impossible to choose any other way. You make my life make sense. I love you.

Finally: neither this book, nor I, would exist were it not for one man, the remarkable brain surgeon, Dr Christopher Kellner. That we had a conversation many months after you saved my life – a stilted, aphasia- and apraxia-hobbled conversation, to be fair, but a conversation nonetheless – and you happened to say, as an aside, that you were reading *Year of Wonder,* and listening to the music, every day, *and that you were looking forward to reading the next one . . .!*

What grace. What astonishing grace.

May I keep your example as a moral touchstone, as well as a source of motivation and robust hope, for whatever comes next.

Thank you.

Notes on Sources

vii. Walt Whitman, 'Democratic Vistas', *Walt Whitman: Poetry and Prose* (The Library of America, 1982); https://www.worldcat.org/title/complete-poetry-and-collected-prose/oclc/8034382&referer=brief_results

January

3. Note on Messiaen's chords from Allen Forte, 'Messiaen's Chords', in *Olivier Messiaen: Music, Art, and Literature*, edited by Christopher Dingle and Nigel Simeone (Ashgate Publishing Limited, 2007), p. 91.
Lines from the Latin prose text '*O sacrum convivium!*', attributed to Saint Thomas Aquinas; www.cpdl.org/wiki/index.php/O_sacrum_convivium

4. Composer's programme note from www.wisemusicclassical.com/work/19135/Asteroid-4179-Toutatis--Kaija-Saariaho/

7. Poulenc as quoted in Edwin Romain, *A Study of Francis Poulenc's Fifteen Improvisations for Piano Solo* (University of Southern Mississippi, 1978), p. 48.
Stravinsky as quoted in *Francis Poulenc: Selected Correspondence 1915–1963*, edited and translated by Sidney Buckland (Victor Gollancz, 1991), p. 94.

8. '*Weirdo . . .*' as quoted in https://www.articulateshow.org/articulate/david-lang-vanguard-of-the-un-cool
Composer's programme notes taken from his website: https://davidlangmusic.com/music/again-after-ecclesiastes

12. *Pitchfork* review quoted from https://pitchfork.com/reviews/albums/anna-meredith-anno/

13. Debussy as quoted in *Debussy on Music* by François Lesure, translated by Richard Langham Smith (Random House, 1977), p. 84. Cited in Mimi Stillman, 'Debussy, Painter of Sound and Image', *The Flutist Quarterly* 33 (1), pp. 41–46 (Fall 2007).

14. Composer's words taken from her website: http://www.musicsalesclassical. com/composer/short-bio/Angela-Morley

18. Chabrier as quoted in Denis Arnold and Roger Nichols, 'Chabrier, Emmanuel', *The Oxford Companion to Music* (Oxford University Press, 2011).

19. Composer's words as quoted at http://www.kennedy-center.org/artist/ composition/5070

20. '*A meditation on violence . . .*' from the liner notes for his album *Blue Notebooks* (Decca [UMO] Classics, 2018).
'*protest*' from Max Richter, 'Millions of us knew the Iraq war would be a catastrophe. Why didn't Tony Blair?', the *Guardian*, 8 July 2016: https:// www.theguardian.com/commentisfree/2016/jul/08/iraq-war-tony-blair-creativity-chilcot-inquiry
Elisabeth Moss as quoted in Tom Huizenga, 'Max Richter's "Blue Notebooks" Offers Moving Portrait For Elisabeth Moss', *Deceptive Cadence*, 21 June 2018: https://www.npr.org/sections/deceptivecadence/ 2018/06/21/622283030/max-richters-blue-notebooks-offers-moving-portrait-for-elisabeth-moss?t=1590682533696

23. Lines from 'Sure on this shining night' by James Agee provided courtesy of Oxford Lieder: https://www.oxfordlieder.co.uk/song/2678

24. Composer's words taken from his website: http://olagjeilo.com/ sheet-music/choral-satb-a-cappella/ubi-caritas/

26. Saint-Saëns as quoted in the entry for Reber in *Grove Music Online*, 2001: https://www.oxfordmusiconline.com/grovemusic/view/ 10.1093/gmo/9781561592630.001.0001/omo-9781561592630-e-0000023006

27. '*intention . . . to create music . . .*' originally from the composer's website, as quoted in ' "Alt-Classical": Is This the Future?', *Standpoint*, 17 November 2009: https://standpointmag.co.uk/alt-classical-is-this-the-future/
'*It was in a dusty old case . . .*' and '*On the anniversary of my mother's death . . .*' from http://www.boosey.com/cr/music/Anna-Clyne-The-Violin/101256

28. Lines from '*What power art thou . . .*' by John Dryden taken from the libretto to *King Arthur* on OperaGlass: http://opera.stanford.edu/Purcell/ KingArthur/libretto.html

30. From the entry on 'Native American music' by Bruno Nettl, revised by Victoria Lindsay Levine, Bryan Burton and Gertrude Prokosch Kurath, in

Oxford Music Online: https://www.oxfordmusiconline.com/grovemusic/view/10.1093/gmo/9781561592630.001.0001/omo-9781561592630-e-1002251909

February

5. Nicholas J. Conard, Maria Malina & Suzanne Münzel, 'New flutes document the earliest musical tradition in southwestern Germany', *Nature*, vol. 460, 24 June 2009: https://www.nature.com/articles/nature08169

6. Charles Koechlin, *Gabriel Fauré*, translated by Leslie Orrey (Dennis Dobson Ltd, 1945).

8. Composer's words taken from her programme notes on the Piano Trio: http://www.jenniferhigdon.com/pdf/program-notes/Piano-Trio.pdf

10. Composer's words as quoted in http://www.antonin-dvorak.cz/en/romantic-pieces

11. Composer's words taken from his interview with Thomas Huizenga, 'The Silence And Awe Of Arvo Pärt', *Deceptive Cadence*, 2 June 2014: https://www.npr.org/sections/deceptivecadence/2014/06/02/316322238/the-silence-and-awe-of-arvo-p-rt

12. Composer's words as quoted in Craig Wright, *The Essential Listening to Music* (Schirmer: Cengage Learning, 2013), p. 163.

13. Composer's words taken from her website: https://sarahkirklandsnider.com/2013/05/the-currents/
    Lines by Nathaniel Bellows taken from the album *Unremembered* by Sarah Kirkland and Nathaniel Bellows.

17. Lines from 'Will there really be a morning?' by Emily Dickinson.

18. Robert Schumann's words as quoted in the publisher's note for the Carus edition of Psalm 42: https://www.carus-verlag.com/en/choir/sacred-choral-music/mendelssohn-wie-der-hirsch-schreit-der-42-psalm.html
    Composer's words as quoted in Michael Cookson's review on MusicWeb International of the 12-volume recording of Mendelssohn's *Complete Sacred Choral Music* by Carus: http://www.musicweb-international.com/classrev/2009/Apr09/Mendelssohn_complete_carus.htm
    Extract from Psalm 42 taken from Martin Luther, *Devotional Writings, Vol. 42 of Works*, edited by Jaroslav Pelikan, Hilton C. Oswald, Helmut T. Lehmann (Concordia Publishing House, 1969), p. 176; English translation by Tara Wondraczek.

19. Composer's words as quoted by Pamela Blevins in her biographical note for MusicWeb International (2002): http://www.musicweb-international. com/classrev/2002/Jun02/Grace_Williams.htm

20. From the liner notes for Einaudi's album *Le Onde* (Ricordi, 1996).

21. Extract from Patrick Gale, *Take Nothing With You* (Tinder Press, 2018), pp.123–124.

22. Lines by Joseph von Eichendorff from *Verschwiegene Liebe*; English translation © Richard Stokes from *The Complete Songs of Hugo Wolf. Life, Letters, Lieder* (Faber, 2021).

23. Composer's words on receiving an honorary degree from the University of Birmingham, 13 November 2015, English translation by Robin Blanton, from her website: https://karin-rehnqvist.se/eng/as-a-composer-i-am-the-consummate-listener/

24. Italian text by Giacomo Rossi; English translation by Tara Wondraczek.

27. Composer's words as quoted in *Schubert: Memoirs by His Friends*, edited by Otto Erich Deutsch (A. & C. Black, 1958), p. 100.

March

1. Composer's words taken from 'Interview: Karl Jenkins, composer', *Church Times*, 9 December 2008: https://www.churchtimes.co.uk/ articles/2008/12-december/features/interview-karl-jenkins-composer and 'Facing the Music: Karl Jenkins', the *Guardian*, 28 March 2016: https://www.theguardian.com/music/2016/mar/28/facing-the-music-composer-karl-jenkins

2. '*inspired lunacy*' taken from the duo's website: http://www. igudesmanandjoo.com/about-igudesman-joo/

3. Composer's words as quoted in Ashley Jackson, 'Affinities: Margaret Bonds and Langston Hughes', 23 August 2018: http://ashleyjacksonharp. com/lectures/affinities-margaret-bonds-and-langston-hughes
Extract from 'Dream Variation' by Langston Hughes, originally published in *The Weary Blues* (Knopf, 1926).

5. '*a map of Brazil*' as cited in Tom Service, 'Villa-Lobos: get to know Brazil's greatest composer', the *Guardian*, 7 March 2014: https://www. theguardian.com/music/tomserviceblog/2014/mar/07/villa-lobos-brazil-bbc-symphony-orchestra-total-immersion

7. Philip Glass as quoted on the composer's website: http://paolaprestini. com

9. German text from Luke 24, v. 29; English translation by John Rutter, taken from the CD booklet for his album *Lighten our Darkness: Music for the Close of Day* with the Cambridge Singers (Collegium, 2006); https://johnrutter.com/product/lighten-our-darkness.

10. George Bernard Shaw as quoted in Henry Kamen, *The Disinherited: The Exiles Who Created Spanish Culture* (Penguin UK, 2008).

13. Johann Mattheson as quoted in the *Encyclopaedia Britannica:* https://www.britannica.com/biography/Georg-Philipp-Telemann/Legacy

14. Composer's words taken from his website: https://stephenpaulus.com/blogs/news/17806884-work-story-the-road-home
Lines by Michael Dennis Browne taken from Last.fm: https://www.last.fm/music/Stephen+Paulus/_/The+Road+Home/+lyrics

15. Lines from '*Reflets*' by Maurice Maeterlinck; English translation © Richard Stokes, author of *A French Song Companion* (Oxford, 2000); provided courtesy of Oxford Lieder: https://www.oxfordlieder.co.uk/song/3337

18. Bertrand Chayamou's words taken from the liner notes from his album *Good Night* (Warner Music, 2020).

19. '*It takes courage and confidence . . .*' from Pwyll ap Siôn's review of Muhly's Four Studies in *Gramophone* magazine: https://www.gramophone.co.uk/review/glass-in-the-summer-house-muhly-four-studies

20. Jacqueline Riding as quoted in Catherine Milner, 'Handel was gay – his music proves it, claims academic', the *Telegraph*, 21 October 2001: https://www.telegraph.co.uk/news/worldnews/europe/germany/1360091/Handel-was-gay-his-music-proves-it-claims-academic.html

21. '*Bach was a deeply religious man . . .*' from András Schiff, 'After 250 Years, the Piano May Be the Last Bach Frontier', *The New York Times*, 12 September 1999: https://archive.nytimes.com/www.nytimes.com/library/arts/091299ns-bach-music.html

22. '*supreme arbiter and law-giver of music*' and Max Richter's response taken from Tom Huizenga, 'What's Composer Max Richter Listening To? Pretty Much Everything', *Deceptive Cadence*, 5 April 2017: https://www.npr.org/sections/deceptivecadence/2017/04/05/520406762/whats-composer-max-richter-listening-to-pretty-much-everything

23. Richard Dehmel as quoted in Friedrich Haider, 'From Salon to Concert Hall', in liner notes for the CD *Richard Strauss: The complete orchestral songs* (Nightingale Classics, 1994), p. 11.
    German text by Richard Dehmel; English translation by John Bernhoff, from *Five Songs, with piano accompaniment, composed by Richard Strauss, with German and English words* (Robert Berhoff, 1898).
25. '*a deeper understanding of folk style . . .*' from Alex Ross, 'Bartok's Folk', *The New Yorker*, 28 January 2010: https://www.newyorker.com/culture/alex-ross/bartks-folk
26. Composer's words as quoted in Tom Huizenger, 'Steve Reich Wins Music Pulitzer', *NPR Music*, 20 April 2009: https://www.npr.org/templates/story/story.php?storyId=103304036
    Tim Page, '*He is a universal composer*' also as quoted by Tom Huizenger, *ibid*.
27. Italian text by Giuseppe Adami from Act 2 of *La Rondine*; English translation by Tara Wondraczek
28. Composer's words as quoted in Jessica Duchen, 'Man for all the people', the *Guardian*, 30 April 1999: https://www.theguardian.com/friday_review/story/0,3605,296502,00.html
29. From Marina Frolova-Walker, 'Intimate Truths: The private world of Tchaikovsky's Eugene Onegin', *Royal Opera House*, 11 December 2015: https://www.roh.org.uk/news/intimate-truths-the-private-world-of-tchaikovskys-eugene-onegin
31. '*beating heart*' as quoted in Ivan Hewett's interview with John Eliot Gardiner, 'John Eliot Gardiner: "Bach has become my obsession"', *The Telegraph*, 3 October 2013: https://www.telegraph.co.uk/culture/music/classicalmusic/10344175/John-Eliot-Gardiner-Bach-has-become-my-obsession.html

April

1 '*classical polymath*' from https://pitchfork.com/reviews/tracks/14090-anna-meredith-nautilus/
    '*a playground*' and words by the composer taken from Marianne Gallagher, 'Mapping the Unexpected: Anna Meredith interviewed', *Clash Magazine*, 25 October 2019: https://www.clashmusic.com/features/mapping-the-unexpected-anna-meredith-interviewed
2. '*accessible, communicative*' and words by the composer taken from Sebastian Scotney, '10 Questions for Composer Dobrinka Tabakova', *The*

Arts Desk, 9 March 2015: https://theartsdesk.com/classical-music/10-questions-composer-dobrinka-tabakova

3. Amy Beach's mother as quoted in Jeanell Wise Brown, *Amy Beach and her Chamber Music: Biography, Documents, Style* (Scarecrow Press, 1994), p. 16.
   Critics as quoted in *ibid.*, p. 129, p. 198.

4. Kimberly A. Francis, *Teaching Stravinsky: Nadia Boulanger and the Consecration of a Modernist Icon* (Oxford University Press, 2015), p. 79.

5. Composer as quoted in the programme note by Robert Andres, 'An introduction to the solo piano music of Debussy and Ravel' for BBC Radio 3: https://www.bbc.co.uk/radio3/classical/raveldebussy/recital2.shtml#:~:text=It%20became%20particularly%20popular%20through,danced%20at%20the%20Spanish%20court%22.

6. Ralph Waldo Emerson, *Emerson: Poems*, edited by Peter Washington (Knopf Doubleday Publishing Group, 2012), p. 188.

7. Programme note by the composer taken from http://www.musicsalesclassical.com/composer/work/11278

8. Edward Thomas as quoted in Matthew Hollis, *Now All Roads Lead to France: A Life of Edward Thomas* (W. W. Norton, 2012).
   Robert Macfarlane in conversation with CBH for the Open Ears Project, WYNC Studios, 23 September 2019: https://www.wnycstudios.org/podcasts/open-ears-project/episodes/robert-macfarlane-on-a-quiet-kind-of-miracle

11. Composer's words taken from her website: http://charlottebray.co.uk/works/solo/beyond/

12. Colin Matthews' words taken from his foreword to *Imogen Holst: A Life in Music*, edited by Christopher Grogan (Boydell Press, 2007), p. xiii.

17. Filippo Picinelli as quoted in *The Cozzolani Project*: https://web.archive.org/web/20091130230438/http://www.cozzolani.com/chiara

19. Composer's words taken from his website: https://ericwhitacre.com/music-catalog/a-boy-and-a-girl
    'Los Novios' by Octavio Paz; English translation by Muriel Rukeyser from the composer's website, *ibid.*

20. Composer's words as quoted in Amanda Petrusich, 'Julianna Barwick is Using the New York Sky to Make Music', *The New Yorker*, 22 April 2019:

https://www.newyorker.com/culture/culture-desk/julianna-barwick-is-using-the-new-york-sky-to-make-music
'*articulating the ineffable*' as quoted in T. Cole Rachel, 'Julianna Barwick: "I'm Not This Gentle Fairy Creature Person"', *The Fader*, 4 May 2016: https://www.thefader.com/2016/05/04/julianna-barwick-will-interview

22. From the composer's *Autobiographical Account of a Tour Abroad in the Year 1888*, as cited on the website Tchaikovsky Research: http://en.tchaikovsky-research.net/pages/Ethel_Smyth#cite_note-note2-2

23. Michael Pilkington in his programme note for Hyperion Records © 1996: https://www.hyperion-records.co.uk/tw.asp?w=W8568
William Shakespeare, *Twelfth Night*: lines from Feste's song in Act 2, Scene 4.

26. '*almost a public history project*' and the composer's words taken from Tom Huizenga, 'Julia Wolfe Wins Music Pulitzer for "Anthracite Fields"', *Deceptive Cadence*, 20 April 2015: https://www.npr.org/sections/deceptivecadence/2015/04/20/401010330/julia-wolfe-wins-music-pulitzer-for-anthracite-fields

27. Composer as quoted in *Encyclopedia Britannica*: https://www.britannica.com/biography/Aleksandr-Scriabin

29. '*beyond category*' as widely cited, e.g. in Margo Jefferson, 'Ellington Beyond Category', *New York Times*, 15 October 1993: https://archive.nytimes.com/www.nytimes.com/library/arts/101593ellington-jefferson.html
'*parallel to the history of the American Negro*' as quoted in Audie Cornish, Christian McBride, Noah Caldwell, 'A Sprawling Blueprint For Protest Music, Courtesy Of The Jazz Duke', *American Anthem*, 22 February 2019: https://www.npr.org/2019/02/22/697075534/a-sprawling-blueprint-for-protest-music-courtesy-of-the-jazz-duke?t=1591803392867
'*Ellington struggled to achieve acceptance . . .*' as attributed to John Edward Hasse, author of *Beyond Category: The Life and Genius of Duke Ellington*, in Addison Nugent, 'When a Jazz Musician Shook Up Classical Music', *OZY*, 13 February 2018: https://www.ozy.com/true-and-stories/when-a-jazz-musician-shook-up-classical-music/83523/
'*Critics have their purposes . . .*' as quoted in *Book of African-American Quotations*, edited by Joslyn Pine (Courier Corporation, 2012), p. 57.

30. Composer's words taken from Anne Cawrse, 'Why I am a composer', *Loudmouth*, 30 June 2021: https://musictrust.com.au/loudmouth/inside-the-musician-anne-cawrse-why-i-am-a-composer/

May

1. *'insatiable creativity'* from Kian Soltani's liner note for Deutsche Grammophon: https://www.deutschegrammophon.com/en/catalogue/products/dvoak-cello-concerto-soltani-barenboim-12023

4. *'little Mozart'* as quoted in Thea Dark, *I Care If You Listen* online magazine, 1 October 2012: www.icareifyoulisten.com/2012/10/french-composers-names-cecile-chaminade
'*She writers wonderfully . . .*' as quoted in Robert Hillinck, 'The Rise and Fall of Cécile Chaminade', *Listen* Magazine: http://www.listenmusicculture.com/mastery/cecile-chaminade
Ambroise Thomas frequently cited, e.g. in Arthur Elson, *Woman's Work in Music* (BoD – Books on Demand, 2019), p. 89.

5. Composer as quoted in an interview with Ryan Derrick Garrison, 21 March 2013, for the research paper 'A Selection of Choral Works by Ola Gjeilo for SATB Choir: Composition, Interpretation, and Recording of The Phoenix Chorale's *Northern Lights: Choral Music by Ola Gjeilo'* ©2013 Ryan Derrick Garrison: https://keep.lib.asu.edu/items/151773

7. Tchaikovsky's letter to I. A. Klimenko, May 1st (13th) 1870, taken from Peter Russell, *Delphi Masterworks of Pyotr Ilyich Tchaikovsky (Illustrated)*, *Volume 4 of Delphi Great Composers* (Delphi Classics, 2018).

9. '*I listen to Beethoven . . .*' as quoted in George Varga, 'Billy Joel talks life & music in revealing interview', *San Diego Tribune*, 7 May 2016: https://www.sandiegouniontribune.com/entertainment/music/sdut-billy-joel-interview-2016may07-htmlstory.html
'*I grew up listening to classical music . . .*' as quoted in Patrick Doyle, 'The Last Word: Billy Joel on Self-Doubt, Trump and Finally Becoming Cool', *Rolling Stone*, 14 June 2017: https://www.rollingstone.com/music/music-features/the-last-word-billy-joel-on-self-doubt-trump-and-finally-becoming-cool-203477/
'*The classical critics take you apart . . .*' as quoted in David Marchese, 'In Conversation: Billy Joel': https://www.vulture.com/2018/07/billy-joel-in-conversation.html

11. Composer as quoted in Annegret Fauser, *The Politics of Musical Identity: Selected Essays* (Routledge, 2017), p. 158.

12. Graham Johnson's words taken from his programme note for Hyperion Records © 2005: https://www.hyperion-records.co.uk/dw.asp?dc=W168_GBAJY0533408

13. As quoted in Selwyn Tillett, *The Ballets of Arthur Sullivan* (Sir Arthur Sullivan Society, 1998), p. 26.

14. From the composer's interview with Bruce A. Russell, '5 Questions to Errollyn Wallen (composer, performer)', in *I Care If You Listen*, 6 August 2019: https://www.icareifyoulisten.com/2019/08/5-questions-errollyn-wallen-composer-performer/

21. Composer as quoted on the V&A's website page for the installation 'Memory & Light', created for the London Design Festival 2018: https://www.vam.ac.uk/event/kmqeKKm5/ldf-2018-arvo-part-x-arup

22. Hans von Bülow as quoted in Michael Steen, *The Lives and Times of the Great Composers* (Oxford University Press, 2004), p. 540.

24. Lines from '*Pour un baiser sur ta peau parfumée*' by Georges Doncieux; translation by Tara Wondraczek.

26. Composer's words from her interview with Tim Greiving, 'Composer Hildur Guðnadóttir Finds The Humanity In "Joker"', for NPR: https://www.npr.org/2019/10/03/766172923/composer-hildur-gu-nad-ttir-finds-the-humanity-in-joker?t=1592129809759

28. Composer as quoted in Kate Molleson, 'The extraordinary life of Ethiopia's 93-year-old singing nun', the *Guardian*, 17 April 2017: https://www.theguardian.com/music/2017/apr/17/ethiopia-93-year-old-singing-nun-emahoy-tsegue-maryam-guebrou

29. Composer as quoted in Bode Omojola, 'Style in modern Nigerian Art music: the pioneering works of Fela Sowande', *Africa* (Cambridge University Press, October 1998), Vol. 68, Issue 4, p. 455, © International African Institute 1998.

30. Composer as quoted in Emily Mackay, '10 "lost" female musicians who deserve more recognition', BBC Music, 7 March 2018: https://www.bbc.co.uk/music/articles/343718ed-4caf-44a2-8291-4aaa18d48c2c
Claire-Louise Bennett, 'Letter of Recommendation: The Recordings of Pauline Oliveros', *New York Times*, 9 February 2017: *https://www.nytimes.com/2017/02/09/magazine/letter-of-recommendation-the-recordings-of-pauline-oliveros.html?mwrsm=Facebook&_r=1*

31. '*I was very reluctant to go . . .*' and '*It is so, so difficult . . .*' as quoted in Rebecca Mead, 'How the Composer George Benjamin Finally Found his Voice', *The New Yorker*, 10 September 2018: https://www.newyorker.com/magazine/2018/09/17/how-the-composer-george-benjamin-finally-found-his-voice '*based on the pitches . . .*' taken from Faber Music's programme notes © George Benjamin: https://www.fabermusic.com/repertoire/meditation-on-haydns-name-1097

June

1. Leopold Mozart as quoted in Joseph Castle, *Student Piano Classics* (Mel Bay Publications, 2010), p. 74.
2. Composer's and Canon Gorton's words taken from Geoffrey Hodgkins' programme note for Hyperion Records © 1996: https://www.hyperion-records.co.uk/tw.asp?w=W8256
   Lines from 'Song of the Lotos-Eaters' by Alfred Lord Tennyson taken from https://englishverse.com/poems/song_of_the_lotoseaters
3. Composer's words and tombstone epitaph as quoted in Pamela Blevins, 'Dora Pejačević : An introduction to a Croation composer': http://www.maudpowell.org/signature/Portals/0/pdfs/New%20Articles/Dora%20Pejacevic%20for%20Signature.pdf
4. '*like watching the setting sun . . .*' as quoted in Grayson Haver Currin, 'Mary Lattimore's "Hundreds Of Days" Reinvigorates The Imagination', *NPR Music*, 10 May 2018: https://www.npr.org/2018/05/10/609160722/first-listen-mary-lattimore-hundreds-of-days
   '*makes complex and expansive songs . . .*' as quoted in Amanda Petrusich, 'The Seismic Emotion of Mary Lattimore's Harp Music', *The New Yorker*, 15 June 2018: https://www.newyorker.com/culture/culture-desk/the-seismic-emotion-of-mary-lattimores-harp-music
5. Psalm 6 vv.1–4, taken from the website for the Choir of St John's College, Cambridge: https://www.sjcchoir.co.uk/listen/sjc-live/gibbons-0-0-lord-thy-wrath-rebuke-me-not?
6. From Tom Service, 'A guide to Louis Andriessen's music', the *Guardian*, 15 October 2012: https://www.theguardian.com/music/tomserviceblog/2012/oct/15/louis-andriessen-classical-music-guide
8. Composer's words as quoted in Tony Trischka's interview, 'Noam Pikelny' for *Banjo Newsletter*, July 2017: https://banjonews.com/2017-07/noam_pikelny_interview_by_tony_trischka.html

10. Nicholas Wroe, 'Mark-Anthony Turnage: A life in music', the *Guardian*, 22 January 2011: https://www.theguardian.com/music/2011/jan/22/mark-anthony-turnage-opera-composer

11. *'provided . . . a glimmer of hope . . .'*, Dwayne Mack, 'Hazel Scott: A Career Curtailed', *Journal of African American History*, 91 (2), p. 160. *'Considering the times . . .'*, Karen Chilton, *Hazel Scott: The Pioneering Journey of a Jazz Pianist, from Café Society to Hollywood to HUAC* (University of Michigan Press, 2008), p. 128.

12. Composer as quoted in Jonathan W. Bernard, 'Voice Leading as a Spatial Function in the Music of Ligeti', *Music Analysis* 13, nos. 2/3 (July–October), p 238.

15. Composer as quoted by Øivind Norheim in liner notes for Naxos Records: https://www.naxos.com/mainsite/blurbs_reviews.asp?item_code=8.553904&catNum=553904&filetype=About%20this%20Recording&language=English

18. Subtitle as translated in Derek Sayer, *Prague, Capital of the Twentieth Century: A Surrealist History* (Princeton University Press, 2015), p. 345.

19. Composer's words taken from his interview with Dan McHugh for WCPE, The Classical Station, 4 February 2021: https://theclassicalstation.org/news/adolphus-hailstork-interview/

20. Gautier Capuçon as quoted in Inge Kjemtrup, 'Why Do String Players Still Love Schubert's "Arpeggione' Sonata?"', *Strings Magazine*, 1 April 2018: https://stringsmagazine.com/why-do-string-players-still-love-schuberts-arpeggione-sonata/

22. Aaron Copland as quoted in Milton Cross and David Ewan, *Encyclopedia of the Great Composers and their Music, Volume 1* (Doubleday, 1962), p. 141. *'a subject very close to my heart . . .'* as quoted in James Conlon, 'Message, Meaning and Code in the Operas of Benjamin Britten', *The Hudson Review*, Autumn 2013: https://hudsonreview.com/2013/10/message-meaning-and-code-in-the-operas-of-benjamin-britten/#.XuYwcoVKg2x *'my parent's [sic] house . . .'* from Benjamin Britten, *On Music* (Oxford University Press, 2003), p. 50.

23. Composer's words taken from Alex Baranowski, 'This is me: The soundscapes of Alex Baranowski', *Campaign*, 7 December 2018: https://www.campaignlive.co.uk/article/me-soundscapes-alex-baranowski/1520256

26. Composer's words taken from her website: https://libbylarsen.com/index.php?contentID=240&profileID=1529&startRange=0

27. Tom Stoppard, *Arcadia* (Faber & Faber, 1993), p. 38.
28. Composer as quoted in Eric Fenby, *Delius as I Knew Him* (Courier Corporation, 1994), p. 181.
29. Helen Bainton, *Remembered on Waking* (Currawong Press, 1960), pp. 66–7.

July

2. Composer's words taken from her notes in *Unsent Love Letters* © Copyright 2017 Boosey & Hawkes Bote & Bock, Berlin. Reproduced by permission of Boosey & Hawkes Music Publishers Ltd.
3. 'Glück das mir verblieb': https://en.wikipedia.org/wiki/Gl%C3%BCck,_das_mir_verblieb#Lyrics; translated from the German by CBH.
5. *'wonders of Rome'* as quoted in Victor Anand Coelho's entry for Kapsberger in Grove Music Online: https://www.oxfordmusiconline.com/grovemusic/view/10.1093/gmo/9781561592630.001.0001/omo-9781561592630-e-0000014695?rskey=6yBbIm
   Athanasius Kircher cited in Paul O'Dette's liner notes to *Baroque Lute Music. Volume 1: Giovanni Girolamo Kapsberger* for Harmonia Mundi (1990/2001).
6. Composer's words taken from her website: https://caroline-shaw-editions.myshopify.com/products/plan-and-elevation
7. Helena Dunicz-Niwińska as quoted in Dr Katarzyna Naliwajek-Mazurek, 'Music within the Nazi Genocide System in Occupied Poland: Facts and Testimonies' in *Musique et camps de concentration*, edited by Amaury du Closel (Conseil de l'Europe, 7/8 November 2013): https://rm.coe.int/090000168047d1948.
8. Colin Matthews' words taken from his obituary of Oliver Knussen for the *Guardian*, 9 July 2018: https://www.theguardian.com/music/2018/jul/09/oliver-knussen-obituary *'a special favourite . . .'* taken from the composer's programme notes for Faber Music: https://www.fabermusic.com/repertoire/requiem-4643
   'It's not a huge work . . .' as quoted by Colin Matthews, *ibid.*
9. Composer's words as quoted by the Genesis Foundation: https://genesisfoundation.org.uk/roderick-williams/
14. *'emotional derangement'* as quoted in Benvenuto Cellini's programme note for National Public Radio © 1999: https://www.npr.org/programs/worldofopera/archives/991002.woo.html
15. *'A great original . . .'* as quoted at https://www.boosey.com/composer/Harrison+Birtwistle

Tim Rutherford-Johnson's words taken from his programme note for the Philharmonia, 10 November 2016; https://johnsonsrambler.wordpress.com/programme-notes/.

17. Composer's words taken from his website: http://www.paulpaccione.com/compositions

18. Liszt and Chopin as quoted in Michael Steen, *Enchantress of Nations: Pauline Viardot – Soprano, Muse and Lover* (Icon Books, 2007), p. 3 and p. 144.
Lines from '*Je suis triste, je m'inquiète*' by Xavier de Maistre; English translation by Tara Wondraczek.

19. Composer's words taken from her website: https://www.evelyn.co.uk/a-little-prayer

20. Alfred Dürr, *The Cantatas of J. S. Bach: With Their Librettos in German-English Parallel Text* (Oxford University Press, 2006), p. 255.

21. György Kurtág as quoted in Mark Swed, 'Kurtag lifts the silence', *Los Angeles Times*, 7 January 2007: https://www.latimes.com/archives/la-xpm-2007-jan-07-ca-kurtag7-story.html

23. Debussy as quoted in Marianne Wheeldon, *Debussy's Late Style* (Indiana University Press, 2009), p.67.

24. Lines from 'An Hymn of Heavenly Beauty' by Edmund Spenser: https://www.poetryfoundation.org/poems/45213/an-hymn-of-heavenly-beauty

25. Composer's words as quoted in Gabríel Benjamin, 'Local Heroes', *The Line of Best Fit*, 4 August 2016: https://www.thelineofbestfit.com/features/longread/olafur-arnalds-on-island-songs
Nanna Bryndís Hilmarsdóttir as quoted in Laurence Day, 'Listen to Ólafur Arnalds' New Collaboration with Nanna Bryndís from *Of Monsters And Men*', *Line of Best Fit Magazine*, 2 August 2016: https://www.thelineofbestfit.com/news/latest-news/olafur-arnalds-collaboration-with-nanna-bryndis-of-monsters-and-men

26. '*a sonic journey . . .*', '*Everything is interconnected*' and '*All music genres . . .*' taken from Arlene and Larry Dunn, '5 Questions to Tania León' (composer, Composers Now), *I Care If You Listen*, 22 September 2015: https://www.icareifyoulisten.com/2015/09/5-questions-tania-leon-composer-composers-now/
'*inner curiosity*' and '*I have been, in a sense, composing myself*' taken from Theresa A. Byrne, 'Artist Spotlight: Tania León', *The Harvard Crimson*, 21 April 2015: https://www.thecrimson.com/article/2015/4/21/tania-leon-portrait/

'*a celebration of contradictions*' taken from 'Afro-Cuban Composer and Conductor Tania León, Nominated for GRAMMY Award, Was Born May 14, 1943', *Africlassical*, 14 May 2013: https://africlassical.blogspot.com/2013/05/afro-cuban-composer-and-conductor-tania.html

28. '*contrasting poetic and philosophical perspectives . . .*' taken from Hélène Grimaud's website: https://helenegrimaud.com/news/new-album-water

   '*serves to conjure atmospheres . . .*' and '*Music peels back the layers of time . . .*' taken from Hélène Grimaud's programme note, 'Meditations on Memory', for Deutsche Grammophon: https://www.deutschegrammophon.com/en/artist/grimaud/

29. Composer's words taken from his website: https://www.earbox.com/hallelujah-junction-solo-piano/

30. Gerald Finzi as quoted in the programme note by Mervyn Cooke for St Matthew's Concert Choir, 1 July 2012: http://smce.org.uk/old/2012/20120701/20120701%20Programme.pdf

31. Dr Oliver Hilmes as quoted in CBH, 'Forget the Beatles: Liszt was music's first "superstar"', *BBC Culture*, 17 August 2016: *http*://www.bbc.com/culture/story/20160817-franz-liszt-the-worlds-first-musical-superstar

August

1. Composer's words taken from the biographical note on his publisher's website: https://en.schott-music.com/shop/autoren/peteris-vasks

2. Composer as quoted in Andrew Burn's liner notes for Naxos records: https://www.naxos.com/mainsite/blurbs_reviews.asp?item_code=8.557146&catNum=557146&filetype=About%20this%20Recording&language=English

3. Leon Botstein as quoted in Gabrielle Cornish, 'She's Rising From the Depths of Soviet Music History', *New York Times*, 27 September 2019: https://www.nytimes.com/2019/09/27/arts/music/galina-ustvolskaya.html

4. Yo-Yo Ma as quoted on the composer's website: https://osvaldogolijov.com/arc/azul

5. Émile Vuillermoz as quoted in Victor Estapé's liner notes for Naxos Records, *Frederic Mompou – Piano Music, Vol. 1 (Maso)*, translated by Paul Jutsum.

   Composer's words as quoted in the description of the work for All Music by Uncle Dave Lewis: https://www.allmusic.com/composition/musica-callada-28-pieces-for-piano-in-4-books-mc0002361679

6. John Keats, Letter to Fanny Brawne, 1820 as quoted in *John Keats: Selected Letters*, edited by Robert Gittings (Oxford University Press, 2002), p. 340.
   Hua Hsu, 'Listening Booth: Rachel Grimes's "The Clearing"', *The New Yorker*, 19 May 2015: https://www.newyorker.com/culture/culture-desk/listening-booth-rachel-grimes-the-clearing
9. Lines from '*Mattinata*' by Ruggero Leoncavallo; English translation by Tara Wondraczek.
10. György Ligeti as quoted in Richard Steinitz, *György Ligeti: Music of the Imagination* (Faber & Faber, 2011), p. 115.
11. From the Marian antiphon *Salve regina*: https://www.liveabout.com/salve-regina-latin-text-and-english-translation-724028; English translation by CBH.
12. Composer's words as quoted by the publisher Universal Edition: https://www.universaledition.com/zoltan-kodaly-378/works/sommerabend-4755
13. Composer's words taken from her publisher's website: https://www.editionpeters.com/product/the-darkness-is-no-darkness/ep71097
14. Lines from Isaiah 26 and Psalm 139, taken from the website for the Choir of St John's College, Cambridge: https://www.sjcchoir.co.uk/listen/sjc-live/wesley-ss-thou-wilt-keep-him
15. Jeffrey Green, *Samuel Coleridge-Taylor: A Musical Life* (Routledge, 2011), p. 182.
   Epitaph from the composer's tombstone cited in Karen Farrington, *Great Lives: As heard on Radio 4* (Random House, 2011), p. 92.
17. Gadi Elkon, 'The Wife: A Review by Gadi Elkon', *Selig Film News*, 31 August 2018: 'http://seligfilmnews.com/the-wife-a-review-by-gadi-elkon/
18. '*meditation and a reverie*' originally from the composer's website, cited in Lin Tian's doctoral dissertation for Louisiana State University, ' The World of Tan Dun: The Central Importance of Eight Memories in Watercolor, Op. 1' (2014): https://digitalcommons.lsu.edu/cgi/viewcontent.cgi?article=2818&context=gradschool_dissertations
   '*diary of longing*' taken from the composer's website: http://tandun.com/composition/eight-memories-in-watercolor/
19. Daniel Hope's words taken from his interview with Cristina Comandașu, translated by Negoiță Roxana-Beatrice, MTTLC, the University of Bucharest, for Radio Romania Music, 3 March 2016: http://en.romania-muzical.ro/articole/art.htm?g=11&c=3271&a=1391421

20. Philip Glass as quoted on the composer's website: https://www.phamiegow.com/bio/

   'I'm so in love with the piano! . . .' as quoted in Margherita Taylor's interview with the composer for Classic FM, 5 July 2013: https://www.classicfm.com/artists/phamie-gow/news/phamie-gow-softly-spoken-interview/

21. *'The human voice . . .'* and *'I use it to describe nature's many sounds . . .'* from the release notes for the composer's album *Illogical Lullaby*, Erased Tapes Records Ltd, March 2018: https://www.erasedtapes.com/release/eratp108-hatis-noit-illogical-dance

   'The sound moved me so intensely . . .' as quoted in 'Spiritual Soundscapes: The global influences of Hatis Noit', *Huck Magazine*, 26 March 2018: https://www.huckmag.com/art-and-culture/music-2/hatis-noit-monday-mix/

   'I didn't understand what the mantra meant . . .' as quoted in 'Hatis Noit on voice, Japanese folk and recording in Fukushima', *SHAPE Platform*, 13 October 2019: https://shapeplatform.eu/2019/hatis-noit-on-voice-japanese-folk-and-recording-in-fukushima/

26. Composer's words as quoted in Laura Volpi, 'Inspiring a new generation of composers: Sally Beamish', *Bachtrack*, 25 January 2019: https://bachtrack.com/interview-sally-beamish-composer-january-2019

29. John Rockwell, 'Leos Janacek: The Vindication of a Composer', *New York Times*, 20 March 1983: https://www.nytimes.com/1983/03/20/magazine/leos-janacek-the-vinidication-of-a-composer.html

30. *'vivid dramatic forms . . .'* and *'Don't do it . . .'* from the composer's interview with CBH for *BBC Music Magazine*, 29 November 2018.

   'It is fulfilment and celebration . . .' from the composer's programme note © Thea Musgrave: https://www.wisemusicclassical.com/work/8426/The-Seasons--Thea-Musgrave/

September

4. Juan Bermudo as quoted in Robert Stevenson's entry for de Morales, revised by Alejandro Enrique Planchart, in Grove Music Online: https://www.oxfordmusiconline.com/grovemusic/view/10.1093/gmo/9781561592630.001.0001/omo-9781561592630-e-0000019078?rskey=dFxdTH&result=1

5. Max Richter as quoted in Jon Falcone, 'Max Richter discusses revisiting Memoryhouse', *Drowned in Sound*, 22 January 2014: http://

drownedinsound.com/in_depth/4147347-max-richter-discusses-revisiting-memoryhouse

John Cage, *Silence: Writings and Lectures* (Wesleyan University Press, 1961), p. 64.

'pardon the intrusion . . .' taken from Maria Popova, 'John Cage's Intensely Beautiful Love Letters to Merce Cunningham', *Brain Pickings*, 9 June 2016: https://www.brainpickings.org/2016/06/09/john-cage-love-letters-merce-cunningham/

6. Nikolai Rimsky-Korsakov, *My Musical Life* (Tudor Publishing, 1935), p. 194.

7. 'Muse of Novara' as cited by Kate Hearne in her programme notes for West Cork Music © Kate Hearne 2016: http://archive.westcorkmusic.ie/details/view/cmf/566

8. Composer's words as quoted in the review on the website Headphone Commute: https://headphonecommute.com/2011/02/15/dustin-ohalloran-lumiere-130701/

11. Composer's words taken from the interview 'How I Wrote . . . Spared – Howard Goodall' for Classic FM, 11 September 2013: https://www.classicfm.com/composers/goodall/guides/how-i-wrote-spared-howard-goodall/

12. Lines from Pierre Joseph Justin Bernard's libretto for *Castor et Pollux* Act 1, Scene 3, taken from Cynthia Verba, 'Dramatic Expression in Rameau's Tragédie en Musique: Between Tradition and Enlightenment', Harvard University: https://scholar.harvard.edu/cverba/pages/castor-et-pollux-act-i-scene-3; English translation by Tara Wondraczek.

13. Rovi Staff, in his programme note for All Music: https://www.allmusic.com/composition/brettl-lieder-cabaret-songs-for-voice-piano-mc0002377965

16. *'I've been a woman . . .'* as quoted in Claude Summers, *The Queer Encyclopedia of Music, Dance, and Musical Theater* (Cleis Press, 2004), p. 29.

Quincy Jones interviewed by CBH in 'The Greatest Music Teacher Who Ever Lived' for BBC Culture, 19 April 2017: https://www.bbc.com/culture/article/20170308-the-greatest-music-teacher-who-ever-lived

Bruno Monsaingeon, *Mademoiselle: Conversations With Nadia Boulanger* (Northeastern University Press, 1988), p. 35.

17. Private interview with CBH, 2019.

18. Caccini as quoted in a programme note by Bristol Ensemble: https://www.bristolensemble.com/notes-for-women/francesca-caccini/

19. From notes by Rupert Gough for Hyperion Records © Rupert Gough 2009: https://www.hyperion-records.co.uk/dw.asp?dc=W12609_GBAJY0979915

20. *sing, applying the music of Bach . . .* from Andy Beta's review, 'Laurie Spiegel: *Unseen Worlds*', for *Pitchfork*, 9 February 2019: https://pitchfork.com/reviews/albums/laurie-spiegel-unseen-worlds/
strangely contemporary . . . from Andy Beta's review, 'Laurie Spiegel: *The Expanding Universe*', for *Pitchfork*, 24 October 2012: https://pitchfork.com/reviews/albums/17067-the-expanding-universe/

21. Dedication taken from the composer's website: https://www.cherylfrancishoad.co.uk/introit-and-blessing-o-come-let-us

23. Frédéric Chopin as quoted in Jessica Duchen, 'Soul sisters: Cecilia Bartoli and Maria Malibran', *Independent*, 21 November 2007: https://www.independent.co.uk/arts-entertainment/music/features/soul-sisters-cecilia-bartoli-and-maria-malibran-758922.html
when the formidable Maria Malibran . . . taken from Patrick Dillon, 'Ladies' Night', *Opera News*, September 2012, Vol. 77, No. 3: https://www.operanews.com/Opera_News_Magazine/2012/9/Features/Ladies%E2%80%99_Night.html

24. Ann-Sophie Mutter's words taken from the official press release for *Across the Stars*: https://www.anne-sophie-mutter.de/en/page/projects/across-the-stars-mutter-williams/

26. From the British Music Collection's biography of the composer: https://britishmusiccollection.org.uk/composer/delia-derbyshire#:~:text=Within%20a%20matter%20of%20months,of%20it%2C%22%20replied%20Derbyshire.

27. From the Respond at Compline on Passion Sunday; English version from *Book of Common Worship: Services and Prayers for the Church of England* (Church House Publishing, 2000).

28. Vladimir Helfert as quoted in Milton Cross and David Ewen, *Encyclopedia of the Great Composers and Their Music, Volume 2* (Doubleday, 1962), pp. 748–9.

29. *'I'm convinced . . .'* Composer's words as quoted in an interview with Kate Molleson, the *Guardian*, 16 May 2015: https://www.theguardian.com/culture/2015/may/16/mark-simpson-immortal-requiem-manchester-international-festival-mif

'*I became obsessed . . .*' taken from Jim Ottewill's profile of the composer for *M Magazine*, 16 June 2016: https://www.m-magazine.co.uk/features/ interviews/interview-mark-simpson/

30. Composer's words as quoted in Anne Goldberg-Baldwin's review of *Hieroglyphen der Nacht* for *I Care If You Listen*, 7 March 2018: https:// www.icareifyoulisten.com/2018/03/portrait-album-valentin-silvestrov-hieroglyphen-der-nacht/

October

2. Private interview with CBH, 2019.

3. Andrew Clements in *Radio 3 Programmes – Composer of the Week, Steve Reich (b. 1936), Episode 1*, BBC, 25 October 2010.
'*emotional magnetism*' Steve Reich's words from a private interview with CBH, 2019.

4. '*as an elegy to a dying marriage*' from Tomas Cotik's liner notes to *Tango Nuevo* for Naxos Records: https://www.naxos.com/mainsite/blurbs_ reviews.asp?item_code=8.573166&catNum=573166&filetype=About%20 this%20Recording&language=English
Composer as quoted in George Predota, 'Tango Passion I: Astor Piazzolla and Dedé Wolff', *Interlude*, 16 July 2017: https://interlude.hk/ tango-passion-astor-piazzolla-dede-wolff/

5. '*other realities . . .*' as quoted in Keith Potter, 'Classical: Finland's serial mystic', *Independent*, 23 July 1999: https://www.independent.co.uk/arts-entertainment/classical-finlands-serial-mystic-1108130.html
'*In both processes . . .*' and '*vivacious and brisk . . .*' as quoted in Timothy Judd, 'Einojuhani Rautavaara's "Autumn Gardens": A Radiant Orchestral Soundscape', *The Listeners' Club*, 14 October 2019: https:// thelistenersclub.com/2019/10/14/einojuhani-rautavaaras-autumn-gardens-a-radiant-orchestral-soundscape/

6. Composer in conversation with Kate Molleson for Kings Place's 'Venus Unwrapped Interview Series': https://www.kingsplace.co.uk/magazine/ interviews/venus-unwrapped-interviews-eleanor-alberga-laura-jurd-anna-meredith/

9. Composer's words taken from an interview with Mike Horanski for the Vienna Choral Society, 28 February 2019: https://viennachoralsociety. org/education/conversations-cecilia-mcdowall-on-composition-cultural-influences-and-commissions/

11. Psalm 37:30–31; English translation: www.cpdl.org/wiki/index.php/ Os_justi_meditabitur

12. *'magical . . .'* Tom Service, 'A guide to Thomas Adès's music', *Guardian*, 1 October 2012: https://www.theguardian.com/music/ tomserviceblog/2012/oct/01/thomas-ades-contemporary-music-guide Composer as quoted in Jon Burlingame, '"Colette" Opens Door to Film Scoring for Esteemed U.K. Classical Composer Adès', *Variety*, 31 October 2018: https://variety.com/2018/music/news/colette-film-score-classical-composer-thomas-ades-1203016828/

13. Composer's words taken from a post on Facebook, 21 March 2019: https://www.facebook.com/Bryce.Dessner/posts/2409396959079356

15. *'possibly the most conservative composer in Europe'* from Martin Bresnick, 'Prague 1970: Music in Spring', *Opinionator*, 25 May 2011: https:// opinionator.blogs.nytimes.com/2011/05/25/prague-1970-music-in-spring/ *'I was always eager to be a communicative composer'* as quoted in Rebecca Schmid, 'Salzburg Pays Tribute to Gottfried von Einem', *New York Times*, 17 July 2018: https://www.nytimes.com/2018/07/17/arts/music/ gottfried-von-einem-rebirth-salzburg-festival.html

18. Christopher Gabbitas's words taken from the composer's website: https://www.patriciavanness.com/

20. Composer's programme note as widely quoted, e.g. in Matthew McDonald, 'Silent Narration? Elements of Narrative in Ives's "The Unanswered Question"', *19th-Century Music*, Vol. 27 No. 3, Spring 2004, pp. 263–286: https://ncm.ucpress.edu/content/27/3/263

21. Susan Josephs, 'A Dream Fulfilled: Women who emigrated from the former Soviet Union are now making a significant mark in the U.S.', *Jewish Woman* magazine, Spring 2014: http://www.jwmag.org/page. aspx?pid=3887

22. Bernstein's words as quoted by the composer in an interview with Kathy Parsons for *Mainly Piano*, June 2003: https://mainlypiano.com/ interviews/craig-urquhart-2003-june

23. Charlotte Gardner's words taken from her review of the composer's album *Baroque* for BBC Music, 2008: https://www.bbc.co.uk/music/ reviews/3dzf/

24. From the programme note by John Gardner (1969), quoted by Samir Savant in liner notes for Hyperion Records, 2010: https://www.hyperion-records.co.uk/dc.asp?dc=D_SIGCD228

26. English translation of Alexei Tolstoy's text from Etcetera Records' note for the album *Youri Egorov: Autumn Songs*: https://www.etcetera-records.com/album/604/youri-egorov

27. Composer's words taken from the programme note on her publisher's website: http://www.musicsalesclassical.com/composer/work/48421

28. '*What then of Autumn . . .*' and '*between its falling leaves . . .*' from Maria Popova, 'Autumn Light: Pico Iyer on Finding Beauty in Impermanence and Luminosity in Loss', *Brain Pickings*, 11 October 2019: https://www.brainpickings.org/2019/10/11/autumn-light-pico-iyer/
'*Wedged between an equinox and a solstice . . .*' from Maria Popova, 'A Beginning, Not a Decline: Colette on the Splendor of Autumn and the Autumn of Life', *Brain Pickings*, 22 September 2016: https://www.brainpickings.org/2016/09/22/colette-autumn/

29. Latin text and translation from the vocal score (Novello and Co., 2011).

30. Titon du Tillet as quoted in the *Encyclopaedia Britannica*: https://www.britannica.com/biography/Elisabeth-Claude-Jacquet-de-la-Guerre

November

2. Composer as quoted in Hyperion liner notes by William McVicker © 1999: https://www.hyperion-records.co.uk/dw.asp?dc=W7376_GBAJY9908712

5. '*insinuating and expressive . . .*' from Anthony Tommasini, 'How Jonny Greenwood Wove the "Phantom Thread" Score', *New York Times*, 21 February 2018: https://www.nytimes.com/2018/02/21/arts/music/phantom-thread-jonny-greenwood-original-score-oscar.html
Composer's remarks about Messiaen as quoted in Helena Asprou, 'Radiohead's Jonny Greenwood has been composing for orchestra – now, he's launching a classical music label', Classic FM, 17 September 2019: https://www.classicfm.com/music-news/radiohead-jonny-greenwood-launches-classical-label/
'*I feel like I'm enthralled . . .*' and '*The principal thing . . .*' from Anthony Tommasini, *op. cit.*

6. Inscription as widely quoted, e.g. in Chandos's biographical note for Thomas Tomkins: https://www.chandos.net/composers/Thomas_Tomkins/3341

8. Words by Julian of Norwich taken from the sheet music (Edition Peters, 2010).

9. Daniel Barenboim's words as quoted in his interview with Simon Usborne for the article 'We finished every bottle!' Berlin's cultural legends on the night the Wall came down', *Guardian*, 5 November 2019: www.theguardian.com/culture/2019/nov/05/fall-of-berlin-wall-cultural-luminaries-remember-wim-wenders-ute-lemper-daniel-barenboim
10. Martin Anderson's obituary of the composer, *Independent*, 18 January 2003: https://www.independent.co.uk/news/obituaries/doreen-carwithen-124778.html
11. Frederick Septimus Kelly, *Race Against Time: The Diaries of F. S. Kelly*, selected, edited and introduced by Thérèse Radic (National Library of Australia, 2004), p. 63.
12. '*icon in sound*' from *The Essential John Tavener: A Guide*: http://www.tavenerguide.com/the-protecting-veil#:~:text=Tavener%20sought%20to%20create%20a,literally%20'God%2Dbearer'.
   Robert Maycock as quoted in James McCarthy, 'The premiere of Sir John Tavener's The Protecting Veil', *Gramophone*, 13 November 2013: https://www.gramophone.co.uk/features/focus/the-premiere-of-sir-john-taveners-the-protecting-veil
13. Catrin Finch's and Seckou Keita's words taken from their website: https://www.catrinfinchandseckoukeita.com/bio
14. '*She plays like a man*' as quoted in David Conway, *Jewry in Music: Entry to the Profession from the Enlightenment to Richard Wagner* (Cambridge University Press, 2011), p. 7.
   Composer's father as quoted from his letter of 16 July 1820 in Sebastian Hensel, *The Mendelssohn Family 1729–1847*, 4th revised edition (Sampson Low, 1884).
   Extract from Felix Mendelssohn's letter to Lea Mendelssohn-Bartholdy of 24 June 1837, as quoted in *Letters of Felix Mendelssohn-Bartholdy from 1833 to 1847*, edited by Paul Mendelssohn-Bartholdy, translated by Lady Wallace (Longman Green, 1864), p. 113.
15. Guy Dammann as quoted in Dominy Clemens' review of the recording by Clemens Records of *Arcadiana* and other works for MusicWeb International: http://www.musicweb-international.com/classrev/2018/Apr/Ades_quartets_261603.htm
16. Paul Hindemith, *A Composer's World* (Harvard University Press, 1952).
17. From Marin Alsop, 'Treasures In The Attic: Finding A Jazz Master's Lost Orchestral Music', 1 February 2013: https://www.npr.org/sections/

deceptivecadence/2013/02/02/170864270/treasures-in-the-attic-finding-a-jazz-masters-lost-orchestral-music

18. Sara Teasdale, 'Stars': https://www.thoughtco.com/sara-teasdale-quotes-2831451

20. *'extended vocal technique'* and *'creating landscapes of sound'* taken from the composer's website: https://www.meredithmonk.org/about/biography/ *'primordial utterance'* from the note by ECM Records describing the album *On Behalf of Nature*: https://www.ecmrecords.com/ catalogue/1473672193/on-behalf-of-nature-meredith-monk-ensemble

21. Composer as quoted in Mary Louise Kelly, 'One Key, Many Notes: Ólafur Arnalds' Piano Rig Fuses Technology And Musicality', *NPR Music*, 19 July 2018: https://www.npr.org/2018/07/19/630111211/one-key-many-notes-lafur-arnalds-piano-rig-fuses-technology-and-musicality

22. Words from Constance Morgan, 'Evensong', from *The LiederNet Archive*: https://www.lieder.net/lieder/get_text.html?TextId=20970

23. Alex Ross, 'Many Voices: Blue Heron brings a hint of the Baroque to Renaissance polyphony', *The New Yorker*, 3 January 2011: https://www.newyorker.com/magazine/2011/01/10/many-voices-alex-ross

26. Composer's words taken from her programme note on her publisher's website: http://www.musicsalesclassical.com/composer/work/3071/47915
Nadia Sirota as quoted in 'Nadia Sirota On Making Music Accessible (Even When It's Weird)', *Classical 91.5*, 2 October 2016, © 2018 NPR: https://www.classical915.org/post/nadia-sirota-making-music-accessible-even-when-its-weird

27. Kate Hearne's words taken from her programme note, 'L'amante segreto "Voglio, voglio morire" Cantate Op.2', West Cork Music Archive, 1 July 2013, © Kate Hearne: http://archive.westcorkmusic.ie/details/view/cmf/298
Italian text anon.; English translation by Tara Wondraczek.

28. Composer's words as quoted in Charlie Robin Jones, 'Nils Frahm: "My music can be quite heavy. Some people faint"', *Guardian*, 28 June 2016: https://www.theguardian.com/global/2016/jun/28/nils-frahm-neo-classical-musician-and-pianist

29. Composer as quoted in Charlotte Cripps, 'Amelia Warner on her new music career and shrugging off gossip about her marriage to Fifty Shades Darker actor Jamie Dornan', *Independent*, 2 March 2017: https://www.independent.co.uk/arts-entertainment/music/features/amelia-

warner-visitor-fifty-shades-jamie-dornan-christian-grey-fyfe-dangerfield-guillemots-ep-eve-a7606896.html

December

2. Text and translation provided courtesy of Oxford Lieder, reprinted with permission: www.oxfordlieder.co.uk

4. Tom Service, 'A guide to Jonathan Harvey's music', *Guardian*, 17 September 2012: www.theguardian.com/music/tomserviceblog/2012/sep/17/jonathan-harvey-contemporary-music-guide

5. Composer as quoted in Susannah Butter, 'Isobel Waller-Bridge on creating the soundtrack for ITV's Vanity Fair: "We used classical instruments in a modern, unexpected away",' *Evening Standard*, 30 August 2018: https://www.standard.co.uk/news/the1000/isobel-wallerbridge-on-creating-the-soundtrack-for-itv-s-vanity-fair-we-used-classical-instruments-a3923616.html

7. Composer's words taken from Crossover Media's promotion notes for the album *Roots*: http://crossovermedia.net/artists/randall-goosby/projects/roots/album/

8. Composer as quoted in Jessica Duchen, 'Max Richter's "Sleep": The longest continuous piece of music broadcast by the BBC', *Independent*, 15 September 2015: https://www.independent.co.uk/arts-entertainment/classical/features/max-richters-sleep-the-longest-continuous-piece-of-music-broadcast-by-the-bbc-10502454.html

9. Mozart and Haydn as quoted in the *Encyclopaedia Britannica*: https://www.britannica.com/biography/Carl-Philipp-Emanuel-Bach#ref169906

11. Private interview with CBH, 2019.

12. Nathalie Stutzmann's words taken from an interview with Peter Dobrin for *The Philadelphia Inquirer*, 19 December 2020: https://www.inquirer.com/arts/nathalie-stutzmann-philadelphia-orchestra-principal-guest-conductor-20201219.html

14. Lines from the Song of Solomon, 8:6, King James Bible.

15. '*global, kaleidoscopic . . .*' from Gloria Cheng, 'Reclimbing the Heaven Ladder', *New Music Box*, 22 October 2018: https://nmbx.newmusicusa.org/reclimbing-the-heaven-ladder/
Terry Riley, '*A lot of intersections . . .*' as quoted by Gloria Cheng, *ibid*.
Angel Deradoorian and Greg Fox as quoted in Mike Rubin, 'Terry Riley's Avant-Garde Sounds Are Still Casting Spells', *New York Times*, 19

435

December 2019: https://www.nytimes.com/2019/12/19/arts/music/terry-riley.html

19. Fred M. Hall, *It's About Time: The Dave Brubeck Story* (University of Arkansas Press, 1996), pp. 16–17.
Composer's words taken from his programme note for Wise Music Classical: https://www.wisemusicclassical.com/work/26544/La-Fiesta-de-la-Posada--Dave-Brubeck/

20. *'don't make it classical'* from the composer's website: https://www.chadlawson.com/pages/about
'mental shower' and *'could be an adversary . . .'* from the video 'Chad Lawson puts his own touch on Chopin', YouTube, 30 August 2015: https://m.youtube.com/watch?v=WLv4Z5sWWsE

23. *'own experience as a human being'* as quoted in Amanda Hooton, 'Peter Sculthorpe: Notes on a Life', *Sydney Morning Herald*, 8 August 2014: https://www.smh.com.au/entertainment/music/peter-sculthorpe-notes-on-a-life-20140808-1024hc.html
'wanted his music to make people feel better . . .' from 'Lesson 3: A Journey through Landscapes', about Peter Sculthorpe, in *The Composers: Fact File*, Liverpool Philharmonic: https://www.liverpoolphil.com/media/295457/introduction-to-composers.pdf

24. Letter of 1514 as quoted in the entry for the composer by Reinhard Strohm and Emma Kempson in Oxford Music Online: https://www.oxfordmusiconline.com/grovemusic/view/10.1093/gmo/9781561592630.001.0001/omo-9781561592630-e-0000051790?rskey=0ZE596&result=6

26. *'acoustic bridge'*, Russian paediatrician Michael Lazarev, as quoted in Nina Perry, 'The Universal Language of Lullabies', *BBC World Service*, 21 January 2013: https://www.bbc.co.uk/news/magazine-21035103
'his mother's lips . . .' as quoted in programme notes for Parlance Chamber Concerts © Jane Vial Jaffe, 2014: https://www.parlancechamberconcerts.org/parlance-program-notes/siete-canciones-populares-espanolas/

27. *Seven thousand people . . .'* as quoted in Mark Hugh Malone, 'William Dawson and the Tuskegee Choir', *The Choral Journal*, vol. 30 no. 8 (March 1990), p. 17: https://www.jstor.org/stable/23547633
Olin Downes' and composer's words as quoted in Tom Huizenga, 'Someone Finally Remembered William Dawson's "Negro Folk Symphony"', *Deceptive Cadence*, 26 June 2020: www.npr.org/sections/

deceptivecadence/2020/06/26/883011513/someone-finally-remembered-william-dawsons-negro-folk-symphony

28. Composer's words as quoted in Verna Arvey, *Choreographic Music: Music for the Dance* (Dutton, 1941), p. 236.

30. Composer's words taken from the interview 'Tina Davidson', by Hilary Hahn, for 'In 27 Pieces: the Hilary Hahn Encores', YouTube, 9 February 2013: https://m.youtube.com/watch?v=z23ABhCS4Q4

Index